Iwan Baan, Baku,
Azerbaijan, 2011

Iwan Baan, Baku, Azerbaijan, 2011

Iwan Baan, Lima,
Peru, 2015

Iwan Baan, Tokyo, Japan, 2011

先祖代々之墓

Iwan Baan, Mumbai,
India, 2018

बृहन्मुंबई महानगरपालिका

Iwan B
Egypt,

Iwan Baan, Port au Prince, Haiti, 2014

Iwan Baan, Dhaka,
Bangladesh, 2017

লা
খী
M/S. LUCKY ENTERPRISE

Iwan Baan, Kampala,
Uganda, 2019

# CONTENTS


see pp. 18–19

## ACTIONS

# THE WRITTEN PAGE

Floris Alkemade

A map represents reality by not presenting most of it; we notice what we see and vice versa. Evolutionary laws determine that we only see what is important to us. Time and again, psychological tests show the stupendous blindness we display with respect to the world around us. What we depict on maps and in drawings is the minute fraction of our environment that we consciously record. Maps are mental constructions and therefore tell us more about ourselves than about the reality surrounding us.

From this perspective, a clean sheet of paper is the ultimate map, free of opinions and distortions, a serene and adequate representation of our blindness. But for designers in particular, empty maps and, by extension, empty sheets of design paper are foremost figments of the imagination, because the elimination, the abstraction of the open field, is not read as the representation of blindness, but as the virgin state in which the lines we draw will create a new reality.

In the spatial environment, of course, nothing exists without cause and effect, no virginity to be found there. Every square metre inside and outside our cities and villages has been cultivated by humans and transformed by nature in a constantly changing rhythm, each time linked to other lives and different objectives. The tabula rasa of a site cleared for building may convincingly present itself as a clean sheet, but we are never the first, never the last, never without a context.

As architects, urban designers, or landscape architects we always write on a previously written page on which no given line is without meaning. Designers are intuitively aware of this, but at the same time unaware of how much of the reading of a site is first and foremost a mental construction in which complexity is generally managed by eliminating it, by side-lining multiple strata. All too easily, assuming to have obtained the right understanding, to do the right thing.

The Tabula Scripta project is a clear demonstration of a mirrored form of hubris, an overconfident endeavour to look at things in a fundamentally different way. It is based on an attitude and method that want to unveil and embrace the myriad aspects of existing complexity and stratification. An attempt to explicitly read *our* time and *our* insights as a stage in an irreducible series of transformations that stretches both towards the future and back into the past, both from our own perspective and from many other viewing points. This approach does not spring from modesty, it is no message to be humble and accept how insignificant we are, but mainly from the realization that outside the realm of our presumptions there exists this rich source of inspiration still largely unexplored by designers. The realization that, from sheer ignorance, designing hands erase layer upon layer, destroying for ever unrecognized qualities. Poor observation leads to landscapes and cities becoming more and more uniform, historical layers becoming more and more unrecognizable, differences eroded, and riches lost. Tabula Scripta is a quest for alternative architectural motives and sources.

The well-manageable, hermetic scope of client, construction site, planning, brief and budget is broken open to allow additional influences and insights in. A recipe for less control and fewer certainties is not exactly something designers eagerly await. But it is this vulnerability—that we instinctively try to avoid—that can facilitate improved perceptions and produce insights that are the outcome of increasingly sophisticated and sensitive studies into the values of that which already exists. Rather than to jump straight to answers and certainties, the first step in the design process ought to be studying the extent of the question.

Designers have an understandable urge to exclude as many restrictive circumstances and complexities from their projects as possible. The research of Tabula Scripta inverts this desire to exclude. Instead, it embraces complexity, gives up control, and studies and builds on stratification, demonstrating how designers are part of an interplay of a wildfire of forces that can only be controlled to a very limited extent. Not reducing the role of a designer out of an awareness of weakness, but from the realization that this approach allows us to tap into a different and more relevant form of design creativity.

This design attitude addresses our current time and age. Our generation should not continue to focus on filling empty pastures with buildings and on designing as if we can afford, in our rich and vulnerable environment, to read project areas like tabula rasas. It is our task to work with care on the existing city, to enrich the already built environment, and to restore and upgrade landscape qualities, ecologically and aesthetically.

With this objective in mind, the question is how to improve the way we read reality and subsequently take things out or add them on the basis of the cultural, social, and historical responsibility that we want to assume. Not to accept that blindness is a precondition to be able to believe in an ideal.

The aim is to design a society in which we, as designers, assume more responsibility for our insights and interventions. Designing is much more than just a spatial, aesthetic profession. Our generation faces a number of questions that touch on the common good: how to deal with climate change, how to initiate a general energy transition, how to sustainably produce food that is currently being produced at the expense of natural values, how to protect sharply declining biodiversity, how to deal with divisive social segregation and a society that is becoming vulnerable due to the ageing of its population. These are fundamental questions, and it is remarkable how strong the spatial component of all these social themes is. The major task our generation faces is finding solutions to these social and spatial design problems. It is time for designers to rise to the challenge. Taking a broader view will enrich the profession by making it more relevant.

The demonstration of stratification that is the research subject of Tabula Scripta therefore includes this social dimension as well as the realization that the ultimate form of sustainability first and foremost lies in better observation and reflection.

This book is a report of observing the complex reality from an inverted perspective: the empty sheet of design paper as a serene representation of blindness, the written page as a source of vulnerability, relevance, creativity, and social awareness.

# LEARNING TO LOVE THE SWAMP

Jarrik Ouburg

'Don't avoid the complexity of reality, let it take you beyond your personal and professional comfort zone.'

Anonymous student Workshop German University Cairo / Amsterdam Academy of Architecture (Cairo, 2017)

## A BAD START

From an economic perspective, 2012 was the worst year for Dutch architects in decades. Architectural firms lost half of their business and many architects found themselves out of work. The crisis which the once so illustrious Dutch architecture found itself in was remarkable and, in my view, had a twofold cause: it was a 'double dip'.

Dutch architects had become very dependent on commercial commissions and, following the 2008 financial crisis, their clients had reached the end of their financial reserves by 2012. There were hardly any investments in building and therefore architects were getting much fewer commissions. It became painfully clear that, through the years, building had increasingly become an economic act and much less a cultural or societal effort. Building had become a goal in itself, a tool for creating square metres, no longer an instrument to raise the quality-of-life, provide decent housing, or create comfortable workplaces. The new offices that had been built and were standing empty, were the clearest illustration of this. By making themselves dependent on a finite economic revenue model Dutch architects had literally and figuratively priced themselves out of the market.

In addition to this cause, which could be argued to lie outside of the domain of architecture, there was a second cause, which was a more intrinsic part of its domain. This was not because of an over-accommodating attitude or modesty, but rather the opposite. During its heyday, the architectural profession had perhaps placed itself on a too high pedestal, as aptly illustrated by the term 'starchitect'. The architect as a pop star performing his trick. In the Netherlands, however, we took this one step further and elevated architecture itself to the same height. In 2000 the book *Superdutch* was published. It presented Dutch architecture as super architecture. This designation was placed over our architectural climate like a glass dome, presenting it as an exhibit, but gradually this climate began to suffer from a lack of oxygen. More and more, designing was about the need to perform. The radical image of a building became more important than its societal or functional qualities. Architecture had become a goal in itself, no longer a means to achieve that goal. Building for building's sake and architecture for architecture's sake. Two bubbles that burst at the same time. From 'superdutch' to 'superditch' in no more than ten years.

2012 was also the year I was asked to become head of the Department of Architecture at the Academy for Architecture Amsterdam, for a four-year term. My task would be to make young students enthusiastic about and prepare them for a glorious career in architecture. It didn't take me long to say 'yes'. The question did however give rise to many subsequent questions, such as 'how' and 'to what end' does one train students in times when the future and the very reason for existence of the field itself are being questioned. That question took a little bit longer to answer.

'L'avenir n'est plus ce qu'il était', the French poet and philosopher Paul Valéry wrote: the future is no longer what it used to be. A thought that may evoke nostalgia or melancholy, but at the same time it can be a source of energy. Education, with all its opportunities and freedom to create a parallel world alongside the intractable practice, proved, on second thought, to be just the place to explore this new future. Especially if one can do so with a new generation of architects for whom this future will soon become today.

How can architecture recapture its social role and—like the Baron von Münchhausen—pull itself out of the swamp by its own hair? The greatest lesson to be learned from the crisis was perhaps that architects, in order to pull off this feat, should be less concerned with their own hair, with the brilliant sketch on the virgin white sheet of paper and with the building as a solitary object surrounded by a tabula rasa. In order to get a grip on this new situation, architects should rather take the swamp as a starting point: the complex reality that we live and work in. A swamp, which after generations of building, demolishing, and renovating has resulted in a layered context that is still too often treated as a parameter that lies outside of the design brief. What we should do is develop an attitude and working methods to see this context, the tabula scripta, rather as inspiration, as motivation, and as a source of architecture—a context that defines the design brief.

How can we improve our reading of this complexity, improve our understanding of it in order to further write about it? In the search for answers to these questions the Tabula Scripta research has defined methods—verbs, actions, and reactions—for how we as architects can add value to what is already there instead of diminishing it. In order to bring each verb into focus, the research draws inspiration from domains outside architecture, such as art, biology, fashion, and psychiatry. This automatically places architecture in broader cultural framework of which it is a part.

The Tabula Scripta research presents exemplary instances of buildings, but also emphasizes educational projects that are complementary to the existing practice, as breeding grounds for new ideas, techniques, and insights. It shows an architecture that is both modest and ambitious. Modest in its careful dealing with what is already there and ambitious as it testifies to the conviction that we are also continuously creating our cultural, social, and historical world. In doing so, Tabula Scripta not only places architectural projects and designs in a broader context, but also places the design practice itself in a broader social context.

## A HAPPY END?

The situation in construction in many countries has been completely reversed compared to the situation in 2012. The economy had been on the rise again for some time, developers were developing again, investors were looking to invest again, architectural firms were working overtime again, and the Academy saw a great influx of enthusiastic students from all over the world again. Business as usual, it seemed.

'Protect me from what I want', Jenny Holzer protested in 1982 on a huge billboard in Times Square, a hotspot of capitalism and consumerism. It's a warning to ourselves. This 'truism' may apply just as well to designers today, so as to moderate their renewed inclination towards more production, and urge them to put quality over quantity, impact over personal ego. The social position of architects remains precarious if they react too eagerly to an economy-driven demand and act less on behalf of the general and cultural interest.

Besides posing the right question, an architect's role is to give the right answer. The surplus value created by an architect—socially, culturally and in economic terms—lies in bringing inspiration through spatial designs that transcend the functional solution. Not just in the seven lean years, but especially in 'fat' years with the most building activity. So, when we are busily sketching again, we should even be more aware of the written page we are sketching on and work with even more awareness of what is already there, who are already there and with what we still have left in terms of natural resources. This requires much more of an architect. More involvement, more creativity, more intelligence. We will need it all for the coming of the next swamp, which, at the time of writing, seems to have emerged.

# HEAVY WORLD

Michiel van Iersel

Look what we have done. We have wrapped ourselves around the world. From the sprawling megacities to the increasingly populous countryside. Humans have produced enough concrete to pave the entire globe with a layer two millimetresthick. Every year, we add more of the same material to cover a land area the size of Greece or England. Scientists have started using the term 'technosphere' to describe the layer of concrete, plastics, radiation, soot, and other man-made materials and waste that are forever ingrained in the planet's surface. An international team led by the University of Leicester has estimated that the total weight of this new sphere is thirty trillion tons, or a mass of more than fifty kilos for every square meter of the Earth's surface, including the world's oceans.

Architecture and the construction industry play an important role in facilitating and accelerating these destructive developments. In the scramble for space and other resources, no stone is left unturned. Globally, human activities move more soil, rock, and sediment every year than all natural processes combined. Whipped up by a staggering population growth and capital flows, we literally move mountains, reroute rivers, turn water into land, and beach sand into skyscrapers. In parts of the world where we have run out of sand for construction, we simply import it. Illegal sand mining endangers coastal ecosystems and turns countries and people against each other. At the same time, we have started to colonize other planets.

But things are changing fast. More and more people understand that land grabbing, large-scale geo-engineering, and private space explorations are symptoms of the same race to the bottom; a zero-sum game with only losers. They know that if we want to avoid falling into our self-made abyss, we need to take a step back and reconcile ourselves with the challenges of our time.

This book is an exercise in embracing and enhancing what already exists. By bringing together a wide variety of voices and viewpoints from very distinct fields and parts of the world, we want to encourage designers, and all others who collectively shape our built environment, to see and cherish the value of re-use and self-restraint. Because despite the mounting dissent, protest, and calls for economic degrowth, we still live in an era of relentless extraction and expansion.

When you look down from a plane, or circle the globe in Google Earth, you no longer can find—to recall the cautionary words of Bruno Latour—a pristine place to land or a territory to occupy without trespassing. The colonial concept of terra nullius, or nobody's land, is not only morally corrupt but also practically impossible. All the land is somebody's and human life has touched and irreversibly changed every corner of the world. The task we face is not to discover and develop new land, but to carefully navigate and connect existing layers of life on Earth.

We cannot undo the harm humans have inflicted on our planet. There is simply no way to untie the Gordian knot that is our world, with all its interconnected challenges and uncertainties. So, to follow Donna J. Haraway's advice, we should, whether we like it or not, stay with the trouble and learn to live on a damaged planet. Only by accepting the mess we have put ourselves in, can we start reassembling our cities and create more just and resilient (urban) environments. Against the reductionism of speculative real estate development, with its sleek renderings and smooth sales pitches that overwrite histories and squander public assets, we have to embrace, nurture, and share the messy world around us. Instead of extraction, autonomy, displacement, and isolation, we have to think and design in terms of value creation, dependency reuse and co-existence.

But where do we start, how do we find allies, and how do we recognize and strengthen existing values? The contributions in this book help us imagine ways of living together on a planet that has run out of unused space and other resources. In addition to architects and urban designers, we have invited people from the world of art, science, and technology to share their stories about the importance of connections and continuity. Each in their own distinct way, using their own specific language, they tell us how existing and emerging complexities can be acknowledged and how new relationships can be developed, or even designed, between the old and new, human and non-human, physical and virtual, mind and matter, and past, present, and future.

This book is not all doom and gloom. On the contrary. There is very little pessimism in the stories and projects that follow. No weeping and wailing, no self-hate or signs of defeat. We might find ourselves in 'a dark woods where the straight way is lost', to borrow from Dante's haunting description of his journey through the nine circles of hell, but there is still hope and inspiration if we dare to look sideways. Just like Dante, who had the poet Virgil and his muse Beatrice to navigate the underworld, we have to team up, keep moving, and find new ways to be in the world.

So let's listen to these voices and open our eyes to the wisdom, beauty, and untapped potential of people, practices, places, and projects within and beyond the realm of architecture. We will hear from artists who incorporate existing elements in their work to reveal and transform overlooked forms of meaning and cultural references. Technologists will tell us how, fuelled by ever smaller and faster microchips and computers, our built environment will become increasingly entangled with virtual reality and other emerging technologies, creating a secondary kind of immaterial architecture that questions the traditional role of design. Others, whether coming from the field of psychology or the realm of urban activism, offer their own variation on the theme of tabula scripta. They make a powerful plea to include the lived experience of people who are often underrepresented in urban planning and design, but whose feedback is invaluable if we want to understand the problems and potential of a place.

If you listen carefully you will hopefully hear, or even feel, their call to action and find inspiration for dealing with a broken world. And if you allow yourself to get lost in the dense and tangled web of references and metaphors, you'll probably come to realize that this book is not a preservationist manifesto or a re-use bible. Quite the opposite, in fact. Many contributors argue that destruction and renewal are not only inevitable, but in many ways indispensable if we want to increase the chances of survival and growth. Here, Dante's dark forest again serves as a powerful parable, as the scene of endless cycles of creative destruction and organic growth where species feed off each other, where lifecycles are interlocked and elemental building blocks mix and mutate over time.

The dynamic nature of forests is not unlike the forces shaping our cities. Whether you look at the gentle layering of architectural styles in places like Amsterdam and Copenhagen or at the violent clash of self- and half-built structures in Cairo and Mumbai and other megacities, they can all be understood as complex ecosystems in which everything depends on everything else.

Intervening in a living ecosystem requires a deep understanding of and respect for the cycles of growth and the interactions between organisms and the environment. Revitalizing a forest, and enhancing its biodiversity and resilience, can be as simple as thinning the trees to bring daylight in, or grafting a young and vulnerable twig from one tree onto the trunk of another, stronger one. Or it can be as complicated as changing the legal framework or raising funds for its protection.

Likewise, to revitalize and enrich the habitats of humans, it is necessary to nurture the life that is already there. To lift a stone and let the light in. Or build on top of, instead of next to. And design the technosphere in sync with the biosphere. Only when we manage to co-evolve with our environment can we continue to co-exist. So read this book, find your allies, and embrace the world.

# ELIMINATE —CREATING BY REMOVING

3

4

5

3 Gert Jan Kocken, *Madonna with Child and Donors, Zwolle, Defacement 16 June 1580*, 2007
4 Robert Rauschenberg, *Erased de Kooning Drawing*, 1953
5 Amie Dicke, *Important Souvnirs*, 2016
6 A firebreak is a strip of open space in a forest to prevent forest fires from spreading.

N-E
ENGELS
WOORDENBOEK
II
NEDERLANDS-
ENGELS
A DICTIONARY
OF ENGLISH
SYNONYMS
AND
SYNONYMOUS
EXPRESSIONS
RICHARD SOULE
WARNE

A DICTIONARY
OF ENGLISH
SYNONYMS
AND
SYNONYMOUS
EXPRESSIONS
RICHARD SOULE
WARNE

6

7 

8

7 Protesters in Durham, North Carolina, knock over a Confederate statue at the county courthouse to show solidarity with anti-racist activists after deadly clashes in Charlottesville, Virginia, 2017.

8 After rising to fame as the teenage star of Disney's television series *Hannah Montana*, Miley Cyrus cut off her long brown hair in favour of a blonde pixie cut that transformed her image into that of a pop idol. 2009/2013

# UNMADE—AN INTERVIEW WITH AMIE DICKE

Mark Minkjan, Jarrik Ouburg

Amie Dicke is an artist based in Amsterdam. She completed her degree in Fine Art from the Willem de Kooning Academy of Fine Arts in Rotterdam. Dicke's work has been shown at galleries and museums and is featured in several private and public collections all over the world. Her work is characterized by reworking, cutting, or removing existing images or objects. Her image from the series *Important Souvnirs*, in which she removed one of two books standing next to each other, revealing the mutual imprint through discolouration and thereby revealing time, was an important reference for this research as it demonstrates how a soft intervention can have a powerful impact. JO

Can you say something about how this image came to be? JO

Removing a book, yes. This particular book was in the studio of a recently deceased artist, at Herengracht 401 in Amsterdam. In order to arrive at the image, you have to do something with the house around it, which is so big and so full of stories. The place has so many layers of history, but sometimes you just mustn't let yourself be distracted by that. I wanted to take away all that from it. But in order to work up the courage to go beyond all these people and this place I had to go through it to feel confident enough to know what it is really all about. It takes time to be suddenly able to say 'it's that folded scrap that concerns me', or something else that you would normally throw away or overlook. AD

I started literally very superficially. I didn't want to touch anything and take my time to walk about the studio and scanning its surface quite seriously, literally superficially. Now and then I made quick sketches with my iPhone, to remember certain moments. Gradually it dawned on me that what really concerned me was how she had lived with all this stuff and also how time leaves its traces, including someone's actions. I believe that you can recognize someone's portrait in objects and things. Especially in her case, as she left so much lying about. It is also a portrait in a sense that many people can relate to it, as we all have a few discoloured books that we dearly wish to keep. We may not have touched them in ages, but still we want them there in our bookcase.

In the end, the only thing I did was taking objects out of their context to photograph them and then put them back again. Those books, for example: they are neatly placed against a white background. I placed them like this to show what I'm concerned with but of course that's not how they were in the house. They were on a full table, among many other things, so you didn't notice them right away: there were picture frames, rocks, feathers, dust. So much dust! I had to blow that first, but not too hard, as I wanted to touch as few things as possible. When I took away one of the picture frames I already saw traces of discolouration in the books. What I especially liked about that was how fresh these traces were. The very moment you find something like that–and this happens to me quite often–it tells you something you can't immediately define yet. But you simply know: 'Hey, here we have one', so you already act. The mind is often slower, coming in later. You've already seen it, you've already felt it, you already understand it but this is all before it can be told in words. It's a different kind of awareness.

JO You work almost exclusively with existing objects or found images.

AD All my work consists of citations. I strongly believe in citing without using words because I think we are filled with that. Nothing is blank. You may sometimes need that blank page as a white background in order to foreground something else. There is a certain contradiction in that, but sometimes it helps to place something. For example, in the cacophony of the table: if I would have taken a photo of that it pretty soon becomes an entire interior. That quickly can become something nostalgic or melancholic. To me, futuristic is almost the same thing as nostalgic; these two are connected somehow, almost sound the same.

JO Longing for the future, or longing for the past.

AD Yes, it expresses the same thing, it's on the same wavelength. What I like about it is that the books are standing there together. If you look closely you can already see a bit of discolouration on the front. These are dictionaries, of synonyms. If you take one of them away for a minute, you see how it is missed; this is very much about missing. These two books have entered into a relationship and they need each other. It was also a little bit of a secret, an almost intimate thing. At the same time, you suddenly see something from the past, but with a fresh colour. That's what this observation is about–that's where things suddenly tipped over and future and past are catching up with each other. You have a look into the past, but it is a fresh moment, as if the book was just now bought.

MM It's interesting that within the exploration of this book we speak of 'eliminating' in the sense of taking out elements. However, what you are clearly also doing is removing context, if even only for a while.

AD Yes, in order to focus. This of course is typical of all my work, the fact that removing something creates an opportunity to take a fresh look at something. Like in one of my scrub works. A man stands against a large column of a building–this is a page from a magazine with an interview with that man. By taking him out of the picture you start looking at other things. And of course, it is immediately also about that man that was taken out because your gaze is drawn to that, but you also see the shadow that suddenly remains and how beautiful it falls between those shoes and those pants. The page number is also very important to me, because if you look closely you can see which magazine the pages from; it is even dated. But all that is only shining through from the back side of the page. I like it if this kind of detail can also be given attention when we are not distracted for a moment by the 'name, claim, fame' of the moment. It's the same with Herengracht 401, really, but it took me a very long time before I realised it. There, I also removed the 'name, claim, and fame'. In the resulting publication *Important Souvnirs*, the names of the place, the artist or myself are therefore not mentioned either. I wanted to see what happens if you take all that away.

MM Is this about making more room for interpretation?

AD This anonymity provides room for continuity. By taking this man out, so many other men can take his place. When I had scrubbed out that man for the most part, I could certainly add five people whom I know very well. It becomes very intimate. This was someone I didn't know and with whom I had no intimacy, but my own memory or history then supplements it. I really like it when that becomes possible. A great many images are intended to portray someone or to tell something, but now they can go beyond that and can be supplemented. This creates very much room.

I can really find it regrettable when art is associated too much with 'ego'. It's okay to mention someone and it's okay to know who made the artwork and where comes from, but I prefer it to be about what hits the target at the right moment. If you say 'Picasso' the immediate response is 'yes, then it's good'. But the good thing about those books is that nobody created that image. It wasn't done on purpose; it is unintentional and therefore has nothing to do with ego. That's what I did with *Important Souvnirs*; it is unmade. And to me that is something from which we can derive some solace: it is made by the sun.

# ... removing something creates an opportunity to take a fresh look at something.

Amie Dicke

P-41

## READING AND RESUMING

Jo Taillieu

JO Jo Taillieu has been leading the office jo taillieu architecten since 2004, after having worked with various international architecture firms. In 2009, this practice evolved into a collaboration with Jan De Vylder and Inge Vinck, with whom he has been leading the office architecten de vylder vinck taillieu for ten years. In 2018, 'advvt' won the Silver Lion for Promising Young Participant at the 16th Biennale of Venice and was one of the five finalists for the Mies van der Rohe Award 2019. Since 2019, Jo Taillieu shifted the main focus back to jo taillieu architecten again, in addition to joint projects at 'advvt'. Many of jo taillieu architecten and advvt's projects acquire their form by drawing, but just as many are formed on the construction site, precisely by lack of drawing: 'on the spot' and 'with the spot'. The layered history of the building that becomes a new starting point for a project. But in new construction and writing as well he abides by the principal of reducing things to their essence. Peeling off layers right to where architecture reveals itself.

JT Accepting the non-useful, the existing as new meaning.

Three ways of thinking, the theory after the practice, the reflection following the practice.

1 Accepting that what cannot be controlled as a form of control. Or, how are cut out establishes the space.

Cutting out a floor on the building site unites the various rooms. While the cut-out was a purely pragmatic intervention in order to realize the original design, it became the design itself. Cutting out a floor to provide a perspective on the rooms and inside into the building. To realize the interchangeability of the floors and differences in height. To mix up the floors and bring them together. Elimination that enriches. To review what no longer needed to be designed. It is rather like the revealing of what was already there, but was not seen before. Insight as the result of the making. Or as a conscious act to reunite what had been separated. A kitchen and an exhibition space, where the kitchen as kitchen also had to be an exhibition space. Cutting away the bottom metre of a wall. Without losing the kitchen as a kitchen and still be able to create one exhibition space. Taking things out in order to add something.

2 The unconventional as starting point. Or, how aesthetics is the result of pragmatism.

A front house and a back house. Separated by an inner courtyard, but in need of becoming one. Making the connection, with a floor, walls, and a roof. Or, almost. But eventually yes, with the light as additional perspective. Not conceived in the vocabulary of architecture but as the pragmatic answer to a question. A simple tube, suspended between the two outer walls, the ultimate connection. Conceived from industrial standardization, a mass product reducing the energy of making a floor, walls, and a roof to a fraction of what it would have been in the conventional manner. Aesthetics as result, never as cause. Leaving out conventions to be really able to answer the question.

3 Undermining in order to support. Or, how cutting a span really constitutes a spanning.

A traditional roof construction. The attic of a former farm house that is to be converted into a living space. A tension rafter that is too low for the space to be usable. Built from the logic of construction, not from the logic of the life that might take place there that was never imagined. Cutting the tension rafter as an undermining of the construction. Substituting it with a metal prosthesis that gives new life to the functionality of the construction. Intervening where necessary, allowing where possible. Not the wood itself as ultimate structure, but this steel prosthesis as possibility of the ultimate structure.

This text was prepared in dialogue with Bart Decroos.

# ... it's making space without building it.

P-54 Gordon Matta-Clark

REMOVING A FLOOR. CREATING A SPACE. An eighteenth-century townhouse, a listed building, is being converted into a fashion shop. The rooms and floors that once provided intimacy and privacy are now at odds with the openness that is required of a shop. Some spatial elements are added; because of safety regulations, an extra staircase is added to the facade at the back, and large mirrors are placed in the rooms, so that clients can change clothes behind them. For an important part, however, the transformation consists of eliminating elements. Wallpaper is removed to reveal the aged wall hidden behind it as a new finish. Doors that were added over the years are taken out again while preserving the openings, which are accentuated with fluorescent orange paint. The biggest spatial impact is created by cutting out a floor in one of the rooms between the ground floor and the basement. The result is a surrealistic image of a mantelpiece, a door, and an opening that seem to hover on the wall. The low, intimate space is transformed into an open space providing many views through the building, like in a 'Carceri' drawing by Giovanni Battista Piranesi.

Twiggy, Ghent, Belgium
architects de vylder
vinck taillieu (2012)

Exterior

Shop interior

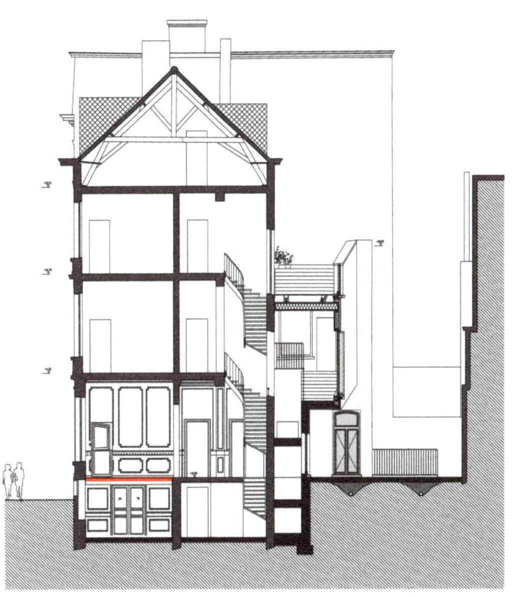

↑ 'Double high' space
Section

architects de vylder
vinck taillieu
Twiggy, Ghent, BE

MvI

**ECHO OF A HOME** *House* was a temporary public sculpture by British artist Rachel Whiteread, consisting of a life-sized replica of the interior of a condemned terraced house in London's East End. The meticulous process involved pumping 193 Grove Road full of liquid concrete. The artist then removed the exterior of the house ('brick by brick', she told *The Independent*), leaving only the hardened concrete visible to passers-by. The work memorialized not the facade of the Victorian house, but the more intimate, private details of its interior. An essentially hidden, private space became, by an act of inversion and erasure, a highly visible public place. Every day large crowds gathered, touching the walls, kneeling down to see the details—the exposed shapes as echoes of the fireplaces, lintels, windows and doors that were once there. After three months of intense debate about its value as an artistic intervention, *House* was completely demolished.

House, London,
United Kingdom
Rachel Whiteread (1993)

Rachel Whiteread,
*House*, 1993

THE VALUE OF DESTRUCTION Detroit has gone through a major economic and demographic decline in recent decades. In an attempt to fight further urban decay, the city runs the largest demolition programme in the United States. Since 2014, contractors have taken down approximately 20,000 vacant buildings across the city and rehabilitated more than 8,000 buildings. One quarter of all structures in Detroit are still in need of intervention in order to restore neighbourhoods, attract investment, and stabilize the decline. If the demolition programme keeps up this pace, the city can remove 40,000 blighted structures in about eight years. A recent study shows that Detroit's approach to clustering demolitions in target areas resulted in an average increase in property value of ninety percent.

Detroit Demolition
Programme, Detroit,
United States
City of Detroit (2014–)

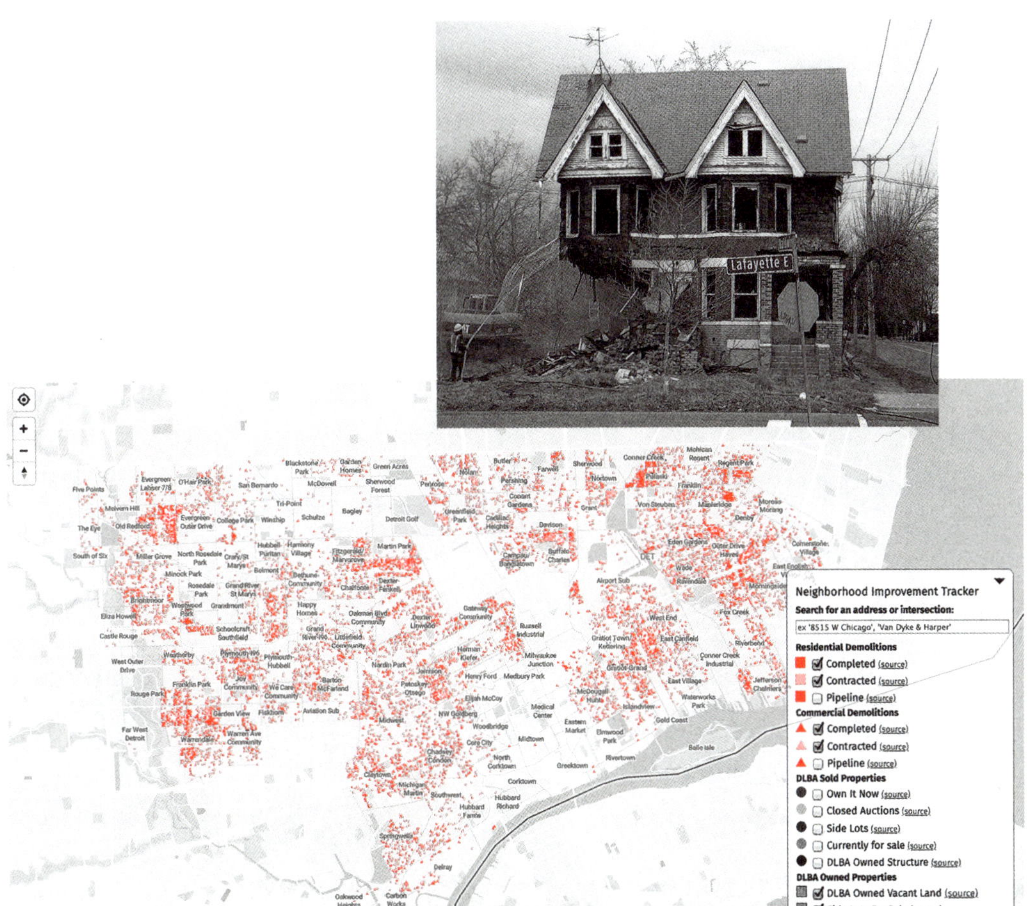


Demolition of a house

Detroit Neighborhood Improvement Tracker
↓ Downtown Detroit as seen from the north

Detroit Demolition
Programme, Detroit, US

J0

## CARVING SPACE

For the Biennale de Paris in 1975, Gordon Matta-Clark, together with friends, cut a large cone-shaped hole at an angle of 45 degrees out of two seventeenth-century townhouses that were to be demolished for the construction of the new Centre Georges Pompidou. By a single intervention the interior of the fifth floor was connected to the exterior of the building and the public space of the street. With the large construction site as a backdrop he showed how destruction can also be a way of creating a new spatial experience. Shortly after they finished the work, at the other side of the same building construction workers began demolishing the building with a bulldozer and thereby also the space created by Matta-Clark. Same act, different tools, different purpose, different outcome.

Conical Intersect,
Paris, France
Gordon Matta-Clark
(1975)

Documentation of the action Conical Intersect

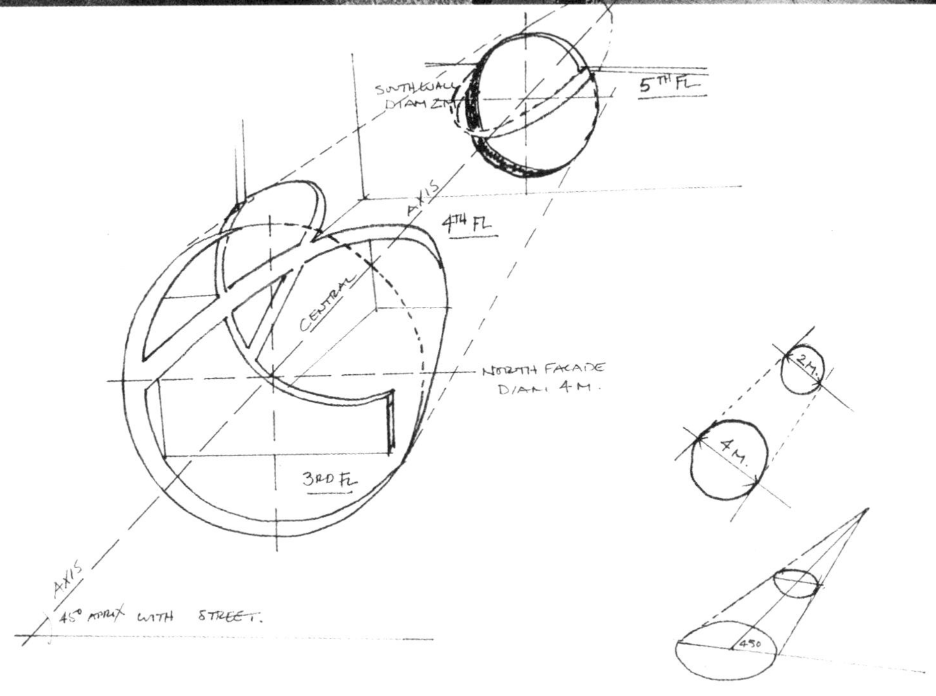


→ Documentation of the action Conical Intersect

Scheme of the intervention

JO

## A WALL THAT BECOMES A RIVER AGAIN

In Northern Ireland, the conflict between the Catholics and Protestants, the so-called 'Troubles', resulted in Belfast in a social and spatial segregation in the city. Metres-high walls, known as 'peace walls' physically separated antagonistic neighbourhoods and were erected along existing barriers—the industrial zones on the riverbanks. Today, decades after the peace agreement heralded an end to the conflict, Catholics and Protestants are still living apart from each other on either side of these high walls of many kilometres. In this project the meticulous demolition of parts of the peace walls has a catalyzing effect on the transformation into a unifying urban landscape in which the neglected rivers are again given a central role. An intervention in the present in order to give the past a role again in the future.

Common Ground, Belfast, Northern Ireland
Gert-Jan Wisse, graduation project (2015)

Situation before
↓ New qualities

Interventions

Common Ground, Belfast, UK

URBAN SHORTCUT The Raadhuisstraat in Amsterdam was formed in 1895 when the increase in traffic necessitated a new breakthrough between Herengracht and Keizersgracht. Dutch painter George Hendrik Breitner became fascinated with the sudden view between the two canals created by this development and depicted it in a number of his works. The new street acquired its meandering form because the adjacent streets were not in line. In the process, a number of listed canal houses were torn down and replaced with a new shopping arcade, designed by A. L. van Gendt & Zonen. This arcade would become a listed structure itself. Listed buildings being replaced with listed buildings.

Raadhuisstraat Break-
through, Amsterdam,
the Netherlands
The City of Amsterdam
Public Works Department
(1895)

Georges Hendrik Breitner, *Construction site of the Raadhuisstraat*, 1898

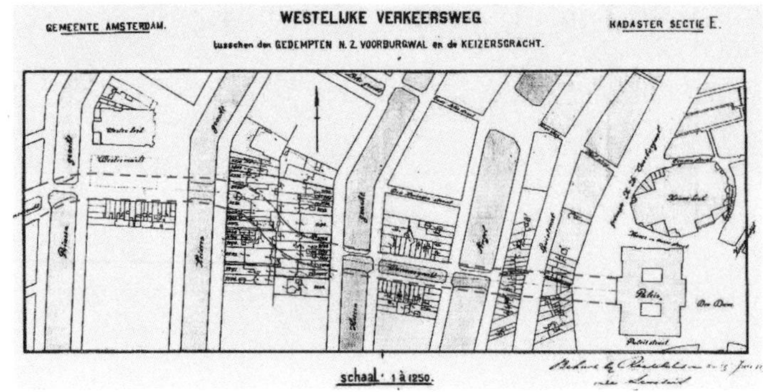


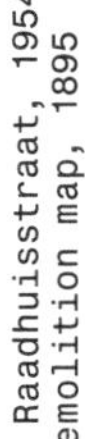

→ Raadhuisstraat, 1954
Demolition map, 1895

MvI

CUT-OUT CHURCHES In a mountainous region in the heart of Ethiopia, some 645 kilometres from Addis Ababa, eleven medieval monolithic churches were carved out of volcanic rock. Dating from around 1200 AD, the churches in and around Lalibela in the Amhara Region, are now a World Heritage Site and still serve as a pilgrimage site for members of the Ethiopian Orthodox Tewahedo Church. The Church of Saint George is among the best-known and and was the last one built of the eleven churches. The construction of the church involved excavating a free-standing block of stone out of the bed-rock and then removing all the waste material from around it. The stone-masons then carefully chiselled away the church outline, shaping both the exterior and interior of the building as they went. They fashioned a simple yet exceptionally beautiful cruciform structure approximately twelve metres high. This gigantic work was completed with an extensive system of drainage ditches, trenches, and ceremonial passages, some with openings to hermit caves and catacombs. Using only pre-modern tools and manual labour, an estimated 3,400 m³ of rock was removed to create the basic form and another 450 m³ to carve out and decorate the interior of the church. These rock-hewn churches provide powerful proof of the potential of inverse architecture.

Church of Saint George (and others), Lalibela, Ethiopia
Architect unknown
(around 1200 AD)

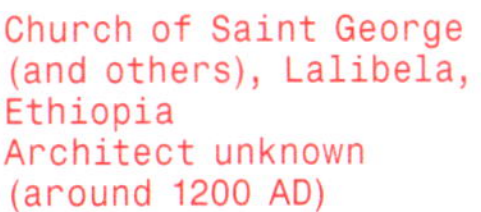

Bete Giyorgis (Church of St. George)

Ethiopian Christmas (Genna) celebration at the rock-hewn churches of Lalibela

Church of Saint George, Lalibela, ET

MvI

## NATURE AFTER DEMOLITION

In the city of St. Louis, various types of trees and bushes have formed an urban forest on the site where once stood the homes and apartments of the Pruitt-Igoe public housing project, before their untimely demolition in the mid-1970s. Built in the early 1950s, the slow deterioration, abandonment, and demolition of the 33 eleven-story buildings became a powerful symbol of racial segregation in the US and the failure of urban renewal and of public-policy planning. Where once more than 10,000 people lived, you can now see birds nesting in the trees and hear the wind blowing through the dense canopy. Trees as an antidote to human failure.

Pruitt-Igoe, St. Louis,
United States
Minoru Yamasaki
(1954–1976)

The Pruitt-Igoe public housing complex in St Louis, shortly after its completion in 1956.

Demolition of Pruitt-Igoe, 1972

Trees on the site
of Pruitt-Igoe, 2019

MvI

**HARDCORE HERITAGE** Promoting preservation as an effort towards imagination and activation, rather than conservation, has been the motivation behind RAAAF's radical interventions in the field of heritage. They call this imagination-based approach 'Hardcore Heritage'. The spatial implications of this approach vary per situation and can be achieved by either removing, excavating, erasing, or altering buildings or sites. One manifestation of this is the project Bunker 599 where RAAAF, in collaboration with Atelier de Lyon, cut through a seemingly indestructible bunker that is part of New Dutch Waterline, to open up this defunct water-based defense system to visitors. Ironically, after the intervention the bunker became a Dutch national monument. It took four weeks to saw the passage through the reinforced concrete, laying bare the multiple historic layers and potential for future appropriation and proving RAAAF's claim that well-designed confrontations between 'conservation', 'destruction', and 'creation' can lead to radically new ideas and spatial experiences.

Bunker 599, Zijderveld,
the Netherlands
RAAAF, Atelier de Lyon
(2010)

After a diamond wire saw was used to cut a straight section through the centre of the monolithic structure, a crane lifted it away to create a narrow slit.

The small opened-up interior
↓ A boardwalk cuts through the heavy construction.

Bunker 599,
Zijderveld, NL

RAAAF, Atelier de Lyon
Bunker 599,
Zijderveld, NL

THE PAST AS FUTURE The village of Sint-Oedenrode has a six-centuries-old church. In 1800, a hurricane sent the old spire crashing through the roof and the church fell into disrepair. In order to save its remains, after the storm new walls were erected between the old pillars of the nave. The once grand and proud church became a small one with an enormous tower. To prepare it for a new type of use, in our time, the church has to be adapted once again. The proposal is an intervention by which quality is gained not by adding things, but by eliminating them. A new separating wall between the tower and the nave is to be removed again and after two hundred years the centuries-old columns are to be revealed again by liberating them from their concrete corsets. High, narrow windows on both sides of the columns provide a view of the fragments of the original outer walls, thereby providing a vivid impression of the actual dimensions of the church.

Knoptoren,
Sint-Oedenrode,
the Netherlands
Floris Alkemade
Architect, 2012

Drawing of the bricked-in columns

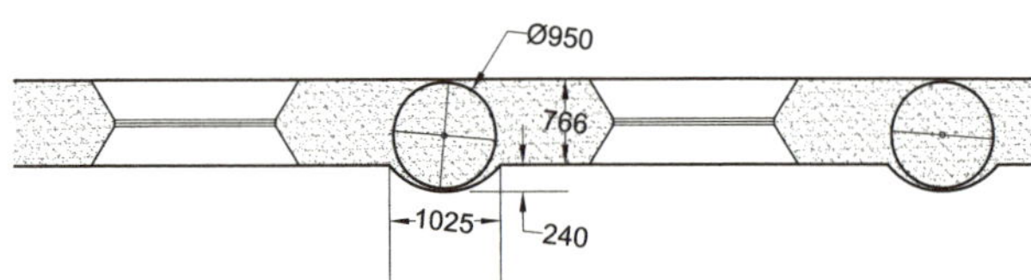


Liberated columns

1 Charles Darwin, 1881
2 Chimpanzee

3

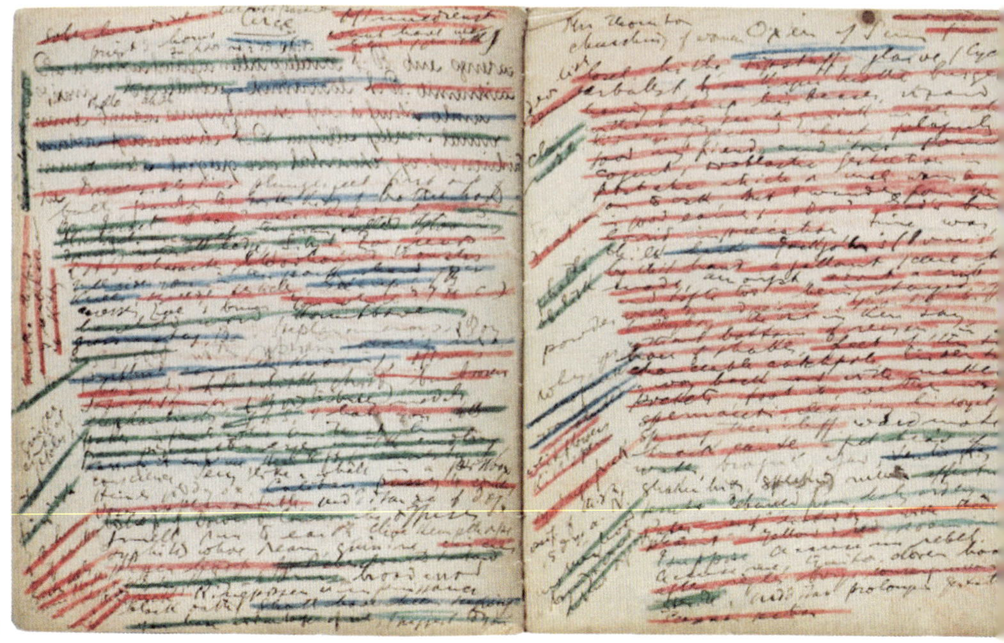

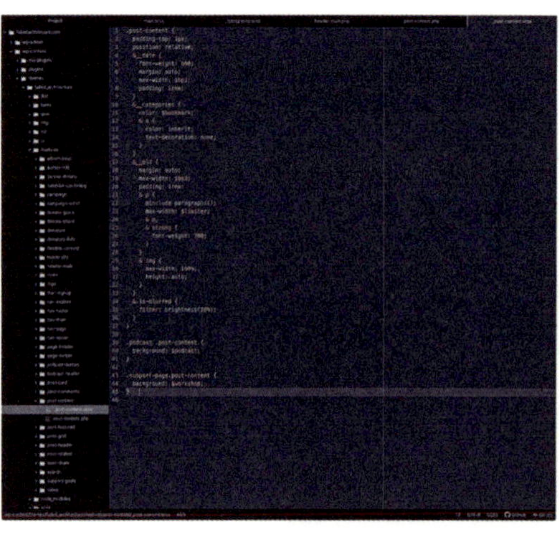

4

3 James Joyce's manuscript for *Ulysses*

4 The coding community continuously develops, shares, uses and modifies languages and systems. This open-source editor Atom shows how one popular website is built using freely accessible and adaptable functionalities including SCSS, SASS, JavaScript, CSS, BEM, Wordpress, Apache and MySQL.

5 André Breton, Jacques Herold, Wifredo Lam, *Cadavre Exquis*, 1940 Exquisite corpse, also known as exquisite cadaver, is a method by which a collection of words or images is collectively assembled. Each collaborator adds to a composition in sequence.

6 Kintsugi is the art of repairing pottery with laquer dusted or mixed with powdered gold.

5

6

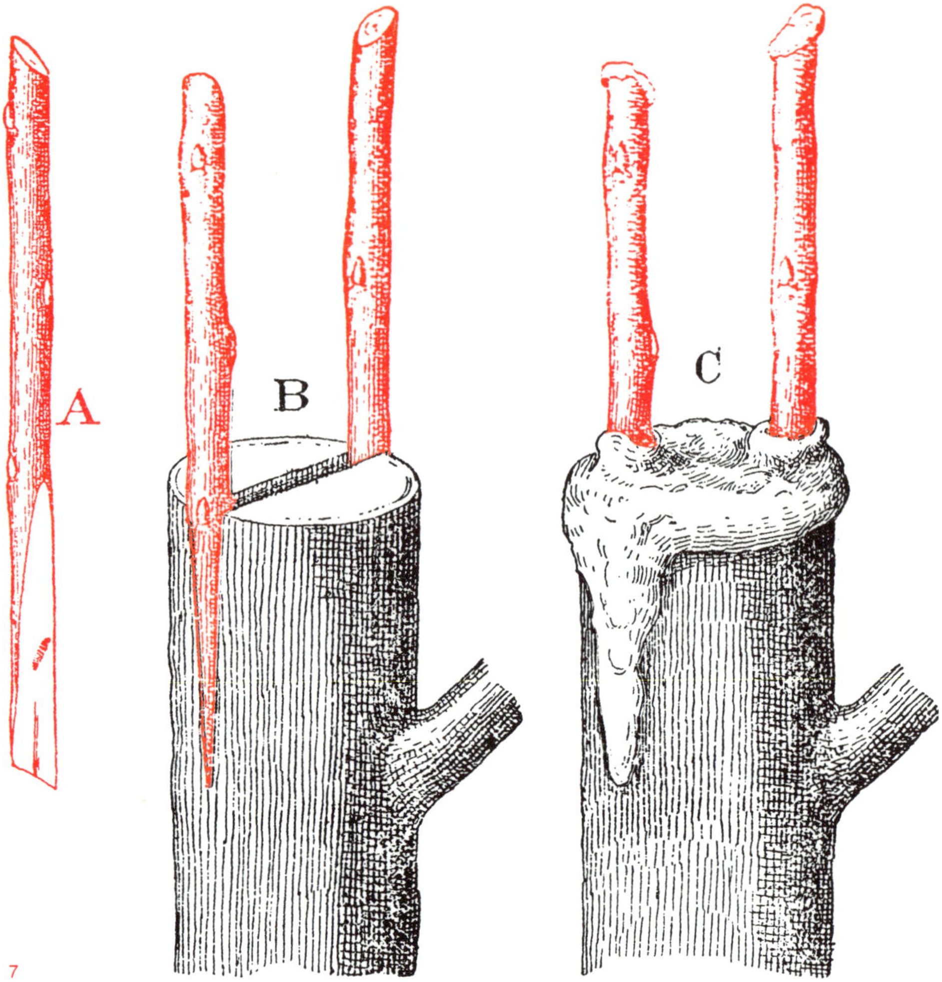

A

B

C

7

8

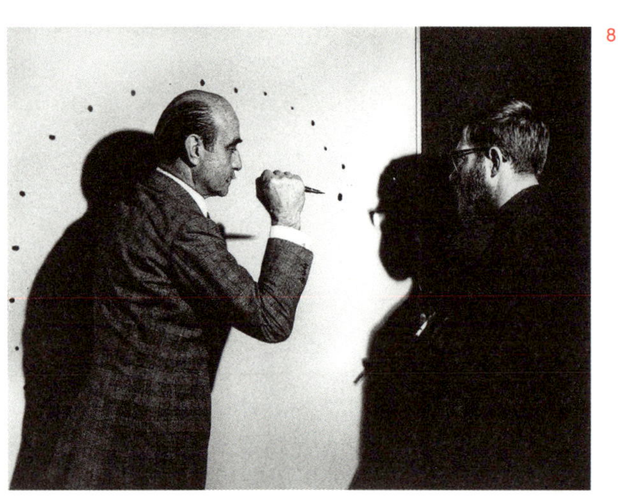

7 Grafting
8 Lucio Fontana
and Jef Verheyen,
*Le Jour*, 1962

# GRAFTING—DESIGNING CONTINUITY IN A CHANGING WORLD

Sean Halloran

Sean Halloran is the plant propagator at the Arnold Arboretum of Harvard University. Occupying 281 acres, the Arboretum's living collections of trees, shrubs, and woody vines are regarded as one of the most comprehensive and best documented of its kind in the world. To ensure that new organic material grows successfully and that the living collections can be shared with other botanical and horticultural institutions, plant propagation is crucial. Propagation is the process of growing plants from a variety of sources: seeds, cuttings, and other plant parts. Grafting is the ancient horticultural technique of joining parts of separate plants in such a manner that they unite and grow together. In this essay, Halloran reflects on the origins and dispersal of plants and grafting as a tool for growth. It provides a powerful analogy for how we think about the origins and development of architecture. MvI

Plant propagation, particularly the art and science of grafting, is integral to our past and future as a species. The artful manipulation of plants is necessary to serve our diverse needs in a rapidly changing climate. Grafting connects us to people of four millennia ago, to our recent history, and provides a continuing connection between plant material and the environment. SH

In their definitive 1975 book *Plant Propagation: Principles and Practices*, Hudson Hartmann and Dale Kester succinctly define plant propagation as '...multiplying plants and preserving their unique qualities'. Grafting is a method of propagating plants, where two or more different plants are joined together to create an apparently singular plant with different characteristics. Grafting may be necessary for maintaining flower or fruit characteristics, speeding up time to fruiting, improving pest or disease resistance, changing size at maturity, or ensuring crop survival in a changing climate.

Some plants are relatively easy to clone via cuttings. New shoots will root from just a section of a parent plant while maintaining their unique qualities. However, many desirable cultivated varieties are not easily replicated or require grafting in order to produce viable clones. Seed propagation



CONTINUE 

would result in offspring that is distinctly different from parent material due to genetic recombination, or 'shuffling' of the DNA resulting in different traits than those of the parents.

Apples are commonly propagated via grafting because the desired attributes (sugar content, acidity, colour, and so on) that have been selected would not manifest themselves if grown via seed. Furthermore, the desired variety, or the apple you would like to eat, could have a predisposition to some detrimental root fungus, so grafting it on to a root system resistant to that particular fungus is improving its ability to survive in the environment.

Let's walk through the grafting of a 'Red Delicious' apple as an example of this process.

First, shoots of a 'Red Delicious' apple are collected from a tree, maybe one growing in an orchard or in your backyard. These shoots, called scions, or the future top of the new composite plant, are selected and placed in a cool place until the propagator is ready to use them. Next, the rootstock, or the future bottom part of the new composite plant, is prepared by removing the top part of the stem and creating a notched tongue that the scion will later fit into.

The scion shoots ('Red Delicious') are then cut down to just a few buds, usually three or four, in such a way that they have the same notching as the rootstock and the plant tissues can be properly aligned.

The tissue of the rootstock and scion are then carefully aligned, tied with a rubber band and sealed with a waxy plastic film to ensure that tissues don't dry out while the two plants form a cellular connection. After a few weeks, the rootstock and scion will form a cellular bridge where water, nutrients, and hormones can be exchanged between rootstock and scion. The resultant plant will always be composed of cells from 'Red Delicious' that make up the top part of the tree, and the root system will be composed of cells from an entirely different plant. If the grafting was done properly, the union will soon become invisible to the untrained eye.

When we combine two different species in an attempt to optimize plant growth in some setting, it is like jamming together two people who speak different languages. If your subjects are amicable, it is likely they will get along well enough to find common ground and work together towards some common goal. Choose incorrectly and perhaps these two plants/people won't be able to survive. The most widely cited example of this occurs when you try to graft specific pear varieties ('Bartlett', for example) onto quince rootstock, and a naturally occurring chemical, prunasin, in the quince becomes toxic to the pear. Without this toxicity, the grafts would be successful. By adding an additional plant, a so-called interstock, which acts as a mediator between the pear and quince, the graft can be long-lived.

Combining two or more plants via grafting is a very complex physiological event with many factors that lead to the resultant plant's eventual success or failure. In plant science, we have only scratched the surface of what makes grafting so complicated. For example, some very interesting research of late has focused on plant-to-plant or forest communication through fungal connections. This is incredible, but further consider that plants also have to communicate within their own organs and tissues. A giant sequoia, for example, has to send signals between roots and tips of shoots up to hundred meters away.

It could be said that the most important technological advancements made in plant propagation happened before most modern religions existed. Grafting is counted among these, and emerged in the realm of two thousand to four thousand years ago or perhaps even earlier. Grafting made possible human domestication of woody plants, where previously our technology only enabled domestication of herbaceous plants, such as grains. We now had the ability to continuously select and propagate trees and shrubs that could bear fruit consistently. This idea of continuity is important when we consider not only the physical connection between the rootstock and scion but also the connection between that resultant plant and its environment.

As our climate continues to rapidly change, so do the ways in which humans can utilize the tools we have available to feed ourselves. Plant breeding programmes have long worked to increase crop yields, but climate change forces us to also focus on perennial crop survival in a rapidly changing world. For example, crops that are now difficult to cultivate in an area can be grafted onto a specially bred rootstock in order to survive the more intense winter. Plants that normally don't tolerate wet summers can be grafted onto more root rot resistant rootstocks to survive changing precipitation patterns. Drought tolerance is another huge focus of plant breeding as rainfall totals may differ wildly from previous trends.

Grafting is one example of how organisms can grow together and how dependencies develop over time that weave through our planet and societies. Not only does grafting strengthen plants, extend their impact indefinitely, and make them more resilient to our changing world–grafting also made dramatic advances in human technology possible.

The world that we live in is founded on propagation. It is likely that all life on this planet exists because of some primordial propagation event. The decisions that have been made since that event have been shaped by an invisible force that provides a basis for all decisions made today. The next time you see a street tree, imagine the multitude of evolutionary and human decisions that resulted in its planting, and all the invisible hands that created that tree's long history and future connections with humans.

# Every existing situation is competent.

P-78 Anne Lacaton

# MAKE DO

Anne Lacaton

Anne Lacaton is a French architect and founded Lacaton & Vassal with Jean-Philippe Vassal in 1989. She is a professor at ETH Zurich and has been a visiting professor at the University of Madrid, EPFL Lausanne, Harvard GSD and TU Delft. Lacaton & Vassals' work is characterized by a huge interest in the existing built environment and a commitment to its users. This attitude is immediately apparent in one of their first commissions, the modernization of Place Léon Aucoc, a small square in Bordeaux. After having thoroughly studied the square, the surrounding buildings, and the trees and having spoken to various residents, they concluded that the square did not really need modernization but that some maintenance would suffice. After much consultation they also managed to persuade the city administration of this. A view of architecture not as homage to one's own ego but as the art of generating the greatest social impact with minimal means. JO

AL In all of our projects, we never assume that what has been built before is obsolete. Rather, we see the existing built environment as an opportunity and use it as the base material for a new project. The existing situation has to be considered as an intelligent, coherent whole. Its qualities should be identified and utilized.

Our attitude is to *make do*, or use what's already there, but never in a conservative way. *Make do* is about taking the qualities and strengths of things as they are. Instead of going against them or denying them, existing qualities should be engaged in a new setup as driving forces for the new project. The design then is invented from the existing situation. An important principle is not to lose anything. Instead of wholesale restructuring, heavy modification, replacement or demolition, our resolute strategy is to carefully add and superimpose. For the transformation of housing projects we consider demolition a mistake because it is very expensive and absolutely not sustainable. Moreover, it does not take inhabitants into account who are generally very attached to their homes. Transforming the existing is sustainable, much more economical and can have a meaningful impact on current residents.

We never consider building restorations to be refurbishments intended to rehabilitate the buildings' original condition. Our approach is to find the right intervention that adds what is missing, repairs what is broken or replaces what is outdated. The aim is to always avoid heavy interventions that go against the building's original design. Altering the existing structure is therefore not an option if it is not an absolute requirement. We always aim to reuse existing materials and properly functioning facilities because they are part of the architecture and the identity of the place. Throughout the process, we pay attention to the various people, uses, trees, soil, and other elements in place. The new project will be recomposed of all these existing qualities combined with everything that will be added. Superimposing two situations, several temporalities and multiple uses, allows for a third space to develop. Ideally, this new space emerges when the design provides increased flexibility and an invitation for new uses, as well as a different relationship with the building's surroundings. The metamorphosis of the existing not only creates a larger space but a new place entirely, because it is appropriated by the inhabitants. This makes the transformation physical and imaginary. The process starts from the interior and aims to extend the space in order to provide more comfort, light, and generosity, especially for living rooms, which are often small in housing projects. We consider it essential to design the projects together with the inhabitants in order to carry out the refurbishment while people continue to live in the flat. A very precise inventory of the site is required to achieve technical and economic efficiency. We identify and classify all the elements fit for reuse and everything that is lacking. This enables us to clearly define what needs to be done on a targeted, case by case basis. Each space is utilized to its maximum capacity by starting from its intrinsic qualities, respecting the heterogeneity of the existing building. This approach requires a lot of observation, attention, precision and rigour. If there is a need to realize more space or new functions, the same attention and precision are required to add new architecture, without re-inventing the building's history and distorting its coherence.

For the transformation of the Grand Parc housing estate in Bordeaux, we started by adding new floor surface, extending the existing spaces. The addition of the prefabricated floor took place from the outside so that inconveniences for the inhabitants were limited. Simultaneously, interior renovations were carried out, including the replacement of electrical installations, bathrooms and sometimes radiators. These works are more disturbing for the users but can be done efficiently within a very short timeframe; a bathroom can be replaced in about five days. The works were planned during the daytime so that at night there would at least be running water. If more demanding interventions were required, these would be tightly planned and the family would spend a night or two in a hotel apartment. To make the project economically and technically efficient, several principles were followed. Early in the process, a very precise construction method was defined to make sure the process could take place efficiently. The project was rationally designed using serial elements and optimal dimensions. No unnecessary complexity–formally or technically–was allowed. Changes to the existing structure were avoided because these would require expensive structural reinforcement. The added floor surface not only enlarged the spaces but also enabled us to improve accessibility and settle technical issues such as acoustics and fire safety without having to modify the internal organization of the house and remove walls or partitions.

Let me conclude with a few of our premises. All places already allow for invention and imagination. Every existing situation is competent. Every constraint can be made productive. It is all about precision, intelligence, and delicacy. Do the minimum in order to turn constraints into something positive, create the extra-ordinary, and breathe new life into the existing situation. Or even do nothing at times when everything is already in place, and all you need to do is notice it.

CHANGING A TIRE ON A MOVING CAR In French social housing, for all types of apartments (single room, two rooms, three rooms, and so on) two things are always decided beforehand: the minimum floor space and the maximum rent. In a practice driven by economic interests this means that the minimum floor space automatically becomes the maximum floor space. Only one aspect of apartments is not mentioned in the relevant legislation: the size of the outdoor space. How this legal lacuna can become the source of spatial quality is demonstrated by this project. Instead of demolishing the three buildings with 530 apartments and constructing new ones, the money was spent on stripping the existing facade and adding a new one with large winter gardens and balconies to give each apartment more space, natural light, and freedom of movement. Each apartment, each family, suddenly seems to be able to breathe and the winter garden becomes a natural extension of the apartment's interior. The blocks were transformed in such a way that all families could stay in their homes during the construction work and no increase of rent was applied after the transformation. This project builds on both the physical and social structure of a building.

Grand Parc Bordeaux,
Bordeaux, France
Lacaton & Vassal
architectes, Frédéric
Druot Architecture,
Christophe Hutin
Architecture (2017)

Adding the winter gardens and balconies.

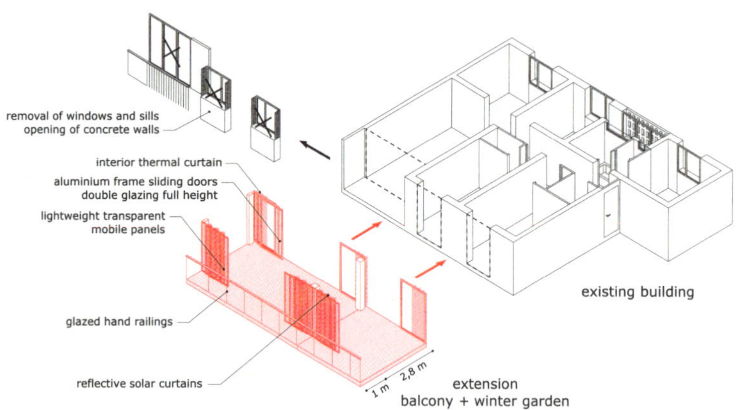


→ New extended facade for existing apartments

Winter garden

Winter garden

Lacaton & Vassal architectes,
Frédéric Druot Architecture,
Christophe Hutin Architecture
Grand Parc Bordeaux, Bordeaux, FR

FROM STATIC TO DYNAMIC The underpass under the A10 ring road connects the city centre of Amsterdam with a new business and housing district and is used by thousands of commuters every day. It is transformed from a dark and unpleasant place into a space worth a detour, by reacting to its existing qualities: the rhythm of the structure and the dynamics of its use. In one direction, the front side of the V-shaped concrete columns are clad with panels with retro-reflective film, a material used for traffic signs that reflects the light back to the light source. In the other direction the columns are covered with mirroring panels, making them lose their heavy and massive appearance. Mirroring cassettes on the ceiling take over the rhythm and length of the existing beams. The design makes a static space dynamic and an everyday experience special. A modern city gate is created whereby the cyclist, pedestrian, and tram itself become part of the project; actor and spectator at the same time.

Mirror, Mirror,
Amsterdam, the
Netherlands
HOH Architecten,
Children of
the Light (2019)

A tram passing by

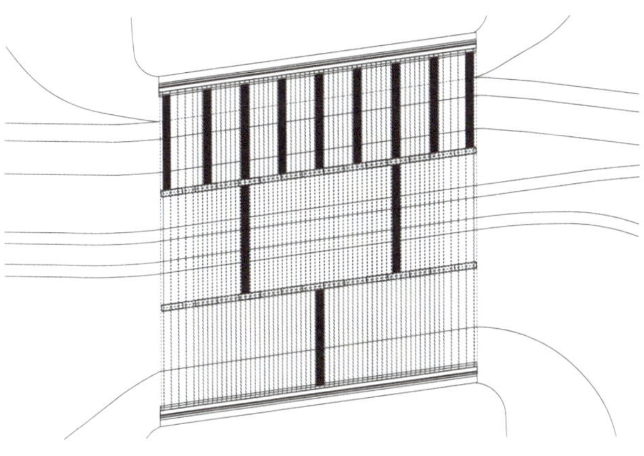

→ The view when crossing the underpass from the city centre by bicycle
Roof plan

## FROM HOUSE TO CASTLE

Now a ruin, Crichton Castle was originally built around 1390 as a fortified house by John de Crichton. It began as a simple rectangular tower, three stories high. Successive rounds of construction over the next two hundred years added a massive gatehouse and residential dwellings resulting in a square courtyard. The last construction phase includes an Italianate diamonded facade on one side of the courtyard, built by Francis, Earl of Bothwell, who found his inspiration during the time he spent in Spain and Italy.

Crichton Castle,
Crichton,
Midlothian, Scotland,
United Kingdom
John Crichton (c. 1390),
Francis, Earl of
Bothwell (c. 1580)

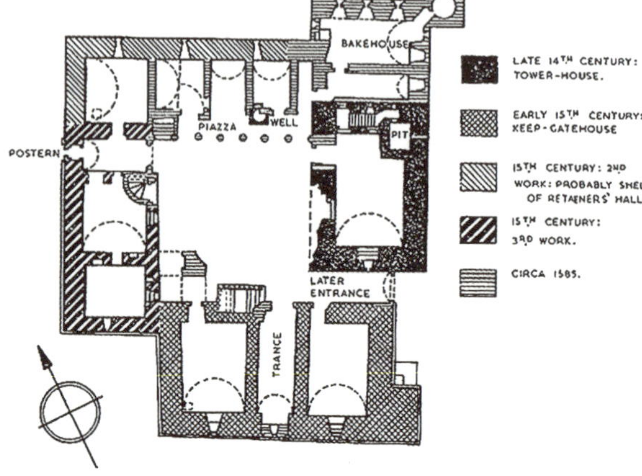


Ground floor plan

Diamond-faced facade and loggia in inner courtyard

Crichton Castle,
Crichton, Midlothian,
Scotland, UK

THE DIALOGUE BETWEEN GENERATIONS 1986 is the year of the Paris revolution. An entire culture is in the grip of an overwhelming longing for radical renewal. The Entrepôt Macdonald, built in that revolutionary year, is one example. In all respects, it is an extreme building, 614 metres long, without any variation. At least as revolutionary is the decision to make the bearing structure much heavier than necessary, making it strong enough to support a second building on top of it. The building is designed as a pedestal for future generations. Forty years on, FAA and XDGA make up the next generation to build on that pedestal, putting forward a proposition aimed at preventing a process of normalization and at showcasing the building's original radical nature by not just putting a second building on top of it, but an entire district.

Entrepôt Macdonald, Paris, France
Floris Alkemade Architect, Xaveer De Geyter Architects
(2008–2016)

The original building upon completion in 1970

Section
↓ New facade

Floris Alkemade Architect, Xaveer De Geyter Architects
Entrepôt Macdonald, Paris, FR

**INCREMENTAL ARCHITECTURE** Elemental has made a name for itself developing simple and affordable 'half-a-homes', which are designed to be added onto by the residents. Providing people with a home that occupies only one half of a given lot, it allows them to adjust and expand the house if, for example, their financial situation or size and composition of their family changes. According to Alejandro Aravena, founder of Elemental, providing a physical space for the 'extended family' to develop, has proved to be a key issue in the economical take-off of poor families. This idea of incremental architecture was first pioneered in the 1970s and 80s by architects like Herman Hertzberger and Charles Correa, who for example designed the Belapur Incremental Housing in Mumbai.

Quinta Monroy, Iquique, Chile
Alejandro Aravena, Elemental (2003)

The original units built by Elemental, which are designed to be added onto by the residents.

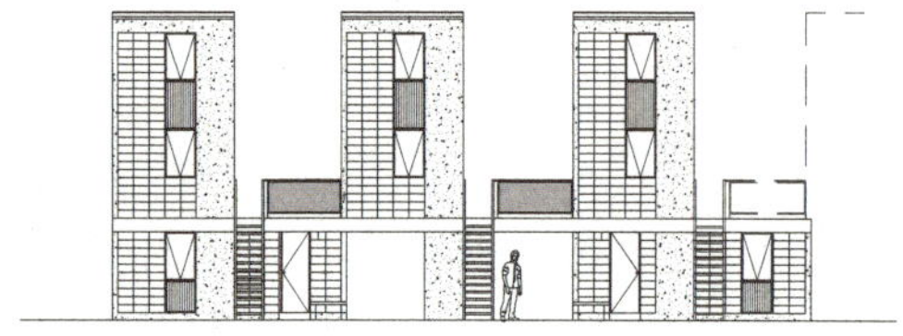

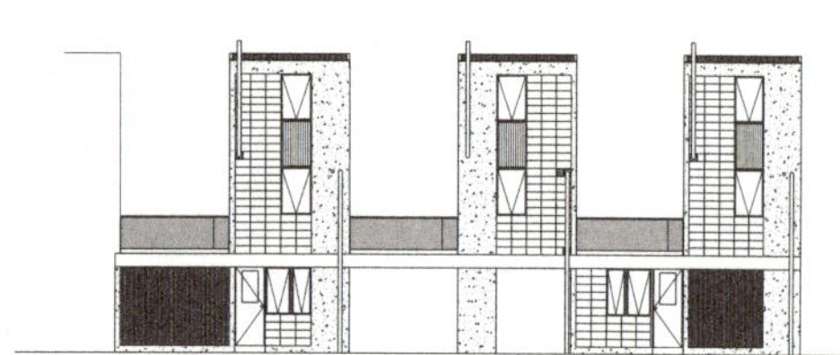

Front and back facade elevations

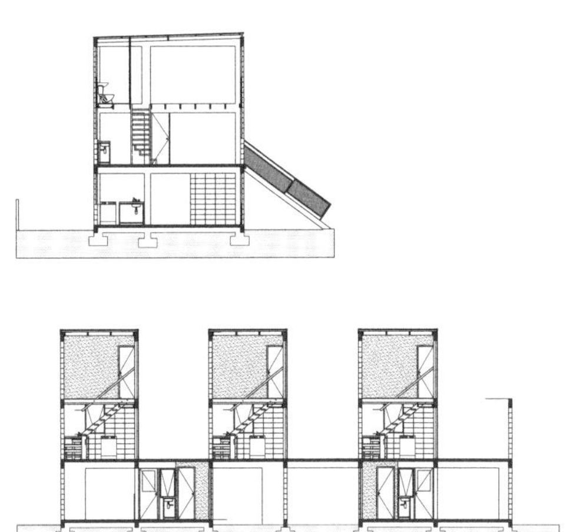

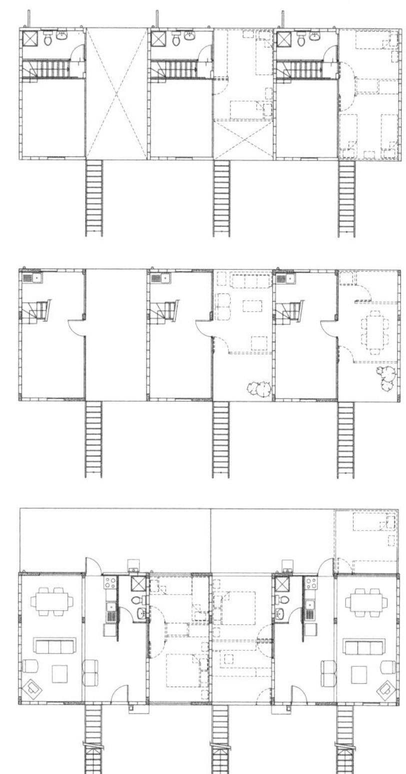

↑ Sections
Ground, first and
second floor

Expansions to
the original units
completed by
the residents.

JO

**REUNITING TWINS** The original buildings in the city centre of Amsterdam were designed as twin houses by architect Philips Vingboons in 1642. The twins were separated at birth, however, and different uses and owners left their traces. The facade of no. 147 was completely replaced in 1882 and the interior of the buildings was basically reduced to a collection of rooms. After three and a half centuries, the two canal houses were reunited into the new home of the Institute for Advanced Study (IAS) of the University of Amsterdam. The project turned the lack of a clear historical style in the building into an opportunity and treated the building as a collection of 'period rooms' whereby each room was designed with respect to whatever specific or generic qualities were found at the start, the wishes of the client, and the surprises that presented themselves during the construction process. Precisely through the cross-fertilization between the different styles, users, and atmospheres, the new institute has acquired its own identity that matches its interdisciplinary research programme.

Institute for Advanced Study, Amsterdam, the Netherlands
HOH Architecten (2017)

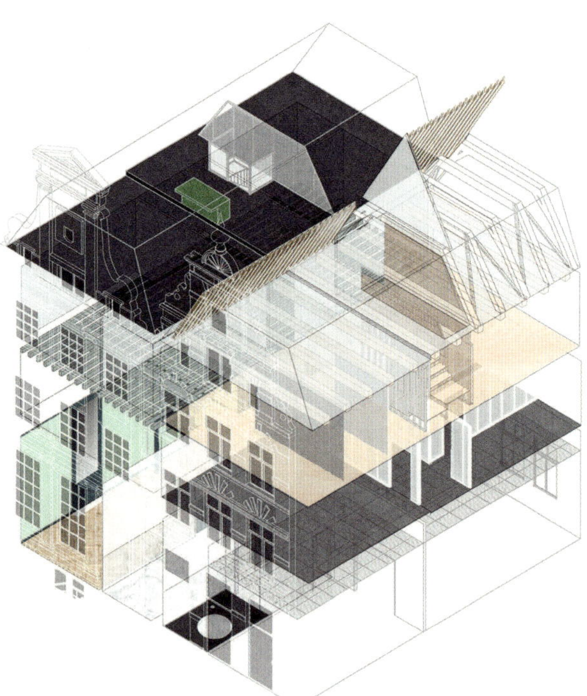

Collection of period rooms

Entrance of
the Green Room

The Wooden Room,
new situation

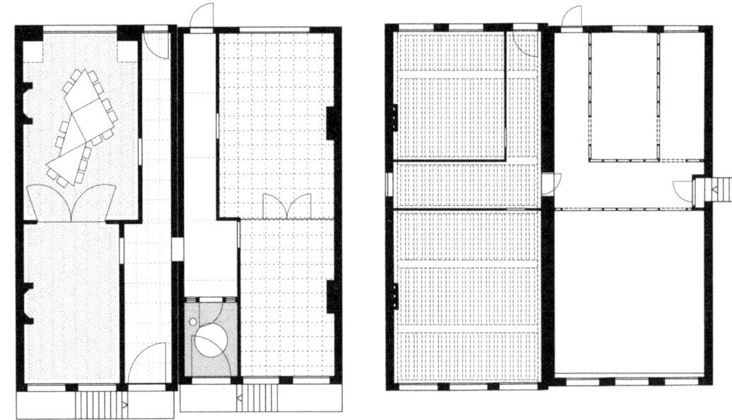

Floor plan piano nobile
and first floor

HOH Architecten
Institute for Advanced
Study, Amsterdam, NL

## TRANSFORMING AN OPEN STRUCTURE

Originally designed as an office building for one thousand people, consisting of sixty tower-like cubes connected by overpasses on each floor. The building was abandoned in 2013 and taken over by a private developer. Hertzberger was asked to make plans for the conversion of the office building into a mix of functions, including housing units for students and for the elderly, and communal spaces for social activities. The transformation had been anticipated in the original design. The architect differentiates between a structure with a long life cycle and infills with shorter life cycles. The redesign aims to keep interventions reversible and leave key characteristics of the spatial idea intact, always keeping visible what is original and what is newly added.

Centraal Beheer offices, Apeldoorn, the Netherlands
Herman Hertzberger
(1968–1972, 2013–)

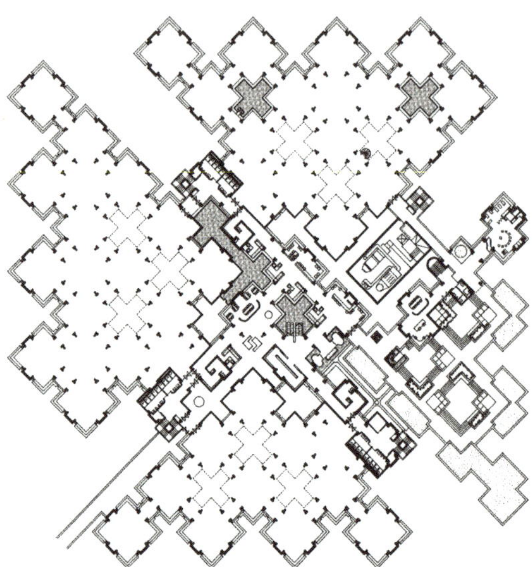

Original floor plan

Aerial view, original situation

→ Artist impression of the redeveloped Centraal Beheer building, which is renamed Hertzberger Park.

JO

## BUILDING UPON A RUIN

On an early New Year's morning, a fireworks rocket landed on the roof of a stately canal house in the heart of the UNESCO listed centre of Amsterdam. The house, dating from 1787, went up in flames. With its two extra floors it had always towered above its neighbours, but now it suddenly was much more in line with the surroundings. Unexpected views and connections between the floors now occurred in the interior. It was the ruins of the building that provided the spatial qualities for further development and for transforming it into an art gallery with apartments for the gallery owner and the artists. It is neither a new building nor a reconstruction of the original one, but rather a new combination of the parts of the building that survived the fire and the new structure, a joining of past and present.

Intervention
Herengracht 132,
Amsterdam,
the Netherlands
Onno Kamer, third-year's student
project (2013)

Herengracht 132
after the fire

Intervention
Herengracht 132,
Amsterdam, NL

**PUBLIC SPACE AS AN EXTENSION** The strategy of this rehabilitation of the public space for the San Pablo Xalpa Housing Unit project was to work with the barriers created by the residents and to open them up, democratize them, and re-signify them to create more unity in the neighbourhood. The residents agreed to remove ninety percent of the barriers, making the recovered public space an extension of each apartment. Like the trees, which were integrated into the new design, the sense of place was preserved through an incremental design process.

Common-unity,
Azcapotzalco, Mexico
City, Mexico
Rozana Montiel +
Alin V. Wallach
(2015–2016)

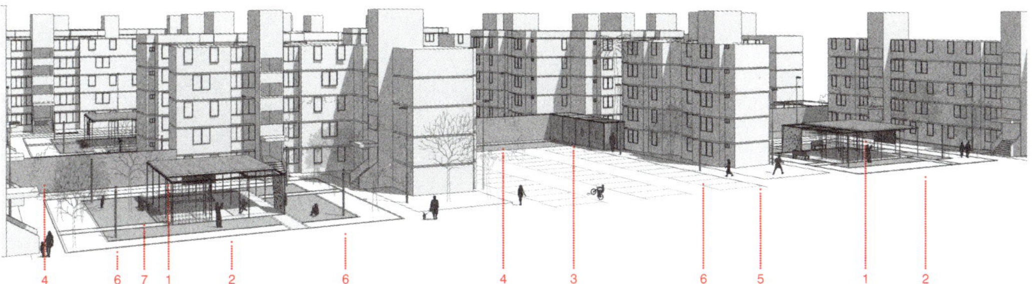


1 Multipurpose ceilings
2 New floors and maintenance of green areas
3 'A library' reconstruction
4 Murals between existing walls
5 Playgroud
6 Lighting
7 Benches and trash cans installation

Common-unity,
Azcapotzalco,
Mexico City, MX

F5

Rozana Montiel + Alin V. Wallach
Common-unity, Azcapotzalco,
Mexico City, MX

**LIVING ON A RUIN** The Theatre of Marcellus was built around 13 BC as an open-air theatre. The theatre fell out of use in the early fourth century and its structural elements were used for the reconstruction of the Pons Cestius bridge around 370 AD. Later, in the sixteenth century, the residence of the Italian noble family Orsini, designed by Baldassare Peruzzi, was built atop of the ruins of the theatre. Now the upper floors are divided into apartments. After two tumultuous millennia, the theatre is now half-alive, with residents living on top of a ruin, like fungus on a dead tree.

Theatre of Marcellus,
Rome, Italy
First architect
unknown (around 13 BC),
later addition by
Baldassare Peruzzi
(sixteenth century)

*Speculum Romanae Magnificentiae*, drawing by an unknown artist

The residence of the Orsini was built atop the ruins of the ancient theatre.

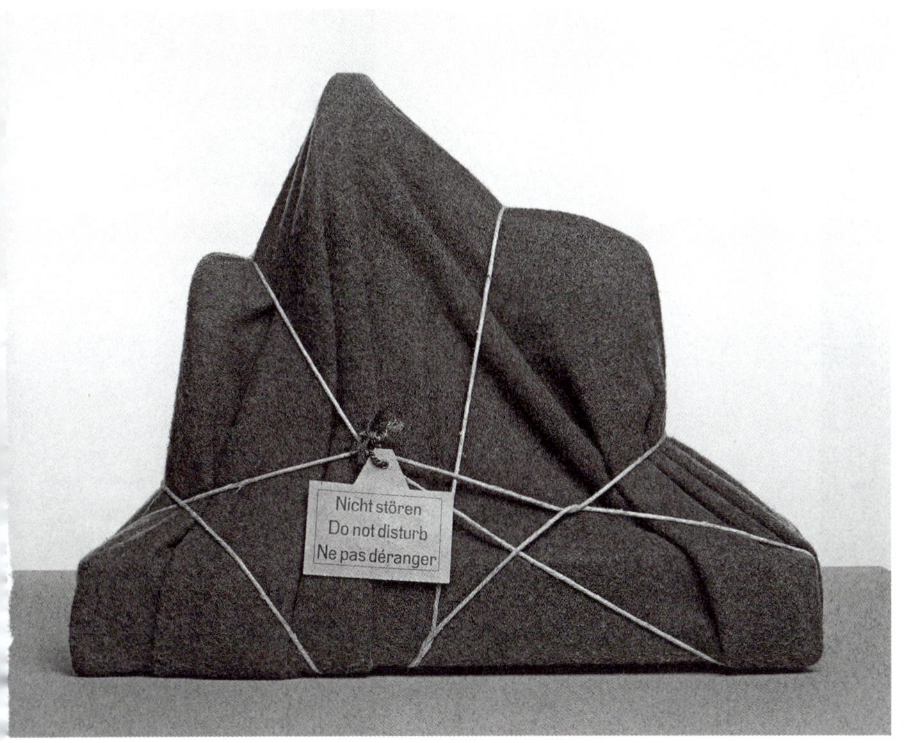


1

2

1 Man Ray, *L'enigme d'Isidore Ducasse*, 1917
2 Jan Gossaert, *Adam and Eve*, 1508

DELL
6814
LAUREL EDITION
60c
OSCAR WILDE'S
most famous novel
The Picture of
Dorian Gray

3

5

4

6

3 Oscar Wilde, *The Picture of Dorian Gray*, 1890

4 Bunraku puppet theatre. In traditional Japanese puppet theatre, Bunraku, the puppeteers are dressed and hooded in black to make themselves invisible.

5 Hito Steyerl, *How Not to Be Seen: A Fucking Didactic Educational .MOV File*, 2013

6 U.S. Air Force fighters disappear against the camouflaged hardstand (disruptively patterned airfield concrete) at Korat Royal Thai Air Force Base, in October 1972.

Form 2413
December 1935

UNITED STATES CIVIL SERVICE COMMISSION

CERTIFICATE OF MEDICAL EXAMINATION UNDER EXECUTIVE ORDER, SEPT. 4, 1924

(APPLICANT MUST FILL IN DOTTED LINES BELOW TO HEAVY LINE)

Richard M. Nixon
(Name)

2706 E. Whittier Blvd. Whittier, Calif
(Post office address)

Male (Sex) Jan. 9, 1913 (Date of birth)

What examination did you take? Federal Bureau of Investigation

In what Department and Bureau are you to be employed? Dept. of Justice, F. B. I.

In what City or Town are you to be employed? Washington D. C.

Rolled print, right forefinger
(Print must be taken to identify person examined)

(Unless the examining physician can guarantee the identity of the person examined, the fingerprint must be furnished. Indelible or stamp pad should be used)

(PHYSICIAN SHOULD FILL IN THE FOLLOWING)

69 1/2 inches. (Height, without shoes) * 162 pounds. (Weight, in clothing) ........ pounds. (Weight, without clothing)

Males, without clothing; females, clothed but without wrap or hat.

*Items checked (✓) were examined and found normal. Deviations from normal are noted. (See instructions on back of sheet)*

1. Eyes: For distance: Without glasses: Right [illegible] Left [illegible] With glasses if worn: Right 20/ Left 20/
(Near vision must be reported in space provided [illegible])
Evidence of disease or injury: Right [illegible]
Color vision [illegible] Method of testing color vision [illegible]
2. Ears: (Consider denominators indicated here as normal [illegible] as numerators the actual distance heard.) Ordinary conversation: Right ear [illegible] 20 ft. Left ear [illegible] 20 ft.
Evidence of disease or injury: Right ear [illegible] Left ear [illegible]
3. Nose [illegible]
4. Mouth [illegible]
5. Throat [illegible]
6. Thyroid (especially in women) [illegible]
7. Heart [illegible] If organic heart disease is present, is it fully compensated? [illegible]
8. Lungs: Right [illegible] If history of tuberculosis, [illegible]
Left [illegible]
9. Inguinal rings (men only): Right [illegible] truss worn? [illegible]
10. Varicose veins [illegible] Varicocele [illegible]
(If "Yes", state location and degree)
11. Flat foot [illegible]
(If "Yes", state extent of impairment of function)
12. Deformities, atrophies, and other abnormalities, diseases, or defects not included above [illegible]
13. Scars of serious injury or disease [illegible]
14. Nervous system (give symptoms and history) [illegible]
15. Urinalysis (see over) [illegible] Venereal disease [illegible]
16. Has applicant ever received [illegible] compensation, allowance, retired pay, or training because of disability received while in military or naval service? [illegible] If "Yes", describe disability and state whether present now [illegible]
17. In my opinion, applicant is capable of performing duties involving [illegible] physical exertion.

544 Wilcox Building, Los Angeles, Calif.
(Place of examination)

7/29/37
(Date of examination)

The examining physician must be in the Federal service

A. O. Shapiro
(Name of examining physician)

Surgeon, U. S. Public Health Service
(Title, and branch of Federal medical service)

*For males, to be taken only upon special written request of the official ordering examination.

This report is to be returned to the official of the U. S. Civil Service Commission requesting the examination

16—1065

7

8

7 Richard Nixon's partly redacted 1937 application file to the FBI

8 Scientology protest in Minneapolis, Minnesota, 2008. Individuals who associate themselves with the decentralized activist movement Anonymous often wear a stylized Guy Fawkes mask popularized by the graphic novel and film *V for Vendetta*, in which an anarchist revolutionary battles a totalitarian government; the masks soon became a popular symbol for Anonymous.

# HIDING IN PLAIN SIGHT—AN INTERVIEW WITH HITO STEYERL

Floris Alkemade, Michiel van Iersel, Jarrik Ouburg

FA, MvI Hito Steyerl is a German filmmaker and artist, also known for her writings on how media and new technologies are affecting our lives. In her 2013 video *How Not to Be Seen: A Fucking Didactic Educational.MOV File* she presents five methods to become invisible in our Information age. Some of her suggestions may seem unrealistic. How, for example, can someone hide in plain sight? Referring to the numerous images created and circulated on the internet, and the impact of social media and surveillance technologies on our lives, she wonders: 'How do people disappear in an age of total over-visibility?' To get a better understanding of how invisibility plays a role in how we interact with our environment, we interviewed Steyerl and talked to her about camouflage, fig leaves and the invisible and intangible architecture that shapes our world. Our interview took place in a restaurant in Rotterdam. A big shock upon entering: the place was extremely noisy. Horror. We finally managed to meet Hito Steyerl in person but, in this clutter, it would be impossible to even try to have a conversation. Hito didn't seem to notice the chaos, didn't even raise her voice when talking. Apparently, her voice found a bandwidth no one else was using, the conversation took place in the eye of a storm raging around us.

HS Most people are just not seeing what is visible, right? Their attention is being drawn to certain things, while other things—even though they are absolutely visible and obvious—do not get noticed at all or are not perceived. So, there seem to be additional options related to this game of visibility and invisibility. It's not just a property of the object itself—whether it's visible or not—but also of the viewer, whether he or she wants to see what's there to be seen.

JO So, you only see what you want to see or what you expect to see?

HS And you also 'unsee'. That's even more fascinating: the ability of people to unsee things. How can they unsee so many things every day? The story 'The City & the City' by China Miéville is a tale of two cities that are basically in the same location. Everything's plainly visible, but the inhabitants of the one city are taught to unsee the other city, and vice versa. So, they live completely parallel lives and they can only transition at certain points, and so on. So, I think the interesting thing is how people manage to unsee, or how they are taught to unsee things that are there and visible?

FA An intriguing theme in your work is how automation will outpace or outsmart us. You talked about how our photos are constructed. Generated by software that manipulates the image through some algorithmic calculation based on photos that we've taken before. Or that the machine finds things in databases and stitches together views making us believe that these are representations of the reality that we experience. We think we do take the photos, but they take us.

HS There is this patent by Amazon, it's not realized, it's just a patent. It's a wrist band for the human workers in the warehouse. Did you see it?

FA I think the V&A bought it at or acquired it.

HS No, that's the old one. The new one is for the shelf workers and it's to make them more efficient. So, they wear a wristband. Whenever their hand goes in the wrong direction it starts to shudder. This is a next level shock. So, it's to guide the hand of the human. To make their movements more efficient. That's automation.

FA A real nightmare. I think that it's not only external forces that are manipulating our movements but that we ourselves are responsible for manipulating our perception of the real world. I like the idea that we are here together now but that each one of us is sitting in a different restaurant.

HS So, what kind of camouflage do you need then? It's not necessary. The idea of camouflage already presupposes that there is a shared space where people see more or less the same thing and one wants to hide from the other. So, already by intervening in this space itself, you can create that effect.

JO As a Westerner, the Japanese Bunraku puppet theatre has always fascinated me. The puppeteers are not hiding at all, they are simply covered head to toe in black fabric. But after a few minutes you only focus on the puppets and no longer see the people operating them even though they are in plain sight. Your film *How Not to Be Seen* struck me in the same way. Both show that we see a mental representation of the world, not the reality. While in the West, like in the Muppet Show, the operators are under the table, we still feel the need to really physically hide.

HS I was thinking the same recently when the Cambridge Analytica scandal broke, because they are like the Bunraku puppet master. They have been doing this in plain sight. Everybody knows about it all the time, but in the aftermath everybody thinks: 'Oh, this guy should have been in the picture while doing this.' It's really exactly the same. It's not a secret. Everybody knew that. I mean, not the details. But now there's a narrative to it and now everyone can see; now there's a face.

We're being played like a puppet that doesn't even know it's a puppet. JO

Exactly. I was really thinking about that, about hiding in plain sight. That this is actually the best message to camouflage, because if you tell everyone that this is how it should be, they won't see it. Just a pictorial convention. HS

To what extent do you think this metaphor of the puppeteer and the puppet can be applied to modern architecture? In the way that also is described in your film, the calibrations, the manipulation, and the denial of reality and responsibility. There's for instance a lot of physical space needed for the cloud and for the internet. We cherish the virtual worlds but the real world in real time is being neglected. Architects are responsible for this too. Are they the puppets or the puppeteer? MvI

I think both. I think you're overstating. I think mostly architects try to solve some kind of commission. HS

Maybe they are not directing the camouflage, but I do think that they are producing the fig leaves that we all, in our position of Adam and Eve, need to hide our shame. Architects are producing the acceptable image to comfort the unacceptable question and therefore evading the need to address reality. If we fail to recognize the consequences of our behaviour it probably is because we are trained to be blind to it. FA

No, it's the secondary kind of architecture, which is not necessarily physical architecture in the sense of buildings, which is not only of course the infrastructure data. It's this bureaucratic regulatory or non-regulatory level, standards of terms and conditions, litigation, corporate language. All of that starts adding layers to architecture. There is more than just architects involved. People who are writing these horrible legal documents, they too determine what architecture is all about. HS

The determining layer is the invisible architecture. Architecture that's not seen as architecture.

# Most people are just not seeing what is visible …

P-107 Hito Steyerl

# TRANSGRESSING WITH SENSITIVITY—AN INTERVIEW WITH MONA EL MOUSFY AND SHARMEEN AZAM INAYAT

Michiel van Iersel, Jarrik Ouburg

Architect Mona El Mousfy and architect and researcher Sharmeen Azam Inayat have both been engaged as architects in the Al Mureijah Art Spaces project. It is the Sharjah Art Foundation's principle venue located in the historic centre of the city of Sharjah. It stands out by staying invisible, in a region known for its eye-catching architecture. Inaugurated with the Sharjah Biennial 11 in 2013, the new buildings provide flexible, climate-controlled spaces for the presentation of works in various media and at different scales. They are nestled in a network of coral stone enclosures, narrow alleyways, open squares beneath an interconnected roofscape. Largely invisible from the outside, the simple white buildings and stone walls blur the boundaries between old and new, in- and outside, open and secluded spaces and between more traditional and contemporary building typologies. The contemporary art galleries are part of the Heart of Sharjah, a cultural heritage project that aims to preserve and restore the old town of Sharjah, which is one of the United Arab Emirates. As advisors to the Sharjah Architecture Triennial, which launched its inaugural edition in 2019, both architects are working to create awareness about the architectural value of structures built in Sharjah in the 1960s, 70s, and 80s, with the aim of eventually preserving them. In this interview El Mousfy and Azam Inayat reflect on the ideas and forces shaping the Al Mureijah Art Spaces project and how it seems to hide in plain sight. MvI

Maybe we can start by zooming out. If you would look at Sharjah's skyline from the sea, there would be a sort of void somewhere in the middle, right? If you look at the silhouette of the city, what is literally called the Heart of Sharjah' is actually a hole in the skyline, because of its low-density and low structures. If you would compare that to the neighbouring emirates, you would see the inverse situation, I think. Or not? MvI

Sharjah, almost like European cities, has grown in a concentric way. So, it expands into the desert in a radial form. And there are actually a lot of commercial areas with high-rise architecture, and we're surrounded by it. And then further inland is the residential zone, where you have villas and low-rise buildings. Abu Dhabi is the one that doesn't have much variation, no historical centre. It is an example of a city where everything was demolished and then rebuilt on a grid. This wasn't done in Sharjah. SAI

MvI So, could we go so far as to say that Sharjah has embraced the idea of obscurity? When I describe it to other people and bring up Abu Dhabi or Dubai, they immediately have a mental image of the skyscrapers, the spectacle. When I say Sharjah, they often don't know of its existence, let alone that they have an idea of what it looks and feels like. But maybe this self-chosen obscurity fits into a bigger scheme or a larger strategy of the emirate to be different from the others?

MEM Although there's the 'Heart of Sharjah' project, in general the United Arab Emirates don't have mega plans; they are reactive. This is interesting, because that's where you find leeway to do things. There's never a fully comprehensive approach.

SAI We should also keep in mind that Dubai, Sharjah and Abu Dhabi are twenty-first-century cities. They are cities that are developing under capitalism, so economic needs come before anything else. It's very different from cities that grew at another time.

MEM Sharjah is probably the most shielded from that, because the emirate doesn't want to engage as much in that capitalist approach. It tries to not borrow, it's more conservative. It almost wants to make a counter proposition compared to Dubai or Abu Dhabi. It's 'closer to our historical past', or, 'we don't want to develop as fast'. The not-borrowing is deliberate.

SAI The context of the Emirates–where in the 1980s and 90s urbanization was happening so fast–was that when there was finally a kind of a pause to consider historically significant architecture, this opened up a completely new discourse around heritage in the region. So, the 1990s reconstruction was a way of making sure that not everything that was there was demolished for the sake of progress: the idea was to reclaim that urban, historical area, to keep it and be sensitive to it.

MEM And celebrate it.

SAI If things had moved according to what was happening from the 1960s onwards, it would have only been concrete high-rise buildings. So, in some ways this focus on our heritage helped to retain the morphology.

MEM There were many different ways in which the city interfered in this neighbourhood in the 1990s. I think it bought the land from the people that owned it and partly had left these neighbourhoods. Some buildings were left as ruins, others were renovated, some were grouped. The interventions from the 1990s created a layer that celebrated the area as a nostalgic museum-like site where heritage or history is fixed, celebrated, and reconstructed, not as a dynamic site. The artists we worked with since then in the Sharjah Biennial have shown a very different approach. They thought about the site as transformable. So, I think this was a strong inspiration for the Sharjah Art Foundation.

Maybe you can talk about the origins of the Al Mureijah Art Spaces: how did you get to know the site, what was your focus, and how did that influence the design? MvT

We were always interested in engaging with this urban fragment, a layered parchment that traces Sharjah's past and draws attention to its present cultural possibilities as a cohabited, co-produced, and simultaneous space. We conceived our intervention as a continuation of the fabric rather than as an incision, disruption or imposition–one that can exist with the successive heterogeneous social layers that precede it and surround it. This desire was coupled with a more urgent motivation, the need for fluid yet abstracted spaces with breadth and flexibility to support contemporary art. MEM

Before the Sharjah Art Foundation started working on the site, and involved us, it became government property, and it was used for multiple things, ranging all the way from museums to storage, to just 'we'll figure out what to do with it'. it was called the 'heritage area', so the city wanted to program it with things that could relate back to the identity of Sharjah. SAI

We first worked in the area during the second biennial, when people were no longer living there, although there were some cultural initiatives active. Some artists used storage and other spaces in the historic district, and in a way, we claimed this part of the city, the enclosures that had remained of these houses. All the other parts of the historical area were completely dilapidated. Afterwards, we were told that we could explore this area further and make a plan for permanent exhibition spaces. The foundation emerged from the Sharjah Biennial, and had an evident need for spaces to accommodate the extended programming, education, and outreach projects. We were told to use specific spaces and to design and build in MEM the manner of the old. Obviously, that was not something we were ready to do.

SAI The heritage department was not very happy with what we did. There was an open, but difficult conversation. We were still operating within a heritage area, which came with certain expectations of what it means for a building to be heritage. But because the Biennial and the Sharjah Art Foundation had a history with the area, they were given a little bit of leeway to come up with an alternative. There was an openness to add a layer and to interact with the previous layers, and not to think of the existing situation as fixed or frozen. And to engage with the question of how to make a framework for contemporary art that also helps a little to transgress the type of aesthetics that might have been expected of the building.

MEM Knowing the area very well was crucial so that we could transgress with sensitivity. We started cartographically and through aerial views, and analyzed the whole history of the development. Based on this we made the argument that this urban fragment has changed so much every decade; every five years there's a big shift and transformation. So, which layer do you actually want to preserve?

SAI I think when we started talking about this urban fragment in this manner, there was more openness to thinking of creating contemporary art spaces as just another layer.

MvI Could you talk about some of the considerations when you were conceptualizing the spaces? Where in the design can we see some of the defining elements of the concept?

MEM A very important conceptual decision was to make the site accessible from many points and create a fluent movement.

SAI Having it remain an inviting space, not something that would close off from any point. Not gated. It was a conscious decision to attract the...

MEM ... the non-museum goers, like people that are from the neighbourhood. Some of these open spaces, like the courtyard, but also the Mirage City Cinema, existed historically but have been reconceptualized as an open-air performance and cinema space. The cultural events organized here now work really well and are very inviting.

We discussed how much we wanted the complex to be accessible and connected to the surroundings. Some venues and buildings are related to the context. When you're in the courtyard, for example, you're really aware of where you are. Some artists are interested in exhibiting in spaces that are directly connected to their context. But some artists' work is not directly related to the context and they prefer to exhibit in a more abstract space. So, there are also more museum-like spaces, which could have been anywhere, because you cannot impose the context on just any artwork. But there's also a whole variety of more or less contextual spaces, where we worked with a lot of traces of older structures that disappeared. Not only literally, but sometimes in a more suggestive way. For example, by creating a dropped ceiling, or an open, central skylight, which suggests an older typology.

SAI Looking at elements of these older typologies, including the courtyard, we found inspiration for lighting strategies that we just used for the purpose of exhibiting artworks and for ways to let natural daylight in. It was not a strict interpretation of the courtyard typology, but it helped us with the spatial organization.

MEM We mediated between the scale of the surrounding urban fabric and the scale of the newly added spaces. There was a lot of reflection on what type of spaces creators and artists and visitors would engage in. Not only interior spaces, but a kind of weaving between exterior and interior spaces in a very fluid manner. This also manifests itself in retractable facades that are perfect for the weather in Sharjah and allow you to merge the in- and exterior for certain activities.

SAI Closer to the north of the site is where the majority of people would enter, and the height of the building was also lower. All of the buildings that are directly adjacent to the existing fabric were kept lower in height. As we get further and further isolated, we also go higher, for larger scale projects. The abstracted building or galleries are more in the isolated areas within the project. The five central buildings are the newly constructed buildings. And then the L-shape of buildings that surround it on the north and the west is the layer of enclosures we did not touch. Some are from the 1990s and some are older.

MvI When we visited the Al Mureijah Art Spaces a few years ago, we were walking down an alley, going around the corner, and we saw shoes outside. I think it's a mosque, right?

SAI The mosque is part of a layer of existing buildings that wraps around the project and was identified to be retained because it was being used. People from the area were happy with it, so we only fixed a few things in it and left it the way it was.

MvI Comparing the ideas of porosity and obscurity, I think there is a tension between the two. Not only physically, in how you create conditions for certain types of artworks, but also metaphorically, in the sense that contemporary art sometimes represents something that you want to keep away from the more conservative powers on the outside.

SAI The fact that it's set back from any main road makes it a little bit isolated. It's embedded deeply in the urban fabric, surrounded by buildings. It's not something that you just arrive at. If we had been situated directly along the main road, as a point of entry to the heritage area, would we have been able to do this? Maybe not. But the fact that it was concealed in some way, something that you arrive at or navigate through an initial facade, did help us to remain isolated. And this idea of isolating and layering is something we carry through in the design as well. For instance, when we started with these smaller buildings, which are more based on the courtyard typology, and subsequently made bigger gestures and higher spaces, that happened only once we were safely within the core of the fabric. It was also because they were aligned, and we didn't want to demolish something that was working, or change something that was used. So, there was a very conscious effort to identify the buildings that had use value for either inhabitants or the foundation. And not to touch them as such. We sometimes take photos from the creek, looking from the water towards Sharjah, and you just see a little light thing.

MEM You see the wall of the cinema, a little peep of it.

SAI And then on the other hand, when we are in the buildings, all of the windows are framed to have views of the creek and of all the surrounding buildings. In that sense it is very hidden, yet you can see everything from it. In some ways we were testing and negotiating boundaries. We were overt in marking our intervention as another interpretive, adaptive layer, while trying to remain contextually sensitive to the existing social and urban fabric.

Some places are secluded and some are more open. I think we created a spectrum. MEM

There is also the negotiation and dialogue about what is public or what needs to be protected or isolated versus what we projected. But it's a really interesting tension, because we've had a history in the spaces. But the porosity is a direct response to the immediate neighbourhood. It might be a maze to people who are not familiar with the area, but it's something that the neighbourhood can familiarize, take over, make use of these roofscapes, and so on. So, I think it's also the proximity of the user or the relationship of the user to the spaces that determines how forced it is. SAI

It seems that your project stands out because it doesn't want to stand out. It seems very much to obscure itself. You kept it so local that, even if I look at aerial photos of the Heart of Sharjah, the old and new buildings blur into one urban ensemble. Then I find it interesting that it was a discussion that it was almost too local. There should be a difference in order to say 'this is old, and this is new'. It should stand out, right? How did you deal with this tension between the old and new? JO

Yes, we decided that we were going to redefine the specific ways in which we're going to retain qualities, experiential qualities, and urban qualities of the area; we'll react to the footprint and we'll respond to it. But a fixed representation that is accurate does not exist. SAI

Also, the way we thought about how to interact with the courtyard typology was important. You can work with the typology because it has a lot of merit, but then it cannot be a space that is completely enclosed and is only used to enter other spaces. So, we created a more fluid form, which slightly subverted the typology. MEM

This fluid occupancy of historical structures and use as cultural clubs, museums, cultural tourism, and spaces for contemporary art creates a simultaneous yet distinct presence. If these 'islands of coherence' can coexist without annihilating each other, and as long as they are sensitized to the social and programmatic needs of the people living in the neighbourhood, we can anticipate and help to create continuity, in some form, of a historically multi-ethnic, multi-layered area.

# Knowing the area very well was crucial so that we could transgress with sensitivity.

P-114 Mona El Mousfy

STANDING OUT BY STAYING PUT Sharjah Art Foundation's contemporary galleries are located in Al Mureijah Square, a historical area of Sharjah dating back to the beginning of the nineteenth century when the United Arab Emirates consisted of just a string of small coastal settlements. The spaces are located amidst a series of restored buildings and ruined enclosures and are part of the Heart of Sharjah historical preservation and restoration project. Inaugurated with the Sharjah Biennial 11 in 2013, the contemporary galleries occupy 65 percent of the site allocated to the Foundation. Carefully embedded in the urban fabric and opening up in multiple directions, the five new climate-controlled galleries provide a range of interiors to present and experience art in various media along with a variety of exterior spaces including courtyards, alleyways, open squares, and an inter-connected roof-scape. The roof becomes an extension of the urban space providing views into alleys, courtyards, and exhibition spaces, as well as views across urban layers, the nearby Creek, and the Gulf beyond. Additionally, the project managed to preserve three existing reconstructed courtyard houses and six ruined coral stone enclosures as traces of the past and outdoor and as spaces for site-specific installations. Largely invisible from a distance, the vast complex incorporates everyday functions, including a small mosque and an open-air cinema, which focuses on films not shown in mainstream cinemas. In a region known for spectacular skylines, the Al Mureijah Sharjah Art Spaces stands out by staying put. By mixing tradition and innovation it symbolizes the cultural fluidity of a historically multi-ethnic city. MvI

Al Mureijah Art Spaces, Sharjah Art Foundation, Sharjah, United Arab Emirates
Mona El Mousfy and Sharmeen Azam Inayat, in collaboration with Hassan Ali Al Jidah (Engineer), Godwin Austen Johnson Architecture (Engineering Consultant) (2010–2013)

→ Sharjah Art Foundation Spaces, Sharjah Heritage Area
Site plan with existing and new buildings

Mona El Mousfy and
Sharmeen Azam Inayat
Al Mureijah Art Spaces,
Sharjah Art Foundation,
Sharjah, AE

THE INVERTED CITY The inner city of The Hague suffers from too much traffic, leading to excessive congestion at certain points. For Grote Marktstraat, the only solution was adding a subterranean layer to the city. Tram rails, two underground tram stations, and large car parks were constructed under the ground over a length of 1,250 metres. To prevent having a rich historical city above and a meaningless infrastructure underneath, the architects chose to design the 'underworld' with the same spatial ambitions as the world above it: the underground tram stations are lofty spaces with many views and connections. The surface level as the dividing line between two complementary worlds.

Souterrain Tram Tunnel, The Hague, the Netherlands OMA / Rem Koolhaas, Floris Alkemade Partners (1994–2004)

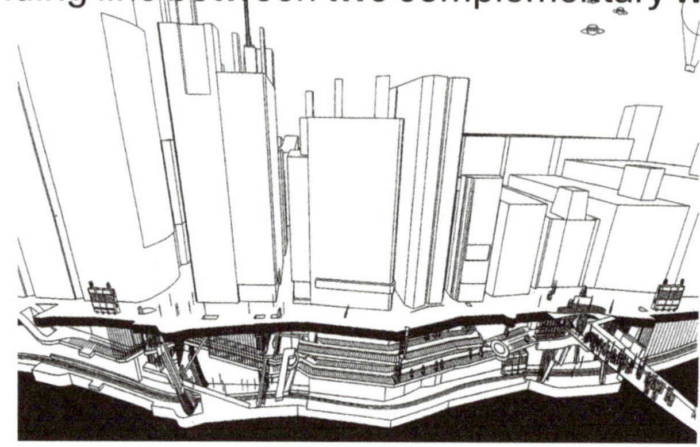

Souterrain Tram Tunnel,
The Hague, NL

KITSCHY COVER-UP OR SYMBOL OF SUSTAINABILITY? Inaugurated in 1971, the Spittelau waste incineration plant in Vienna was largely destroyed by a fire in 1987. It was decided to reconstruct it in exactly the same spot. The Viennese artist and environmental activist Friedensreich Hundertwasser, known for his nature-inspired artworks and organic designs, was invited to redesign the facade of the plant. He refused at first, but when Vienna's mayor promised that the plant would be equipped with the most modern emission purification and reduction technology, the artist finally agreed. Criticized by some as a kitschy cover-up of a fundamentally problematic $CO_2$-emitting and 'greenwashing tourist attraction', others praise the colourful facade, the golden ball on the chimney, the roof greenery, and planted trees. The discussion about the Spittelau plant continues to this day. In the meantime, a silent revolution took place behind its much-debated front. In the decades since its inauguration and subsequent reconstruction the traditional incarcerator was slowly transformed into a state-of-the-art waste-to-energy plant, producing three times as much electricity as before, while saving millions of cubic meters of natural gas annually.

Spittelau waste-to-energy plant, Vienna, Austria
Architect unknown (1969–1971), reconstruction with design of facade by Friedensreich Hundertwasser between 1988 and 1992

Spittelau waste-to-energy plant

**NOMEN EST OMEN (THE NAME IS AN OMEN)** Since many years, behind a stately historical facade in The Hague a hardcore pop temple has made its home, under the most appropriate name of Paard van Troje (Trojan Horse). Because of safety and sound regulations the rather run-down building was in need of almost complete renovation. The structure behind the facade wasn't worth saving but the facade itself was on the list of protected monuments. Behind this historical layer room had to be made for two music venues, bars, foyers, dressing rooms, and loading bays. Partly because of financial considerations, the Trojan Horse theme became the leitmotif. On the outside, the monumental facade was carefully restored, while behind it the traces of decades of underground culture were just as carefully preserved. The music venues were designed as individual boxes and were placed on spring blocks, so that a completely different world with completely different aims was realized behind the respectable city facade. The contrast between the building's outer and inner world is so big that the concealing historical layer has been crucial in the music centre's integration in the city.

Paard van Troje, The Hague, the Netherlands
OMA / Rem Koolhaas, Floris Alkemade Partners (1995–2003)

Construction

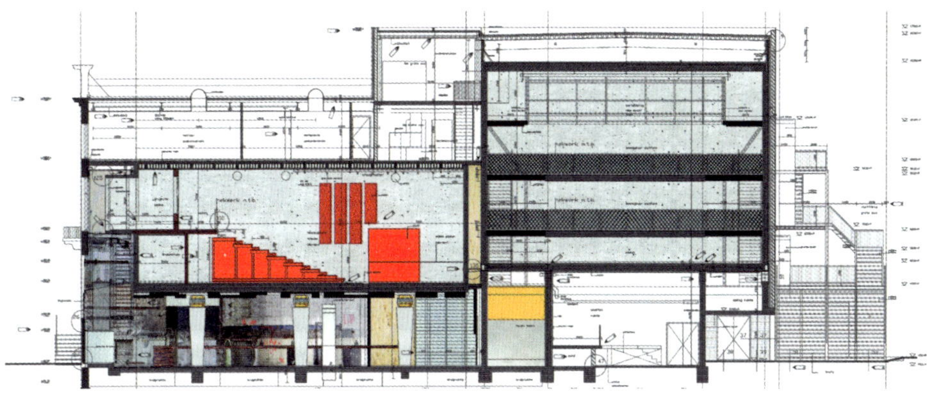

Section

JO

## UNDER CONSTRUCTION

Although they are temporary constructions, scaffolding determines a street view so often that it has become part of the permanent image of the city. This is especially true of historical inner cities where facades of buildings—just like people's faces—demand more maintenance as they become older.   But whereas with people the natural end of this ageing process is death, the view of these buildings is being preserved as if they are expected to last forever. A permanent process of transformation is taking place behind the embalmed facades from the seventeenth century, hiding the twenty-first-century interiors. A mockery of time in which the face does not age and the body is even rejuvenated.   Only at the instant of the cosmetic operation itself, the renovation, does the building synchronize with the present time. Clad in white operating sheets the scaffolding seems to give modern architecture, if only for a brief moment, a place in the historical city after all.

Scaffolding, Amsterdam,
the Netherlands
Anonymous (–)

Singel 388, Amsterdam

**GRANDIOSE DISAPPEARING ACT** Neighbouring the Royal Castle of Kronborg at Helsingør, a Danish national monument and World Heritage site, the Maritime Museum of Denmark had to comply with a wide range of heritage regulations and restrictions when it commissioned the architects of BIG to design a new building. The new museum could in no way compete for attention with Kronborg, one of the most important Renaissance castles in Northern Europe. To avoid (self-)censorship, the architects decided to go underground. In a grandiose architectural disappearing act, they turned a derelict dry dock, which had been used for large-scale shipbuilding, into a hidden world of subterranean bridges and sunken gallery spaces, which are wrapped around the dry dock at a depth of as much as eight metres below sea level. Approaching the museum, only a series of bollards and benches along the edge of the sunken dock indicates the presence of what has been created under ground. Even the handrails have been made transparent in an effort to create the illusion of invisibility.

M/S Museet for Søfart/Maritime Museum of Denmark, Helsingør, Denmark
Bjarke Ingels Group (BIG) (2013)

Diagram

M/S Maritime Museum of Denmark with Kronborg Castle in the background

→ Road leading up to Kronborg Castle

M/S Museet for Søfart/ Maritime Museum of Denmark, Helsingor, DK

Bjarke Ingels Group (BIG)
M/S Museet for Søfart/
Maritime Museum of
Denmark, Helsingør, DK

J0

## A WHITE CUBE HIDING IN A BAROQUE SPACE

The pavilion in the ballroom of Duivenvoorde Castle is the centrepiece of the exhibition that celebrates the museum's fiftieth anniversary. The Louis XIV style interior dates back to 1717 as is evidenced by the life-sized portraits of the successive generations who have lived at the castle. In addition, the museum has a collection of 131 (family) portraits which for the occasion are scanned, reproduced in black-and-white and hung on the bright-lit walls in the pavilion. Several artists are invited to bring a personal portrait and add a contemporary layer to the collection. The hexagonal shape of the pavilion is an extrusion of the central pattern in the existing broadloom carpet. The exterior of the pavilion is clad with a mirroring surface. Because of the mirroring, the interior of the baroque room becomes an even more excessive space whereby the pavilion, ballroom, visitor, and portraits visually merge into one complex image.

Portrait Pavilion,
Duivenvoorde,
the Netherlands
Studio Paulien Bremmer,
HOH Architecten (2011)

Hexagonal pavilion

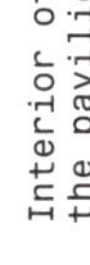

Interior of
the pavilion

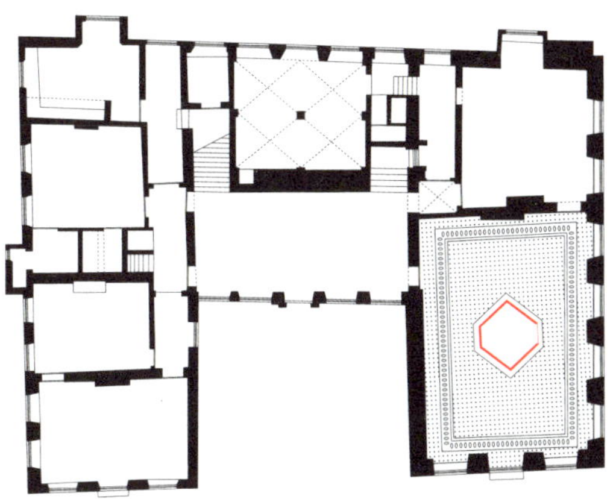

Floor plan

MvI

## GRACEFUL HIDEAWAY

The Star Apartments are a pre-fabricated and purpose-built residential housing complex that caters to the needs of the long-term homeless and mentally ill living in Los Angeles' infamous Skid Row neighbourhood, where an estimated 8,000–11,000 people are living in tents and other temporary structures. Opened in 2014, the mix-used Star Apartments include 102 small living units. Rather than levelling the site completely, an existing single-story structure was incorporated into the new design. Using prefabricated light-weight elements made it possible to lift a multi-storey building on top of the existing structure. According to the architect, one of the first things people do when living on the street is putting up makeshift walls around themselves to try to create some feeling of safety. To compensate for the limited private space and provide residents a sense of safety and belonging after years of (self-)abuse and isolation, a shielded semi-public social space was developed inside the building. The result is an urban refuge that adds a touch of grace to a rough neighbourhood and gives residents a permanent hideaway where they can re-start their lives without feeling exposed and humiliated by the compassion or contempt of others.

Star Apartments,
Los Angeles,
United States
Michael Maltzan
Architecture (2014)

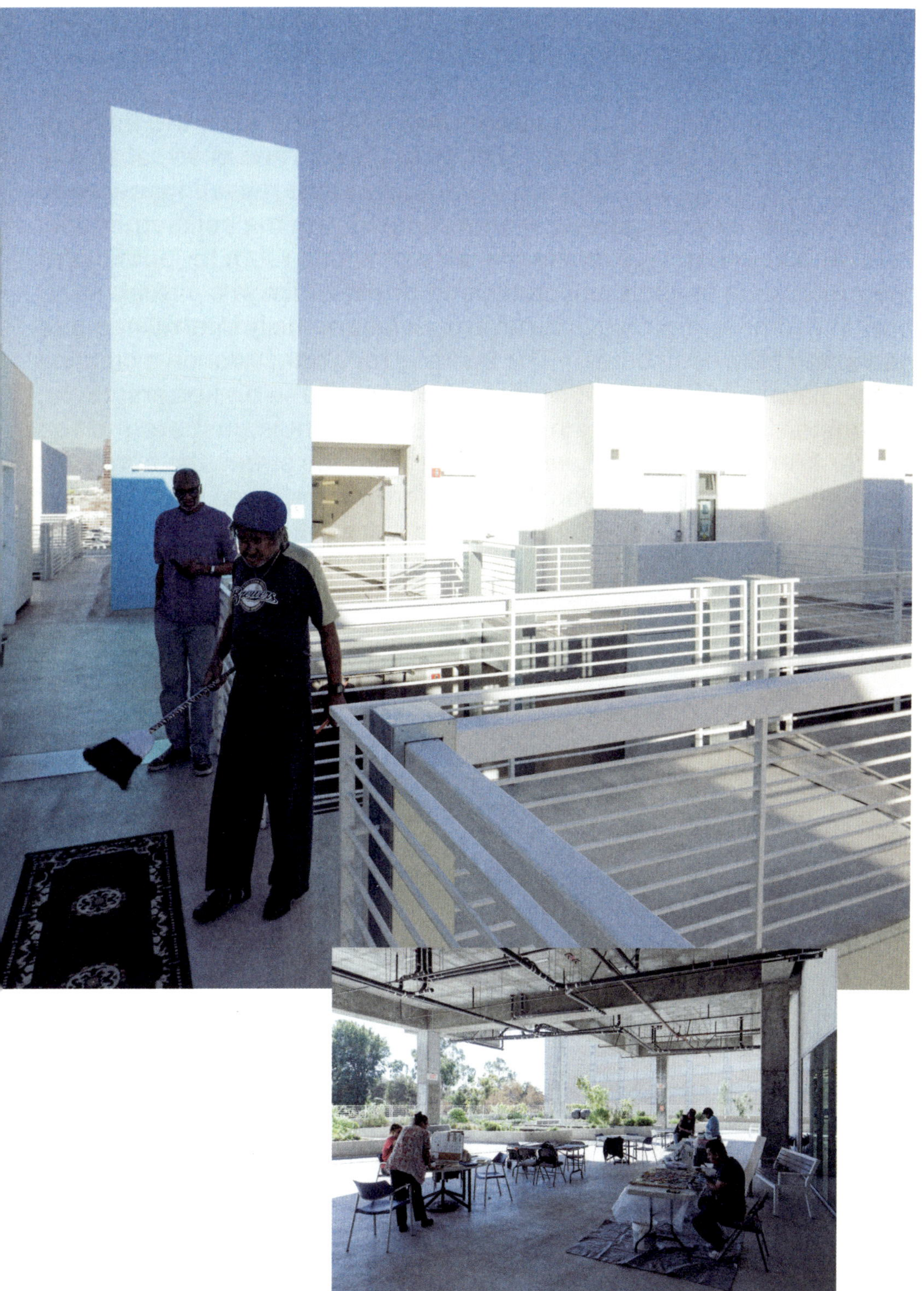

Entrance to apartment on top floor

Communal space on the first floor with public amenities.

**SPATIAL ENCRYPTION** The house for the fugitive whistle-blower Edward Snowden is a physical translation of the political themes raised by the former CIA employee when he revealed the secret and massive gathering of information about private citizens via the Internet by the American government. The virtual world and physical space, privacy and the public domain, concealing and revealing, security and transparency are given a spatial dimension in the building, which, besides being a private residence, also provides room for public programmes such as lectures, study, and debate. Like in a virtual maze, both these programme elements are simultaneously intertwined and separated from each other. The building runs right through a building block, having one facade on Herengracht and one on Keizersgracht, in Amsterdam. Whereas Anne Frank's Achterhuis, just around the corner from this location, wasn't visible from the street, the house for Snowden is there for everyone to see. Here, a safehouse is not created by hiding it physically but by encrypting it spatially.

A place to hide for Edward Snowden, Amsterdam, the Netherlands
Paul Kuipers, graduation project (2019)

Elevation Keizersgracht

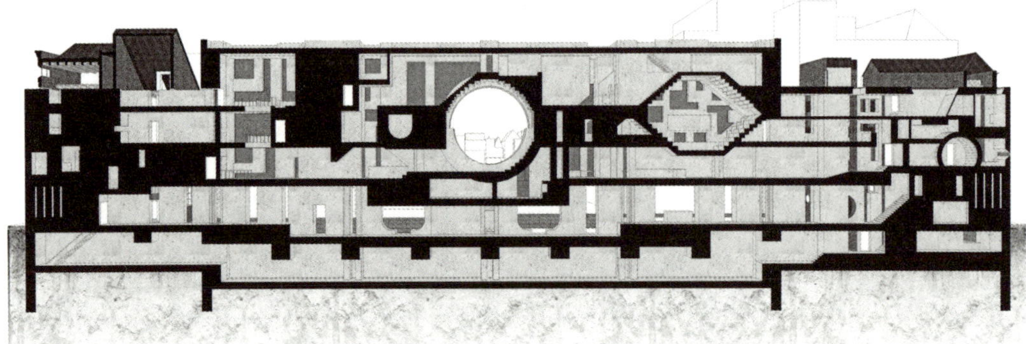

Section

A place to hide for Edward Snowden, Amsterdam, NL

# RECON-
# FIGURE—
# THE WHOLE
# AND
# ITS PARTS

LEGO
Architecture
Villa Savoye
12+
21014
3

4

FROSTA STOOL
4×
1×
3D PRINT
IKEA
5

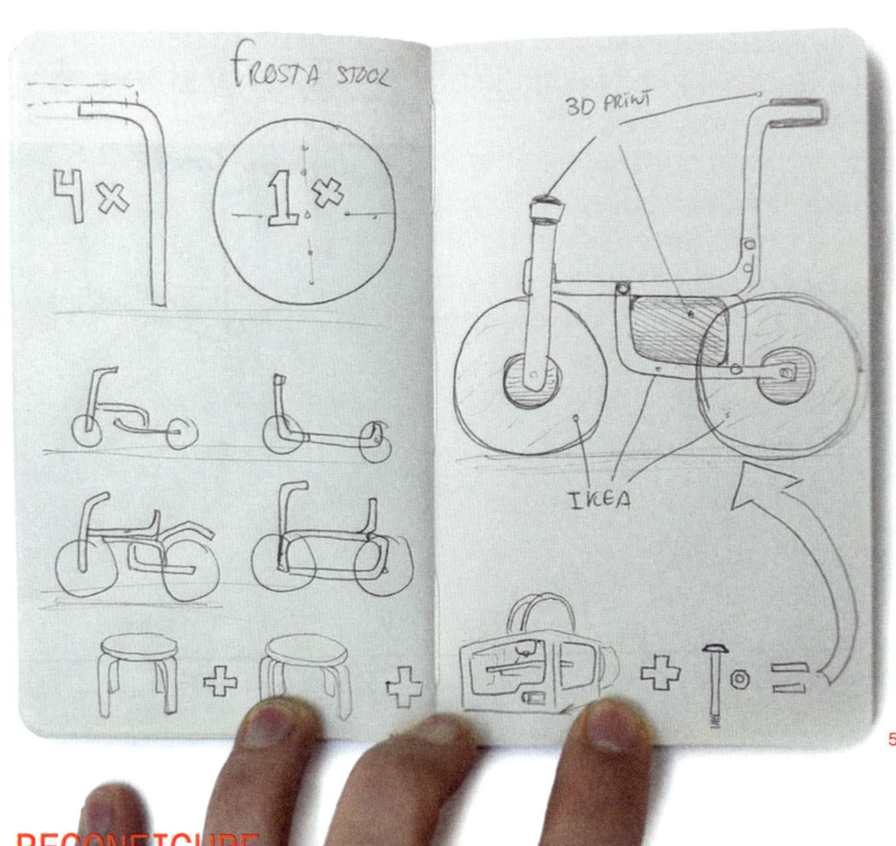

6

7

3 LEGO Architecture®
Villa Savoye
4 A sports floor
converted into
furniture
5 Andreas Bhend
and Samuel Bernler,
*Draisienne.
IKEA's stool Frosta
hacked*, 2013
6 Virgil Abloh,
*Air Jordan I
Off-White™*, 2018
7 Tejo Remy,
*Rag Chair*, 1991

8

8 Marga Weimans, *Floating Building Dress*, Wonderland Collection, 2009

# THE PERFECT DRESS—AN INTERVIEW WITH MARGA WEIMANS

Mark Minkjan, Jarrik Ouburg

Marga Weimans studied Public Administration before graduating as a fashion designer. Since her debut in 2005, she has been one of the most prominent fashion designers of the Netherlands, with high-profile international shows and exhibitions in the Groninger Museum and other venues. By definition, making clothes consists of reconfiguring existing elements, fabrics, and patterns. To this Weimans adds elements that define her personal identity as a modern woman with African roots in the Netherlands. She combines fashion with design, architecture, politics, and technology. The innovative and intelligent way in which she brings together all these elements in new configurations make her designs transcend both function and decoration. JO

MM In your work you often deconstruct existing structures or narratives in order to then reconfigure them in a new way. Can you say something about that?

MW The result of each of my collections is some form of reconfiguration. The method or thinking process is more important than the products or new configurations that I'm showing. I often try to use elements that are overlooked by most people. How can you transform an unseen spot, an untold story or an unused material into something that can exist in Paris on the level of couture? I always try to discover what more can be done in fashion. I also think about the challenges we are facing as mankind and how to work that into my practice. And then I try to show that through very personal work.

JO How do you go about that?

MW Most of the time, my work is about myself and each collection is another page in my diary. The environment or space in which my life unfolds plays an important role in this. For example, it could be Rotterdam and the narrative may be what is going on in the city and how that impacts me. In my last few collections I built the conceptual space 'Fashion House' where I tell my story as a maker. In each space of that fashion house there is something going on and that is then what a particular collection is about. For example, the space 'boardroom' is the business space of the commercial fashion house. I translate that into: fashion is a capitalist system and what is actually my business model? How do I sell? Through reflecting on the fashion trade, I started thinking about my slave past. My life's path is the direct result of the fact that we were once captured to become the means of production in a capitalist system. Especially on behalf of fashion: picking cotton, and so on. I can then make a collection, just like an architect makes a design for a building, but I can also decide *not* to make something, for a change. No product, no statement in a dress. Instead I may want to collaborate with people, make connections, and in that way weave a fabric by reaching out to others who are also concerned with identity, inclusivity, and racism. Weaving the inclusive city that provides room for migrants, refugees, people with low incomes, or people with high incomes who in fact are also victim of the capitalist system in a sense. The structure in which we work simply controls us.

'The Dress' means working on an issue and that issue is the textile that I am creating at the moment. For years I worked in a large studio, with interns and the whole caboodle. At some point I saw where society was heading, with racism and the advent of populism. I started to worry. I thought: collections are not contributing to changing things. Normally I would dress the city, place the fabric, but now I literally wanted to go into the city.

JO You want to change the body itself?

MW And the mentality, by contributing to the debate. When talking to an institute you do a project and you think about what its use is. This of course is an interesting exercise but I always think: what is actually the output? But if you link up with people who have a certain integrity and who wish to change something, then things will actually start to change.

JO And is fashion then a metaphor or do you, as a professional, have certain skills you can apply when faced with a certain question?

MW I also come from a university background, having studied Public Administration. And, if you're from Rotterdam, urban planning is part of your life from a very young age. You see how the city changes and also, I grew up in circles of urban planners—parents of children I knew were directors of urban planning with maps of Rotterdam on their walls. The subject was always Rotterdam or some newly designed neighbourhood. It's just in your DNA as Rotterdammer that there's always work being done on the city, also by the artists working here. I've done many art projects and have played in films. They were always about the city and what we wanted with it. That is also a skill or experience I bring with me.

But it's also simply thinking critically. During debates I always say: 'Guys, what are we talking about? All this stuff about inclusivity is all fine and dandy but what does it bring us?' So of course, at some point I am invited to make that critical remark, which is again a result of my experience. So, do I see fashion as a metaphor? Yes, perhaps I do: fashion is about identity. Sometimes this is the identity of the city, which I'm trying to represent or dress. Or whose complex identity I attempt to reveal.

MM Can fashion be a vehicle for that?

MW You can use it to try to make a coherent fabric of thought or social processes. That's what I'm doing now in the 'Boardroom': I study trade. And earlier I have actually always used symbols from the city in my clothes. In clothing, the city is reflected. For example, in the work *Wonderland* I worked in the image of a high-rise building that I could always see from my old studio. At the time I thought: Rotterdam-Zuid is up and coming now, but still nobody wants to come from the centre to the poorer parts around Zuidplein, where my studio was. I was showing my work in Paris but also wanted to show my own habitat from which I derive so much inspiration. So, it's a tribute but I also added another narrative about Rotterdam.

I really like fashion, high fashion and glamour, but I grew up in a punk, leftist, criticalfeminist family. And each time I see something pretty I think 'but how was it made?' and 'who suffers and who profits from it?' So, I am always deconstructing things. It's always 'yes, but…'. I can't just simply do something, I need to see the context, including the political one. It partly has to do with my background. I do see myself as a descendant of a consequence of that capitalism. I always question wealth: how is it acquired? Everything has multiple layers and shadow sides but I use the beauty of fashion, the prints and the wealth, to lure people in in Disney-like fashion. People tend to quickly think 'Wow! What a pretty dress'. And whenever I can, I then deliver the blow, ha ha.

MM One of the examples we had in mind with regard to reconfiguration in fashion is of course taking elements from elsewhere. Whether they are literally other materials or symbols from elsewhere.

MW I very much did this in the wax print project with the architects Barend Koolhaas and Aura Luz Melis. I came up with the ideas and the images and they would rework them in Photoshop by reconfiguring them and adding colours. Wax print is a printed fabric developed by the Dutch company Vlisco, which is focusing on the West African market. I did my own thing with it.

This is also how many young black creatives work, such as Virgil Abloh and the people around him. Coming from street culture they pictured themselves in Paris in the world of luxury but were not accepted there, also because there weren't any role models in those circles. What they then did was to take high fashion–'a little Helmut Lang, a bit of Raf Simons; they are my heroes I will simply copy them'. At some point they developed an autonomous language. These are fan boys thinking: 'Cool, I'll use that!' In the fashion scene this is frowned upon because things always have to be authentic and original. But if you are just outside of 'the powers that be', reconfiguring can be a good strategy to get yourself in or making yourself felt. And often you are then adopted by the powers that be because it's a very attractive attitude.

Virgil was even interviewed by Rem Koolhaas. But when Virgil starts to say something in very philosophical language to account for it all, Rem says: 'Yeah, yeah, we know all that.' There is still that undercurrent of disdain, whereas these guys are the future. Everyone's wearing sneakers, street culture is now in Paris. Rihanna has her own fashion house and make-up line. It can be very small things, such as the Nike sneakers by Virgil Abloh in which he uses these cable ties. In doing so he elevates the commonplace, the plainness. The fantasies I had about the fashion house I now see take place in reality.

This is something I could not have imagined five years ago. The fashion academy teaches you to think like that: what will people be wearing five years from now?

JO That seems puzzling to me. You have to make do with your experience and what you are seeying now, and then translate that and reconfigure it in a new way into something that will have meaning in five years' time. How do you do that?

MW I'm an information junkie and also suffer somewhat from ADHD. That helps, as you are constantly taking in large amounts of random information just to keep that brain going.

JO And what are your sources of information?

MW Nothing fancy, really. CNN, *The New York Times*, American gossip sites like TMZ. At the moment I am fascinated by weight loss. From all these articles you can glean all kinds of information about society by how they write about it.

JO Can you give an example of this, from the weight loss culture?

MW Yes, it's all very much about the 'journey' to arrive at that seventy kilos. And about not taking powders and pills, but changing your lifestyle. And you always see the same list of products: curly kale, mixed nuts, avocados, and what have you. And if you suffer from diabetes you get the same list. It's just copy-paste. Apparently, these things are good for everything. And then I think: who's behind this? These days it's 'don't look at the scales, embrace your body', that whole body-positivity vibe.

With Vincent de Rijk I made an installation for 'Boardroom' that features a naked figure in a whole field of tubes. This was no longer a dress. I felt like 'I really need to expose myself'. And this pain of racism too. I've always lived above that.

JO So, the perfect dress is transparent?

MW It's not even there, no. It's invisible.

JO Is that your ultimate goal, not to need clothes anymore to communicate your identity to others?

MW Yes, and then to enter into a relationship with each other. Also with people you disagree with. That you do not retreat into a wonder world but look each other in the eye and become truly inclusive.

... recycling boils down to downcycling while entropy and loss of value are accelerated.

P-148 Lionel Devlieger

# REVERSE ARCHITECTURE—THE VIRTUES OF UNBUILDING AND REASSEMBLING

Lionel Devlieger

Lionel Devlieger is an architect and holds a PhD in architectural history and theory from Ghent University. He has been visiting professor at Ghent University, Virginia University and TU Delft, and co-founded Rotor in 2006. Rotor is a design collective that revolves around promoting a more resource-efficient materials economy. It manifests itself through research, curatorial projects, architecture, deconstruction, and material markets. In the Belgium Pavilion at the 2010 Venice Architecture Biennale, Rotor conceived an installation on wear in architecture. In 2016 the spin-off cooperative Rotor DC (Deconstruction and Consultancy) was founded, focusing primarily on the dismantling and reuse of materials from buildings from the service industry that are slated for demolition. In this essay, Devlieger argues why dismantling and reusing salvaged building components is essential, challenging, and pleasurable. MM

For the past fourteen years, Rotor, with different tools, has been hammering the same nail: the importance of material choices in building projects. Back in 2006, when we incorporated as a non-profit organization, we stood pretty isolated–though not alone–in advocating the off-site reuse of building parts. Things have changed since. From a marginal position we moved to the centre of the stage, sometimes receiving more attention than we bargained for. What happened? Well, the arguments in favour of component reuse have gained traction within ever bigger circles. Let's rehearse them quickly. LD

First, reuse helps to reduce the amount of construction and demolition waste. The problem of waste produced by the building industry has only increased, probably due to the shortening of building lifespans. In Belgium, for instance, amounts almost doubled between 2004 and 2016 (from eleven million to almost twenty million tonnes annually, or from twenty to thirty percent of the totality of waste material produced in this country). In the Netherlands, over the same period, the amounts literally doubled (from 49 to 98 million tons, or from

53 to 69 percent of the totality of waste materials produced). Secondly, reuse avoids the production of new building materials and all related environmental impact such as greenhouse gas emissions. Here too, over the recent decades, numbers have not evolved positively (the global production of cement, for instance, more than doubled worldwide between 2000 and 2017), while the effects of climate change became ever more tangible. Thirdly, by avoiding the consumption of new materials, reuse mitigates raw material depletion and destructive extraction practices, such as the logging of tropical forests for old-growth durable wood. Apart from the resulting natural habitat loss, such practices directly contribute to climate change, as they diminish the planet's capacity for photosynthesis. Finally, and on another level, reuse creates local economic activity (ranging from the disassembly, transportation, and remanufacturing to the cleaning and marketing of these goods) that is impossible to delocalize, is less polluting and fit for urban settings: slowly taking a building apart can only happen on site, it is mostly done from the inside of the building, and requires mostly hand-tools. In Brussels, as in other metropolitan areas plagued with high unemployment numbers since the departure of the manufacturing industry, there's a growing body of opinion advocating that at least some productive economic activity involving manual labour is preserved.

Not only are these arguments beginning to stick, authorities and the public alike are starting to understand the fundamental difference between reuse and recycling. Reuse is the salvaging of components for integration in a new structure without altering them substantially. Recycling is the crushing and melting of materials in order to reintroduce them in the production chain. In many cases, such as the 'recycling' of inert waste into aggregates, recycling boils down to downcycling while entropy and loss of value are accelerated. In other cases (e.g. the recycling of metals or glass), it still requires massive amounts of energy.

This growing awareness of the benefits of building component reuse might be seen as a reason for contentment. Yet it failed, so far, to bring about any kind of revolution in the practices on the ground. Our perception is that people, even if theoretically accepting the necessity of a transition to a more circular construction industry, are convinced that the changes need to come from the realm of technology, and that only technologies that are as yet non-existent will help us out. So, all eyes are turning to engineering departments and their research labs.

With this mindset, businesses, scientists, and designers alike are now betting, for instance, on increased automation in the building industry, both during component production (standardization, pre-fabrication) and in the assembly phase on site (think robotic arms piling up neatly fitting bricks). The idea is that a more streamlined assembly will do away with the idiosyncrasies of building sites operated by humans (where each mason has his own work method) and that dismantling could be equally optimized, or even automated. Hence components should be redesigned; new and reversible assembly techniques imagined. Interoperability would be made possible through the introduction of superior system standards, to be gradually imposed on the entire industry.

This high-tech approach to the idea that a building is a bank or a temporary storage of Lego-block-like building materials, available for subsequent uses, implies that tools should be available to do the bookkeeping. Here BIM-models are supposed to do the trick. These virtual 3D models of a building, intended first and foremost to enable architects, engineers, and other consultants to co-design a complex object, are also to become detailed 3D inventories of all building parts, useful for whenever a deconstruction is planned.

Thanks to special sensors in the materials, supported by technology that still needs to be invented, not only the chemical composition, place of origin, travels, dimensions, quantity, and physical properties of every component could be monitored, but also their current condition: working properly or not, in need of oil, paint, repair, replacement, or damaged beyond repair. A never-ending stream of data, running in real time from sensor chips embedded in every single brick, would then generate and endlessly updated version of the BIM dataset, so that everything is known in advance when the deconstruction crew sets to work.

From the point of view of the technocrats, this technology and data driven transformation of the building industry to more circular standards is an engineering challenge to be solved by investing the right resources in the right place. Such an industry-wide project would start from the premise that the required standards will be set objectively and hence meet no resistance from either the public or the industry.

Unfortunately, things are not that simple. The building sector is a complex system combining tangible parts (the existing built fabric, infrastructure, quarries, excavators, brick kilns, building materials outlets, concrete pump trucks, and so on) and intangible elements (building regulations, bidding procedures, specification habits, architects' tics, client tastes, etc.). All in all, it shows enormous inertia. Also, its competitive nature is not exactly conducive to reaching consensus.

If you focus exclusively on the technological superiority of the new-to-be-developed building materials of the future, you simultaneously condemn all that was built before to obsolescence. Not only does that amount to a new form of tabula rasa, it also disregards the vast intelligence embedded in the existing built fabric. The most popular building products available on the current reuse market in Belgium are surprisingly 'old': traditional bricks and hand-carved cobblestones, mostly from the nineteenth and early twentieth century. When starting to consider buildings as material banks one cannot overlook the banks that already exist (they are by far the biggest). Following this, the nature of the building materials extracted from them will continue to impact future building practices, at least for a while.

Many of the challenges encountered by the reuse sector today are not technological but legal: procurement procedures, building material certification processes, insurance policies and other regulations were all written with the linear, not the circular economy as a backdrop. Rewriting these regulations will require skilled lawyers, not architects or engineers. Yet, within our current political system no team of experts, however competent, has the legitimacy or power to impose one certain industrial standard over others. Such unilateralism would come into direct conflict with the principles of the capitalist market economy in which we still function. Discouraging the use of certain technologies through regulation is possible if they prove to be unsafe or hazardous for humans, not just because they are wasteful.

Then there is the problem of the business models in the building industry, which are by nature catastrophically wasteful. From the point of view of component suppliers, the recipe for profit generation remains: sell as much stuff as you can. Or: make your customer/user consume as much building parts as possible. The rest is of secondary importance. Perversions such as designed obsolescence and buildings with a limited lifespan are only logical consequences. Solutions might lie in turning the model upside down, as suggested by the proponents of product-service systems. Here users pay a fixed monthly fee for a service such as lighting, instead of buying the product, i.e. the lamp.

Another complication is the clash of functionalism and human psychology. If engineers were to rationalize the use of resources in the fashion industry, we would all be wearing uniforms. Rationalizing resource use in the building industry would similarly impose standardization and uniformity beyond what most people (certainly in Belgium!) deem acceptable. It all runs counter to the deep-rooted human yearning for individuation (of persons or groups) through the objects and buildings one is closely associated with: clothes, cars, furniture... and buildings. How do we overcome these contradictory pulls?

Finally: since Fordism, we have been taught to cherish the positive effects of mass production and consumerism and to forget about its wastefulness. An early critic was Aldous Huxley, who in *Brave New World* (1932) mocked the cultural indoctrination that favours newness. Youth, in his portrait of a fictionalized totalitarian society, is put to bed with slogans such as: 'ending is better than mending' or 'the more stitches, the less riches'. These mantras of squandering have not always been there. They are successfully inculcated mental habits, but they can be undone. That might be work for philosophers, psychologists, sociologists and advertisers.

Solving the challenges of implementing circular modes of material use will require a joint and coordinated effort in which actors with a variety of backgrounds and expertise will have to play their part. It will also be a political and cultural process: institutions and people's tastes need to change. Rotor has merely tried, in its decade-and-a-half long existence, to outline the shape of these different challenges.

But what about the architects? Let us first not forget that in most cases it is the architect who decides which and how many materials will be used in the recomposed assembly that is the new project. Beyond the implications these decisions have on the project itself (in terms of economy, beauty, functionality, durability, and so on) they also have a direct impact on natural habitats, on humans and non-humans, often in remote territories. Shifting to closed loops and salvaged materials at least allows us to keep a keen eye on these environmental impacts, and possibly generate more positive outcomes.

Architects might start by gradually introducing reclaimed building components in their projects. As they are already composing collage-like assemblies of industrially produced components and systems, the change might be less radical than it seems. Looking closer, however, salvaged components carry along the history of their past use, which opens up the possibility of infusing a new register of meaning in the reassembly.

There are many inspiring examples of salvageable materials. When we found a suspended ceiling in the lobby of the former Générale de Banque building in Brussels, consisting of thousands of downward pointing lacquered sheets of metal (dubbed 'millefeuille' in French), it took us no more than a dismantling test to understand the ingenuity of the flat-pack-prone system. Despite suspended ceilings currently being unfashionable, the system elegantly incorporates all technical equipment in the plenum (piping, cabling, smoke detectors, ventilation, lighting devices) while softly filtering the light. This salvaged ceiling has been in high demand in Rotor DC's shop. There was not much left for ourselves (Rotor) to use. We therefore used it sparsely rather than wall-to-wall in our own projects, for instance as a highlight above the counter in the Dekkera bar in Forest.

For a long time, operators in the second hand building component market have been concentrating on so-called architectural antiques. That is, materials that are pre-Second World War and characteristic of traditional building typologies and techniques: carved natural stone, ancient bricks, oak beams, terra-cotta tiles, wrought iron, and so on. This preference was ushered by a market favouring 'old' things, maybe for sentimental reasons. But it was also supported by the deep-rooted conviction that industrially produced post-Second World War building materials were intrinsically less valuable and durable and hardly worth conserving. The example of the Générale de Banque ceiling demonstrates that this is not necessarily the case. There is a lot of recoverable quality to be found in buildings from the last decades of the twentieth century. But there are no generalizable rules on where or how to find it. It doesn't seem to be the job of architects either, to go and scout for it.

That is where we deem it necessary for trustworthy and accountable operators, specialized in selective deconstruction of contemporary or recent buildings to rise up and do the job. In 2016 we started Rotor DC with the ambition of being such an operator. A professional company developing expertise in scouting salvageable quality in recent buildings slated for demolition, in extracting these materials, and making them available for architects and designers to use.

From what we know, this work is a very personal thing. Every operator in the trade is bound to develop its own, idiosyncratic identity, much like a vintage clothes shop will develop its own style though the assortment of reclaimed clothes put on display. This is no different for Rotor DC. Our selection of materials and goods is the result of a kind of curating process. Three levels of constraints are guiding that process. First, for reasons of economy and space, we have to be highly picky in what we dismantle and bring back to our warehouse. We can only afford to store the best and most profitable materials–because of storage costs everything stored needs to sell at a decent enough price. Secondly, we only have access to a limited number of demolition sites. Geographically, we try to focus on Brussels and there are only so many building sites where we will be able to extract materials. And finally, our team will be attracted by certain materials, because we think they have a certain quality, because we know they are scarce (for instance marbles from already depleted quarries) or because we know they are versatile and can easily be reused. In the end it also boils down to a sense of beauty and personal taste.

Much in contrast with the high-tech circular utopias discussed above, we hope for a future of the building industry in which a wide variety of salvaged materials are made available through a finely developed network of operators active in reverse architecture. Each with their own skills, inclinations, and assortments. As such, they would be the fitting counterparts for those other professionals, architects, who are active in joining these components into new, well-balanced re-assemblies.

FROM BANK TO BAR Dekkera is a bar and shop in Brussels that specializes in local craft beer. Designed by Rotor, who work exclusively with materials salvaged from the interiors of buildings scheduled for demolition, the bar opened in a former grocer's shop in 2017. Most of the materials used in this project are high-quality construction elements salvaged from buildings under demolition in Brussels. The front part of the bar is made from a parquet floor taken from the headquarters of the Generale Bank, showing subtle traces of decades of intense use by bank employees. The ceiling, taken from the same office complex, resembles a cloud of bank notes and helps to diffuse the light more evenly. The rectangular black tiling around the base of the bar was sourced from the nearby Arts-Loi metro station, and the wood-laminate chairs from a decommissioned European Commission building. The basalt floor of the bathroom was once the facade of another office building. The use of recovered building materials reflects the owner's careful selection of mostly locally produced ingredients for his assortment of craft beer.

MvI

Dekkera, Brussels, Belgium
Rotor (2017)

Dismantling of bank's ceiling
↓ Interior of Dekkera

Rotor
Dekkera, Brussels, BE

PLAYING WITH THE WIND The blades of windmills are made of carbon or glass fibre composites and are very difficult to recycle. As wind turbines have an average lifespan somewhere between ten and twenty-five years, it seems contradictory that the sustainable—and growing—wind industry should produce an ever-increasing amount of waste. In this playground, five blades are reconfigured and their new function makes optimal use of the material's properties: it is strong, weatherproof, and ergonomic and with a diameter of 140 cm it is large enough to create staircases and places to play inside the blades. The difference in scale between children and the blades, combined with the strange fact that something that is usually cutting through the air at a height of fifty metres is now lying motionless on the ground, guarantees that the playground meets its most important criterion: stimulating children's imagination.

Playground Wikado,
Rotterdam,
the Netherlands
Superuse Studios (2008)

The spatial intervention creates different areas.

Hiding place

Playground Wikado,
Rotterdam, NL

MvI

**SPOILS OF HISTORY** On the Cycladic islands in Greece you can find numerous examples of *spolia*. The term is used in archaeology and art history to describe the reuse of elements from earlier buildings in more recent ones, most typically the reuse of Greek or Roman buildings in Early Christian or medieval structures. On the Greek island of Paros there are still a number of striking examples of marble *spolia*. In ancient times, Paros was famous for its white marble, which was mainly used to create statues and temples on the island and across the Mediterranean. In the town of Parikia there are many walls and other fragments of a tower that used to be part of a castle, which was built by the Venetians around 1260 when they occupied the island. The ruin consists of column drums of various sizes, extensive parts of a Doric architrave from a Classical temple, building blocks from an Archaic temple, and a circular building, transferred nearly in its entirety from somewhere else. Brought together in a three-dimensional jigsaw puzzle, it raises the question whether this assemblage should be considered an art piece or an act of vandalism.

Castle of Parikia /
Paros Acropolis,
Parikia, Paros, Greece
Architects unknown
(1300 BC–1200 AD)

Spolia on Paros
↓ Castle of Parikia

Detail of R[illegible] /
[illegible]os Acropolis,
Parikia, Paros, GR

RISING FROM THE RUBBLE OTOProjects is a purpose-built workshop and performance space for the experimental music venue Café OTO in East London. The building occupies a disused site in the area of Dalston and consists of a single-storey detached structure that can host a variety of live events. In all their projects Assemble wants to be resourceful and use scrap materials. OTOProjects was built by a team of sixty volunteers, who made use of the dirt and debris found on site. The earth, gravel, and rubble on the seemingly empty site was gathered, sieved, bagged, and compressed: transformed from waste into giant building blocks. Deep rubble walls were finished with a decorative 'rubble-dash' render and topped with a lightweight timber trussed roof. The filled rice bags that were used to build the supporting walls created the right acoustic properties for the programme of workshops, talks, film screenings, and temporary art installations organized by OTO. According to Alice Edgerley, a founding member of Assemble, the structure can be knocked down and all the materials can be reused or go back to the state they were in.

OTOProjects,
Dalston, London,
United Kingdom
Assemble (2011)

Rubble wall

Workshop and performance space

OTOProjects, Dalston, London, UK

J0

# A BORROWED BUILDING

The pavilion was used for presentations and as a meeting point during the Dutch Design Week. With such temporary events everyone usually focuses all their energy on the moment of the grand opening. In this case, however, that principle was radically overturned: the design had in mind the time after the grand finale, with the idea of preventing the applied materials to be degraded to waste after having been used for just a few days. All materials that were needed for the construction of the pavilion were borrowed: the piles that served as columns, a glass roof from a greenhouse builder, wooden beams, facade elements, lighting, and furniture. Because all the borrowed materials had to be returned to their owners intact, drilling, welding, gluing, or sawing was not an option. By applying a temporary way of joining using lashing straps, a very legible structure was made in which the whole was more than the sum of its parts.

People's Pavilion,
Eindhoven,
the Netherlands
Bureau SLA (2017)

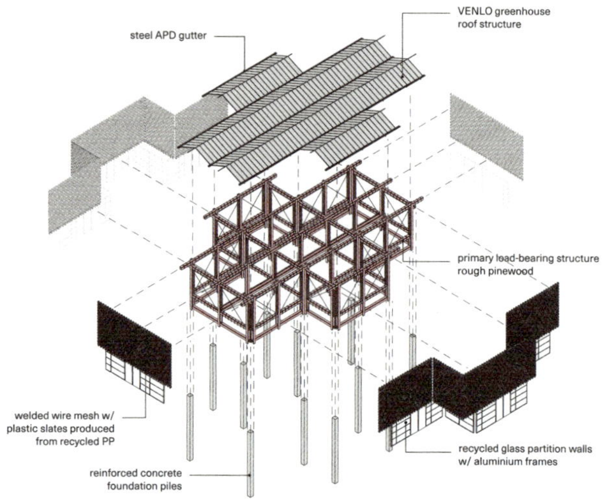


Diagram assemblage

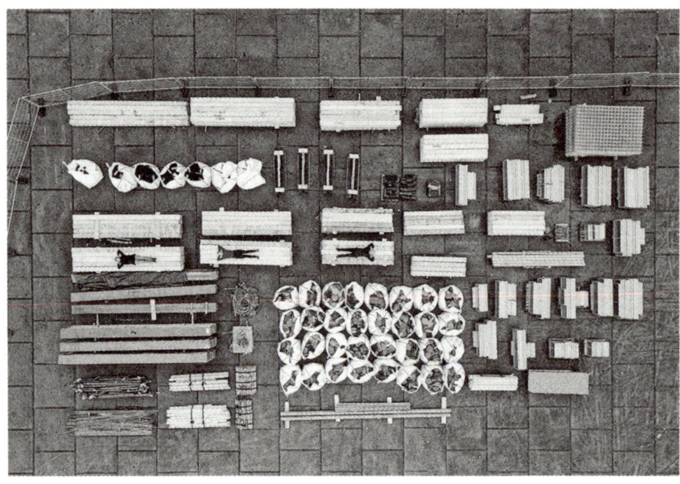

Building materials

Steel straps hold together wooden beams. ↓ Plastic tiles cover the upper facade

People's Pavilion, Eindhoven, NL

Bureau SLA
People's Pavilion,
Eindhoven, NL

MvI

## CONCRETE CONSOLATION

French artist Cyprien Gaillard often juxtaposes architectural elements from different epochs to reflect on and rewrite history, with an emphasis on the socialist experiments of the twentieth century. He combines sculptures, videos, engravings, photographs, and interventions in public space to tell the story of the rise and fall of utopian urbanism and to revisit and rehabilitate certain modernist icons and ruins. For his sculpture *Cenotaph to 12 Riverford Road, Pollokshaws, Glasgow* (1967–2008) he salvaged fifteen tonnes of concrete from the remains of a demolished social housing project. The rubble was brought to London, cast into a four-metre high classic obelisk and put on public display. It became the first of Gaillard's 'monuments to dead buildings'. In the same year he used the crushed concrete remains of a tower block from Issy-les-Moulineaux, a suburb of Paris, to pave the path leading to Château d'Oiron, a majestic Renaissance building in the west of France. In this work, called *La grande allée du Château d'Oiron* (2008), the artist applied the same strategy, merging vandalism with alchemy, to create beauty from decay and turn a trauma into concrete consolation.

Various projects
Cyprien Gaillard
(1967–2008)

Path made from recycled concrete at Château d'Oiron

Sighthill Cemetery
with ruin of
12 Riverford Road,
Glasgow

Cenotaph to
12 Riverford Road,
Pollokshaws, Glasgow

J0

ROOMSERVICE A restaurant is located on the ground floor of a hotel in Amsterdam that is being refurbished. During the renovation the restaurant moves to the adjacent St Olof's Chapel, one of the oldest chapels in the city. Hotel room furniture that became available during the renovation was used to transform the monumental space of the chapel into more intimate dining rooms, imitating the former hotel rooms and turning the restaurant into one big room service. On the ground floor one dines in a surreal world among identical mini bars, nightstands, hanging mirrors, and curtains with the chapel as a backdrop. On the mezzanine level a cocktail bar is located where the guests can oversee the maze of rooms.

Roomservice, Amsterdam, the Netherlands
HOH Architecten (2016)

Available hotel room furniture

Overview of maze

SHUFFLE IN SPACE   Land readjustent is the re-parcelling of land in which land owners swap pieces of land. In Europe and North America, the system is often used to form larger, continuous agricultural fields in order to improve productivity. In Asia it is applied specially to reconfigure irregularly parcelled agricultural land into rational building lots. In Japan, for instance, this type of bottom-up urban planning accounts for thirty percent of the urban area and is called 'The Mother of City Planning'.   In a city like Tokyo the urban area itself is also further developed via this spatial exchange, but in the third dimension, and in addition to land owners, the property owners, tenants and subtenants are stakeholders too. More than five hundred stakeholders were involved in the transformation of a suburban neighbourhood into the 724,000 m² mega complex of Roppongi Hills, featuring a 54-storey office tower, apartments, shops, restaurants, a hotel, and a museum. It took fourteen years to—financially—persuade everyone involved to participate and eighty percent of residents opted for living in a new apartment in the new plan. Although the project aimed at reproducing the characteristic small-scale intimacy of the original neighbourhood, this quality turned out to be not easily scalable.

JO

Land Readjustment
System, Europe,
United States, Japan

Ad agricultural reform, 1946

Roppongi Hills before redevelopment, 1997
← Roppongi Hills after redevelopment, 2004

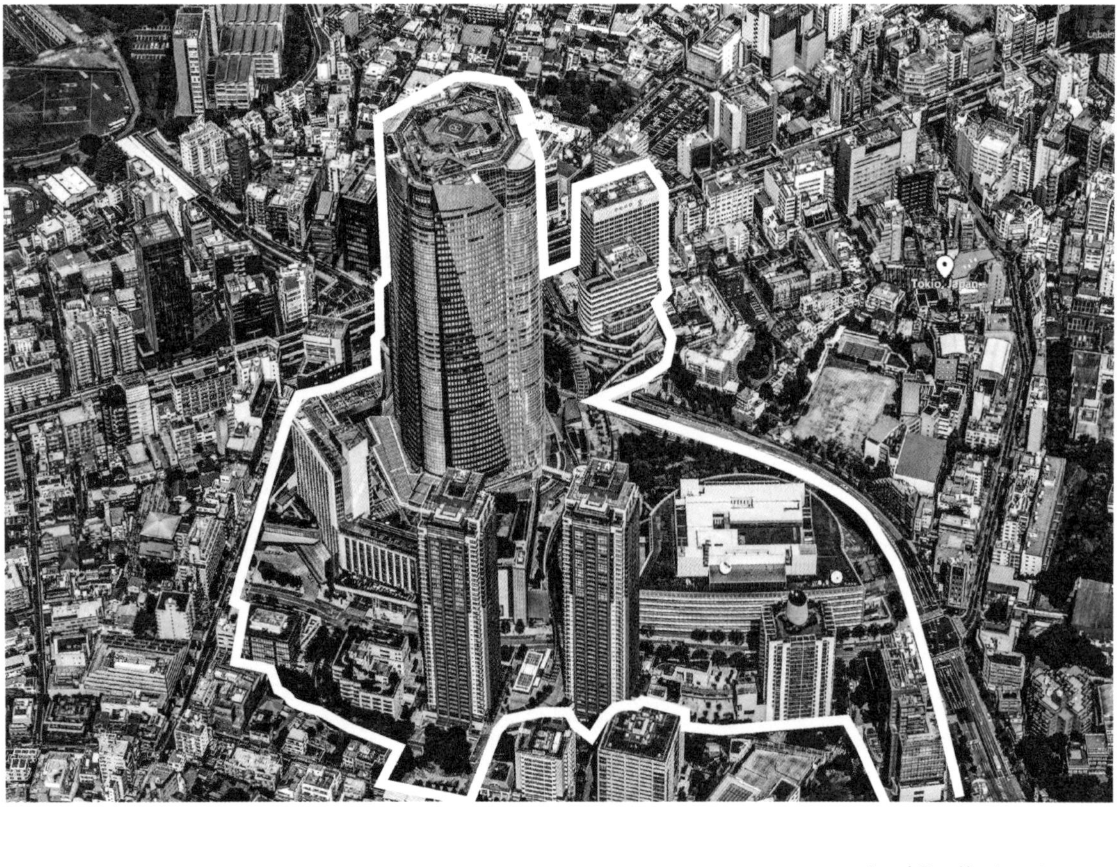

# REPURPOSE —FROM THE INSIDE OUT

3

4

3 Since the 1970s, skateboarders have been using empty swimming pools
4 A satin bowerbird uses plastic bottle caps to decorate its nest
5 Interior of Landbouwbelang, a squatted industrial complex in Maastricht, the Netherlands
6 The yellow vests movement, known as the ‘Mouvement des gilets jaunes’ in French, is a populist, grassroots protest movement for economic justice that began in France in October 2018. Normally used by emergency services and road workers, protesters started wearing the yellow vests because of their high visibility and association with the working class.

5

6

7

8

7 Steel drum band, Barbados, 1970
8 Large water bottle employed as gas mask, Cairo, 2013

# THE ARCHITECTURE OF SQUATTING

René Boer

René Boer works as a curator, critic, and researcher in the fields of architecture, urbanism, heritage, and art. He is part of the Amsterdam-based Non-fiction collective, managing editor at Failed Architecture and involved in various urban social movements. He recently published Architecture of Appropriation with Het Nieuwe Instituut and curated the exhibition 'The Right to Build' at Amsterdam's Architecture Centre. He is building a network of 'Grounded Urban Practices' with the Cairo-based CLUSTER studio, and is involved in the research collaboration 'Contemporary Commoning' together with the Gerrit Rietveld Academie, the Waag Society, and others. In this essay, René Boer traces the spatial practice of squatting as it emerged in contemporary Western culture over the last forty years. In the immediate architecture resulting from this spatial practice, the end user also takes on the traditional roles of 'client', 'designer', and 'contractor'. These roles also coincide in time: from the very first moment, living, designing, constructing, and reconstructing take place simultaneously, resulting in a most direct relationship between users and architecture. MM

Throughout history, the well-to-do have favoured the construction of new buildings over reusing structures abandoned by a previous generation. Erecting new buildings according to the latest fashion, or even introducing new styles and symbolism, have always been important tools in communicating a founder's wealth and power. This fetish for the new has dominated architectural practice well into the twentieth century, as Modernism's tenets continued to strictly prescribe tabula rasa developments. Only in recent decades has there been a gradual shift in which the well-to-do are developing a growing interest in repurposing the remnants of the past. From the 1980s onwards, real estate developers started to transform industrial heritage into loft apartments, while large cultural institutions and the like also began to understand the potential of re-using such spaces. RB

Repurposing existing buildings wasn't a totally new phenomenon however. In many countries, society's poorest never had any choice but reusing the spatial leftovers of others, often by making structures inhabitable that weren't originally meant for living in.

The most direct source of inspiration for contemporary (and often commercial) forms of 'adaptive re-use' dates from the mid-1960s. With the rise of countercultural movements, youngsters in European and American cities started to experiment with giving derelict buildings radical new functions, by converting churches into nightclubs and schools into housing. They sometimes initiated their projects out of necessity, but increasingly also out of appreciation for the irregular, spontaneous, and poetic forms that can result from repurposing urban and architectural spaces.

These experiments preceded the advent of a global, often clearly politically motivated squatting movement, which specialized in occupying and repurposing properties without the permission of the owner. Within a short period of time, squatting became a well-known and visible phenomenon in large cities such as Berlin, London, and New York, but it also took root in smaller cities and even rural communities. Local squatting movements have initiated some famous, early examples of bottom-up redevelopments, such as the transformation of Copenhagen's military barracks into the Freetown Christiania commune, and they continue to fuel new experimental transformations to this day.

The squatting movement in the Netherlands is particularly interesting, as it has over time developed a set of institutions, protocols, and rituals, such as weekly consultations, squatting manuals, and specific methods to research vacant properties. These tools were made available to any group who wished to collectively take over space and repurpose it according to their needs and desires. By doing so, squatting from the 1980s onwards has increasingly become a widely accessible, 'open source' spatial practice, allowing many to experiment with their own visions of bottom-up transformation.

For decades, squatting a property that stood empty for more than one year was legal in the Netherlands, which has been crucial in mainstreaming the phenomenon.

Throughout this period, applying this open-source spatial practice according to your own ideas was a normal way to house oneself and realize other social, economic, and cultural programmes, resulting in thousands of squatted properties during the movement's heyday in the 1980s. The 2010 criminalization of squatting has made it considerably less common, although some complex legal procedures have allowed for its limited continuation. In Amsterdam, a movement of homeless refugees is just one of the many groups who continue to use the tools of this spatial practice today.

Squatting has also been important for the broader normalization of adaptive reuse, by familiarizing many with the possible outcomes of unexpected transformations. Over time, it has also been a key source of inspiration for the development of various alternative (but closely related) tactics and methods. In the 1990s, organizers of raves would scan for suitable locations and make deals with owners for weekend-long parties, while over the last decade a new kind of socially inclined organizations have started to lease abandoned office buildings to temporarily transform them into affordable artist studios. Together with individuals buying atypical structures to transform and inhabit them, all these diverse tactics represent an avant-garde movement that has, in more recent times, been extensively copied and sanitized by the conventional real estate sector.

While real estate developers tend to retain control of the entire transformation before allowing the user in at the very end, bottom-up repurposing generally starts with the (future) user gaining access to a new space. In most instances, squatters breaking down a door or a new group of temporary occupants arriving on the scene don't know what to expect inside. Without the opportunity to make a comprehensive plan, they often have to install themselves in the very first spaces they encounter. These spaces are immediately used and inhabited and from there interventions in the rest of the place can be coordinated. Funds for a comprehensive makeover are mostly lacking, which often results in a gradual transformation and using found or recycled materials. As the place is already taken in use while being repurposed, lessons learned at an earlier stage might inform later developments. In any case, people experiencing the simultaneous habitation and transformation tend to develop a strong bond with such spaces, as their way of life over time materializes in the emerging architecture.

This gradual, grounded transformation process results in very specific spatial qualities, including a certain unexpectedness, a sense of spontaneity and authenticity. Spaces often retain traces from their past and remain in constant flux, while their uses are generally not specifically prescribed by the new occupants. At the same time, the original typology often comes with a set of spaces that are hard to translate one-to-one to the new setting, resulting in leftover rooms and in-between voids. The impossibility to reach 'full efficiency' in such a transformation adds a certain breathing space stimulating one's imagination of how it might further transform in the future. These qualities are the particular result of the conditions created by a low-cost, gradual, and open-ended redevelopment carried out by the users themselves. They are difficult to achieve using conventional design methods characterized by stricter timeframes and fixed visions.

Squatting, rather than legal forms of adaptive reuse, inevitably comes with the underlying condition of a constant eviction threat on either the short or long term. This situation gives all spaces an immediate sense of urgency. It both emotionally charges and strongly politicizes any physical intervention. Something that has been constructed today, may be gone tomorrow. Additionally, the ideological preference for collectivity is sometimes translated into the creation of public spaces and amenities, such as neighbourhood gardens or free shops. This results in a certain porosity in the boundaries with the surrounding environment, allowing other people to enter and take ownership of these spaces.

Part of the Dutch squatting movement has over time sought to 'regularize' their squats by officially renting, leasing, or buying the property from the owner. The addition of this specific tactic to the squatter toolbox was often met with opposition by the more radical fractions of the movement, who rejected the notion of property in its entirety. A 'legalization' of a specific squat would take the immediate threat of eviction away, but at the same time introduce a process of normalization. Having to meet building regulations and monthly payments, and being able to plan for the years ahead creates a radically different relation to a space. Over the last decades, hundreds if not thousands of squats have been legalized in the Netherlands, and still exist today as collective housing arrangements or cultural venues.

The architectures that emerge as a result of repurposing spaces bottom-up, from scratch and with the users on-site are unique. Conventional real estate developers have tried to mimic such spaces extensively, for instance by copying the aesthetics that are otherwise the result of years of collective labour, and use them in the commercial transformation of existing buildings into housing or hotels. While knock-offs might sell, it has proven impossible to simply emulate the particular spatial qualities of gradual, bottom-up redevelopment.

Rather than appropriating the tactics, ideas, and aesthetics of social movements, cultural entrepreneurs, and visionary individuals for commercial ends, architects and other spatial professionals should use their professional expertise to support emergent developments where needed. This could take the form of proposing and stimulating bottom-up, open-ended, and gradual transformations in adaptive reuse projects in which they have the lead. It could also mean lending political support to self-initiated appropriations even if they are against the law, and offering affordable, professional advice to such projects where needed. By doing so, they will continue to make it possible for people from all walks of life to repurpose the spatial remnants of the past according to their hearts' desires.

# DESIGN IN DIALOGUE

Freek Persyn

Freek Persyn is an architect and founding partner of the Brussels-based practice 51N4E and Full Professor of Architecture and Urban Transformation at ETH Zurich. Since its founding in 1998, 51N4E have done multiple repurposing projects in various countries. In this article, Persyn describes the design approach behind a shared cultural space inside the repurposed submarine base of Saint-Nazaire on the French west coast. The aim of the process was to shape a narrative together with future users, from which the architecture followed. By doing so, the potential meaning and spatial possibilities of the place were revealed. The proposal also enables further appropriations in the future. MM

Built by the Nazis during the Second World War, the submarine base of Saint-Nazaire was the only building left standing after the whole city had been flattened. The base is monumental, but not a monument. It is still standing there, not because people like it but because it is almost impossible to destroy. After the war, the limited resources were used to rebuild what the city really needed, rather than to destroy what it didn't. As a result, the submarine base was left standing, in all its bulky oppression. A long, deep and high structure, with very thick walls of more than two metres at the base and close to eight metres for the roof. FP

Repurposing this building was never a desire, or even a choice. It had simply become unavoidable. After Saint-Nazaire's centre had been rebuilt, the moment had come to deal with the rotting corpse of a building in its midst, right between the city centre and its port. Unlike other such bases along the Atlantic, like the one in Bordeaux, the base of Saint-Nazaire could not be ignored: it was too central, too close by. Facing this challenge required imagination and courage, and that is exactly what Joël Batteux (the then mayor of Saint-Nazaire) and the Spanish urban designer Manuel de Solà-Morales have shown. Their idea was to see the base as an artefact that could become a public destination by making sparse openings and giving access to the roof to allow incredible views on both the Loire estuary and the Atlantic Ocean. The interventions of Solà-Morales were limited and that is precisely where their strength lies. In a most delicate way, a public route has been carved through and over this mountain of concrete, turning it into a public experience and making its interior accessible by opening up a few large but unobtrusive holes in the facade.

With these openings the structure of the building was exposed in all its banal simplicity: a row of long and narrow rooms built for submarine boats to dock and be protected. A series of slots, as generic as any other parking garage or industrial allotment, basic in form but dramatic in scale. Being exposed, the simplicity of the allotment took over and the slots were made available to the city. One by one, programmes have been fitted in those very slots, organized by the logistical internal street and loosely connected by a theme of tourism and culture including an experience centre for transatlantic travel, an experimental art space, and a music club. Step by step, a cultural programme was invented for or reassigned to the base.

The question we got involved in was to relocate a multi-purpose hall for local cultural initiatives. Think bingo nights, tango events, large-scale dinner parties, concerts by the local music academy, fairs, cabaret, and so on. If even we had difficulties understanding how to bring together such a diverse programme in the submarine base, imagine the people that make up all of these cultural initiatives—how would they feel about having to move into the most glaringly neglected part of town? They are people from a city with a largely working-class culture, not specifically intrigued by the romantic drama of decay that the base is conveying. It was evident that it was not to be taken for granted, despite the fact that we ourselves were clearly being drawn by the drama of the place.

Inspired by that tension we presented not a project, but an approach: to design in dialogue. This approach meant that we did not start by talking about architecture, but to try and envision how the base could be used, and why. The question we asked ourselves was: how could occupying the base become appealing? This approach got us selected, and we entered a process where nothing was to be taken for granted, not even the assumption that they really wanted to do this.

'They', it turned out to be, were a loose faction of administrators and third-party service providers, a mayor at the end of his mandate and his future replacement, some local politicians, one or two experts, a representative sample of the associations and the future users, and a noble, almost retired project manager. What held them together was a certain ambition to make something of their city, and to take care of the people living in it. What we did as a group was to talk about that ambition and how the project at hand could be of added value on multiple levels. It could strengthen the base as a destination and turn it into a real cultural infrastructure where the different parts would benefit from each other's presence and proximity. We imagined common facilities and talked tirelessly about pragmatic issues such as water infiltration, corrosion from the sea salt, and fire escape schemes. We invited the group to come and visit other cultural facilities, in Belgium, ranging from the socialist people's palace Vooruit in Ghent to C-Mine in Genk, the repurposing of former mining facilities we designed ourselves. It made them, and us, see how a building can shape a culture and contribute to the welfare as well as the pride of local citizens.

A diverse palette of tools was used in the design approach, which allowed us to look beyond the building and the project's perimeter in a double movement of both zooming out and zooming in. Zooming out, we created a new discourse, clarifying and naming the different ambitions and scales that this intervention would have an impact on. Terms and words were formulated for the project, structuring how the various parties involved talked with each other. An urban reality drawing of the city was created to evaluate the urban impact of the project. The drawing allowed everyone to see the intervention in relation to the other venues that were already in place, and discuss how all of them would work together. Beyond the perimeter of the base, the drawing showed how future routes could go, and how the big dock on which the base is sitting could transform into a port facility that was also a public space. We reframed and redrew this drawing gradually, meeting by meeting, to highlight the ongoing projects and future ambitions of the city and its port. The representation of the project's impact gradually grew by simultaneously projecting and analyzing, and it was literally visible to all, in a process of reading and writing at once.

Zooming in, we made models that allowed us to get close to the future action and envision various scenarios of use. Very simple models allowed the future users to test and discuss how the layout of the space would work for different occasions. We could stand by and watch them imagining things and play around, almost like in a children's game. Overhearing these discussions, for example, led us to propose not one single entrance, but seven possible entryways. Another example of how these dialogues steered the design: to make the space not only suitable for large programming on weekends, but also for smaller gatherings during the week, we designed a large, mobile, soundproof screen that can be lowered from the ceiling in one single sweep. This makes it possible to separate a fraction of the space and activate the basin on a daily basis. By looking closely, the interventions became very precise, and were evaluated based on the real difference they would bring to the future experience.

Not once did anyone ask where the architecture was. The architectural proposal emerged in the relation between the city and the users. Quite naturally, the imagination shifted towards the way they would use things, where the sunlight would shine, but also what kind of city they would like to inhabit in the future, and how this project could help them move in that direction. Interesting discussions on how much the city administration should control or intervene, how much the associations could organize and appropriate themselves, are concrete examples on what a welfare state should be. In the social welfare state of the postwar years, people were taking care of but somehow also patronized. Discussions on self-organization and autonomy of future users reflect a larger shift this working-class city is grappling with. Another discussion was the relation to the port: should it remain productive or become touristic? This paved the way for a different understanding of what the facades of the building could be, belonging to the port as well as to the city. These open discussions were framing the future, not as a decisive choice but as a growing common awareness.

By challenging all people involved, but also by simply helping them describe what it means for them to spend their money —on what, and why—we had managed to shift the occupation of the base from an industrial allotment to an indoor urban district. A place where things don't stand coldly together, but where they activate each other as well as the public space between and around them. Rather than seeing the building as an object inserted inside the base, we developed a device offering potentials, an infrastructure activating a broad range of possibilities for various future uses and users. This is an interpretation of sustainability in architecture that is largely overlooked or forgotten: beyond material sustainability, we aimed for a spatial configuration that generates resilience and openness in the way it can be used by current and future generations of users.

We did not change the base but the perception of it, by focusing on the discourse and the use. Beyond repurposing, we made the future users appropriate the base and imagine the potential it offers. This is a work that is as much about understanding and revealing as it is about drafting a proposal. It requires tools and a process that develops a spatial solution as well as a commonly shared narrative. It is about creating trust and inviting people to exceed their initial expectations. Key to that process is showing how the infrastructure could be so much more than what was initially asked for. The strength of this common process of reframing is that the result gains in rootedness and potential. By designing in dialogue, we were able to verify the design from many different viewpoints. We have tried not to cater to every specific demand separately but to develop a framework that translates these inputs with a semantic openness: a spatial configuration that anchors the building into the site and is not predestined for one single type of use. Through the process, we have imagined a building beyond its initial use, able to respond to an open and unpredictable future.

**BINGO IN A BUNKER** During the Second World War, the occupying forces built a large fortified submarine base in Saint-Nazaire, on the French Atlantic coast. When the city was flattened towards the end of the war, the concrete submarine base—measuring 295 × 130 m—was one of the last remaining buildings. Demolition of the base was considered several times, but this idea was finally abandoned because of the sheer size of the building and the high demolition costs. Gradually, the building started to host various functions: a restaurant, a space for public gatherings, an centre for experiencing (former) transatlantic travel, a roof garden, a concert hall, and a venue for experimental art. The architects of 51N4E and their collaborators were commissioned to conceptualize and design the rehabilitation of units 12 and 13 of the bunker that could provide space and facilities for both existing and new activities. The final design, for which the architects consulted many members of the local community, is a deliberately simple project. It functions more as an urban district or piece of infrastructure than as a single building, providing a surplus of space instead of a predefined programme and offering a broad range of possibilities for various future users. The architecture of the project is very basic, adding simple elements while exposing traces of the tumultuous past, while connecting the space to the context of the bunker and to the local community.

MvI

Les Alveoles, Saint-Nazaire, France
51N4E in collaboration with Bourbouze & Graindorge (2013–2018)

The former submarine base of Sainte-Nazaire

Fragment of urban reality drawing
↓ Exterior of the Jacques Brel Festival Hall

51N4E icw
Bourbouze & Graindorge
Les Alvéoles,
Saint-Nazaire, FR

**A CITY, A MUSEUM** In the summer of 1986, the Ghent Museum of Contemporary Art, now S.M.A.K., did not have its own building but it did have a pioneering curator. Jan Hoet called upon the citizens of Ghent to open up their houses for the exhibition 'Chambres d'Amis' (Rooms of Friends). He then invited 51 international artists, including Sol LeWitt, Daniel Buren, Dan Graham, and Mario and Marisa Merz to each create a site-specific work for one apartment. Hoet's criterion for selecting the artists was: 'They had to work with space, be able to deal with space.' Walls became works of art, living rooms became studios, gardens became exhibition spaces and the city itself became the museum.

'Chambres d'Amis',
Ghent, Belgium
Jan Hoet (21 June–
21 September 1986)

Daniel Buren, *Le Décor et son Double*, home of Annick and Anton Herbert, Ghent, 1986

JO

**A NATURAL ALTERNATIVE** Banker Dirk Scheringa commissions architect Herman Zeinstra to design the Scheringa Museum of Realism. With the financial crisis, the banker goes bankrupt in 2009. Construction of the building, eighty percent finished, is put on hold and the art collection is sold. What remains is a surreal spectacle; a large, empty museum building in the middle of agricultural countryside. The proposed transformation of the building starts with opening it up to the elements: air, light, and moisture. Careful openings and tears are made in the construction for plants to colonize, in order to stimulate and manage the process of constructional decay. Over a period of fifty years, the building will gradually transform into an ecological haven for plants and animals that are threatened by intensive agriculture in the surrounding area. By being a place for both decay and growth, both life and transience, the building will become a true Museum of Realism after all.

Second Nature, Opmeer, the Netherlands
Hannah Schubert, graduation project (2015)

Existing exterior

Interventions

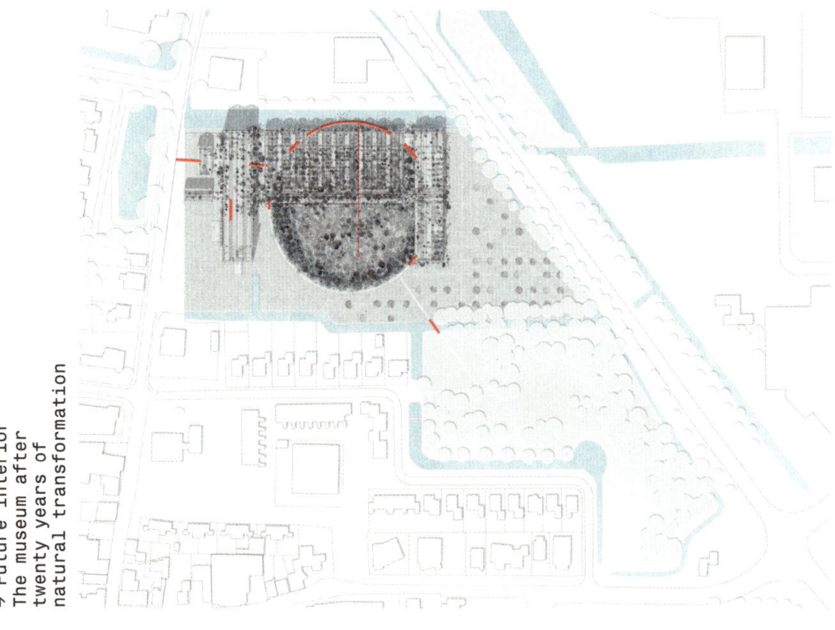

→ Future interior
The museum after
twenty years of
natural transformation

Hannah Schubert
Second Nature,
Opmeer, NL

**CHURCH, MOSQUE, MUSEUM, ...** The Hagia Sophia was constructed 1,500 years ago at the orders of Byzantine emperor Justinian. During the first millennium, the building served as an Orthodox Christian cathedral. It became an important site of Muslim worship after Sultan Mehmed II conquered Constantinople in 1453, renaming the capital city Istanbul and designating the Hagia Sophia a mosque. In the 1930s, Kemal Atatürk, the founding father of modern Turkey, ordered to turn the building into a museum, as a symbol of the secular republic that replaced the Ottoman Empire. However, the decoration on the exterior walls remained a blend of Islamic motifs and symbols of Christianity. And now, almost ninety years later, another political leader is eying the building. Ever since President Recep Tayyip Erdogan started promoting a more prominent role for Islam in Turkey, there have been calls to convert the historic structure back into a practicing mosque. In a recent appearance on national television he officially declared that 'Hagia Sophia will no longer be called a museum. Its status will change. We will call it a mosque.'

Hagia Sophia,
Istanbul, Turkey
Isidore of Miletus
(532–537 AD)

Islamic motifs painted on top of a Christian cross on the ceiling of Hagia Sophia

**UMWERTUNG ALLER WERTE (THE REVALUATION OF ALL VALUES) – FRIEDRICH NIETZSCHE** Between the two World Wars, Germany built an impressive industrial culture. In that era, two architects, Schupp and Kremmer—both students of Mies van der Rohe—designed the Zeche Zollverein: a coalmine with emphatically architectural allure, radiating not just functionality but also pride. When the mines closed in 1985, decay set in. However, demolition plans evoked such a strong feeling of loss that, in a reverse movement, the entire complex was listed and eventually even classified as world cultural heritage. OMA created a masterplan for reusing the old industrial buildings and also designed the visitor centre and museum in the former Kohlenwäsche. An exercise in the art of the most minimal intervention; clearly recognizable escalators are the only intervention to give the former industrial building a new meaning and identity.

Zeche Zollverein,
Essen, Germany
OMA/Floris Alkemade
Partner, Heinrich Böll
Architekt (2001–2007)

Aerial view, 1933

Zollverein in 2002

Zeche Zollverein,
Essen, DE

↑ Staircase
Coal conveyor and
new escalator

+40.15
Visitor Centre / Office

+37.30
Restaurant

+30.30
Visitor Centre / Exhibition

+24.30
Visitor Centre / Exhibition

+31.30
Education

+17.30
Exhibition

+11.30
Exhibition / Library

+06.30
Preparation / Studios /
Depot / Exhibition

+00.00
Metaform

-05.00
Exhibition / Depot (optionally )

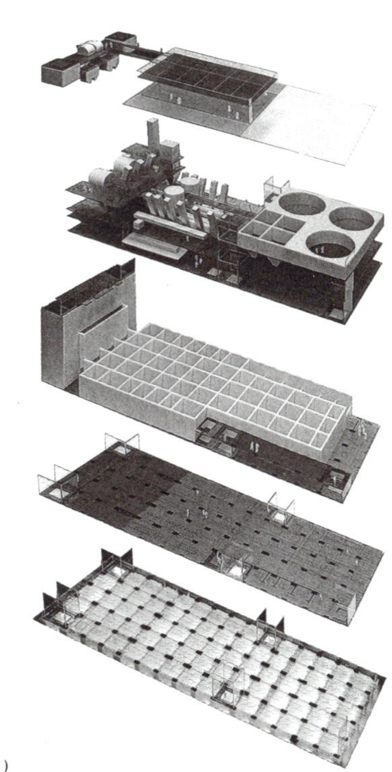

OMA/Floris Alkemade Partner,
Heinrich Böll Architekt
Zeche Zollverein, Essen, DE

J0

MIND THE GAP The Tussen-ruimte (Dutch for in-between space) project stimulates new activities and use in the otherwise conservative canal area of Amsterdam, a UNESCO World Heritage site. The project does not focus on the buildings itself because those are subject to strict regulations. Instead it focuses on the 56 small spaces found between those buildings, which were historically used as back alleys or access to a stable but have nowadays lost their function. As a network, these small spaces have the potential to introduce a different kind of architecture, use, and users to the rich history of change in the canal area. The first intervention focused on the smallest Tussen-ruimte: ninety cm wide, ten metres deep and twelve metres high, on Herengracht. Fifty perforated curtains that vary in length were hung between the two neighbouring houses in order to enclose a small space. The space functioned as a small public retreat to escape from the hectic city life on the canals.

Tussen-ruimte,
Amsterdam,
the Netherlands
HOH Architecten /
Non-fiction (2013)

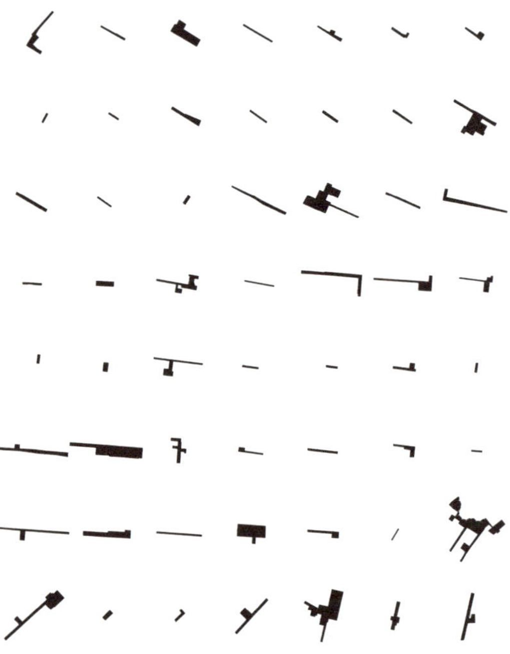

The plans of 56 mapped spaces

Exterior of the first intervention

Section of the
first intervention

Tussen-ruimte,
Amsterdam, NL

MvI

## THE ART OF FRAMING

In the Belgian city of Ghent, a 160-metre-long complex of concrete storage pits along the Handelsdok canal was earmarked as a new public space. The so-called 'Grindbakken' were formerly used to transfer sand and gravel between ships and lorries, but were cleaned up and painted white to create space for events and exhibitions. When the team of Rotor visited the site before the makeover, they were struck by the graphic quality of certain elements in the concrete structure: the colour gradients, traces of use, graffiti, weeds, the omnipresence of iron oxides and the freshly made holes and cuts in the walls. They decided to interfere in the whitewashing process. After selecting and documenting the most interesting sections of the wall, plastic-covered frames were put in place to prevent these sections from being painted over and become lost during the cleaning operation. Instead, the freshly painted walls turned the Grindbakken into an outdoor art gallery, accentuating the untouched and often overlooked traces of industrial activity and the colourful graffiti.

Grindbakken, Dok Noord,
Ghent, Belgium
Rotor (2012)

Plastic-covered frames

Detail of Grindbakken
↓ Grindbakken from above

Grindbakken, Dok Noord,
Ghent, BE

J0 A PUBLIC PALACE The Palace in Dam Square was designed in 1648 by the architect Jacob van Campen as Amsterdam's town hall. The public building included a court, a prison, an exchange bank, the mayor's residence, a wedding room, and offices for the city's administration. Rembrandt's *Night Watch* hung there too at some point, and the painting was even trimmed to make it fit between two doors. In 1806, the Emperor Napoleon Bonaparte appointed his brother Louis King of the Netherlands, at which point the town hall was converted into a private palace. Ever since, the building has served as palace, now the property of the Royal family who uses it a few times a year. The new plan shows that with a number of precise interventions this closed-off, introvert building in one of the most public places of the city can be transformed again into a public building of significance for the city. The original exchange bank is to become a food bank, the former cellblock a day nursery, the *Night Watch* is to return to its original location, and the mayor's residence will be the King's apartment. Maximum social effect with minimal architectural intervention.

Huis van de Stad
(House of the City),
Amsterdam,
the Netherlands
Ramon Scharff, graduation project (2017)

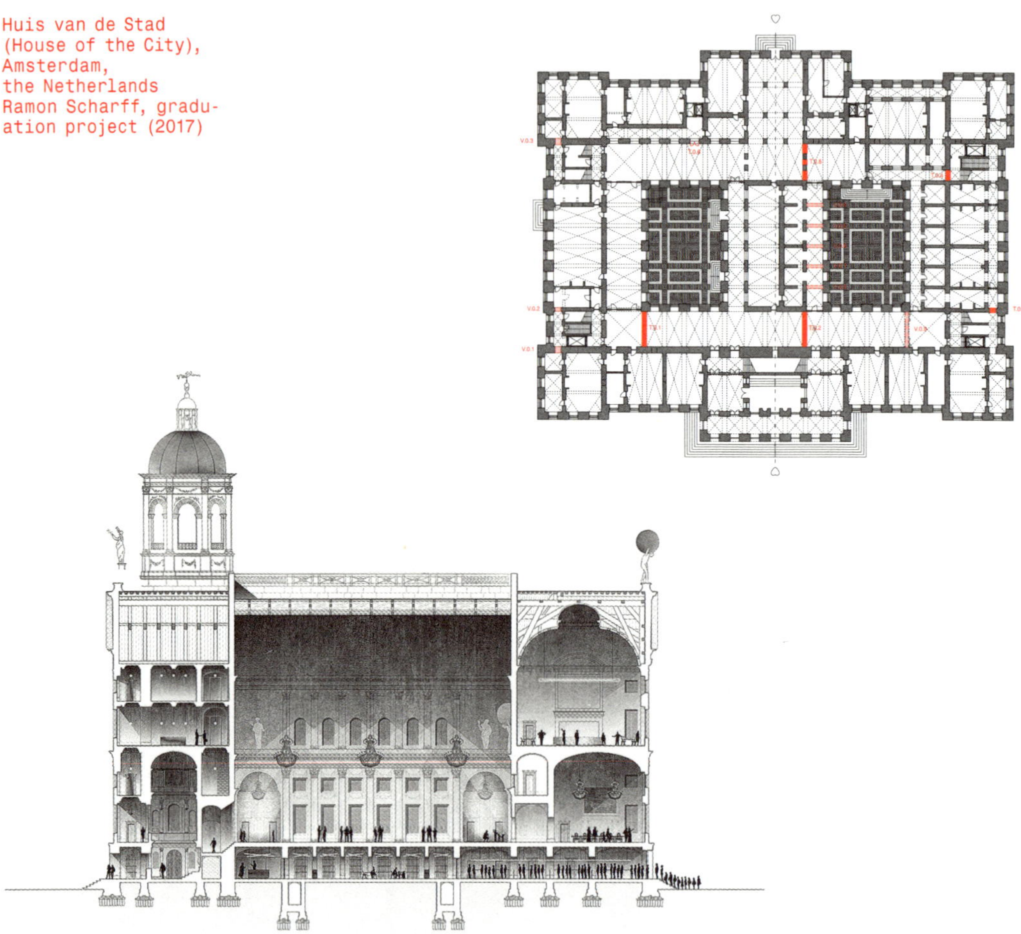

Floor plan showing interventions

Section

ARCHITECTURE FOR ALL SESC Pompéia is a leisure and cultural centre in an old steel drum factory located in the heart of Pompéia, a traditional working-class neighbourhood in the northwest of São Paulo. Designed by Lina Bo Bardi, the vast complex of renovated factory buildings and two new towers combines facilities for sports, theatre, and other leisure activities. It was sponsored by the non-profit Serviço Social do Comércio (SESC), a non-governmental organization providing workers with health services and sporting and cultural activities. Even before Bo Bardi started working on the design, SESC was already providing cultural and sporting activities and local residents used the buildings for playing football, for dance and theatre, or to just have drinks and barbecues together. After visiting the site, she came to the conclusion that 'what we want is precisely to maintain and amplify what we've found here, nothing more'. Instead of demolishing the old factory to build a new complex, SESC and Bo Bardi decided to preserve and upgrade it, adding only the most necessary elements as cheaply and robustly as possible.

SESC Pompéia,
São Paulo, Brazil
Lina Bo Bardi
(1977–1986)

Repurposed factory buildings with new-build concrete towers

Street connecting in- and outdoor spaces
↓ Lounge area with curvilinear pool

Lina Bo Bardi
SESC Pompéia,
São Paulo, BR

JO

## ALL WITHIN THE WALLS

Designed by Karl Bonatz during the Second World War as a bombproof air raid shelter for the passengers and staff at Friedrichstrasse railway station, with a sheltering capacity of 1200 people, 180 cm thick exterior walls and a 320 cm thick concrete ceiling (1942). Used as a shelter during the last months of the war for up to 4000 local residents (1944). Used as a prisoner-of-war camp by the Red Army (1945). Used as a textile warehouse (1947). Used as storage for tropical fruits from Cuba and therefore called the 'Banana Bunker' (1957). Used for techno parties and named the 'hardest club on earth' (1992). Used as a theatre (1994). Used for the erotic trade fair 'Sexperimenta' (1995). Used for illegal S&M party 'Overture der Lust' (1996). Used for the art exhibition 'Files' (1996). Converted to house the private art collection and used as residence of Christian and Karen Boros (2008). From shelter to sex, from communism to capitalism. The moment when freedom of movement within a building is practically impossible, the flexibility of people and their use becomes apparent.

Boros Collection
and Residence, Berlin,
Germany
Karl Bonatz (1942),
Realarchitektur (2008)

Ground floor

The converted
bunker, 2017

# DENSIFY —EXPAND INWARDS

3

4

3 The Large Hadron Collider ATLAS at CERN
4 Tartan weaving
5 An intricately carved ivory tusk
6 Francesco Ungaro, *Unsplash*

5

6

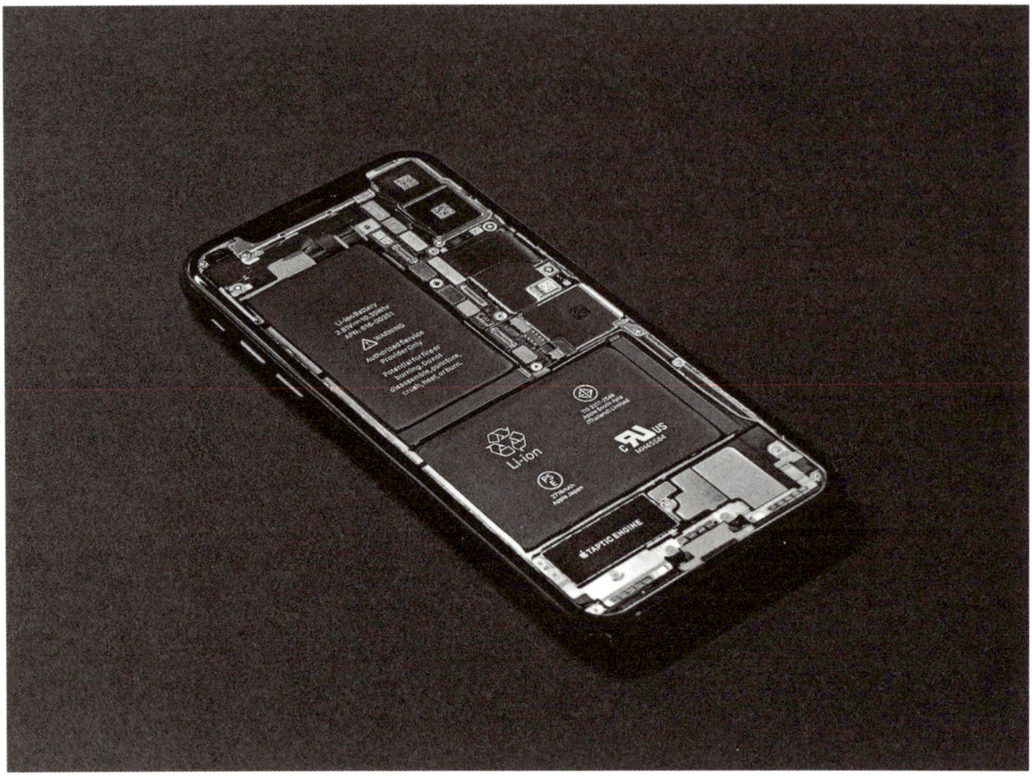

7

8

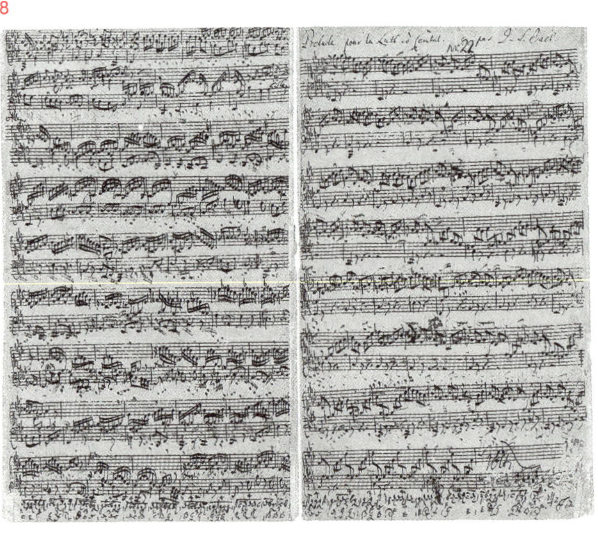

8 The inside of a mobile phone
7 Writing down *Prelude, Fugue and Allegro in E flat BWV 998*, Johann Sebastian Bach ran out of space for the final movement and had to squeeze the last nineteen bars onto the bottom of the fourth and first sheets.

# DIMINISHING, FOR GREATER RETURNS

Tom Simonite

Tom Simonite is a senior writer for *WIRED* magazine and was previously the San Francisco bureau chief at MIT Technology Review. He covers emerging technologies and their effects on society, including machine learning, artificial intelligence, and computer hardware. Thinking about urban and architectural densification challenges, integrated circuits, or chips, emerge as a useful analogy. Simonite traces the history of chip densification and the race for continuous innovation to squeeze ever more functionality in ever smaller spaces. All of this to enable ever more complex processing to fuel a digitizing world. MM

One of the most powerful inventions of the twentieth century is also one of the smallest and it continues to get smaller. The story begins in Murray Hill, an unremarkable looking suburb in New Jersey, with an unremarkable looking corporate campus on its southern edge, where many remarkable things have happened. It is home to Bell Labs, an industrial research and scientific development company, founded at the end of the nineteenth century in New York, and named after Alexander Graham Bell, who first commercialized the telephone and pioneered the hydrofoil. For decades after the Murray Hill site opened in 1942 it seemed haunted by his polymath inventive spirit. Bell Labs was the birthplace of cellular telephony and the first communications satellite, and no less than nine Nobel laureates won the prize for work done there. The lab's most consequential invention of all can be found in a historical display off the main lobby: a palm-sized object in gold, plastic, household glue, and germanium crystal, which looks more like a modernist sculpture than a technological wonder.

That sculpture was made, by hand, in 1947. It is, in fact, the first transistor, an electronic device that helped fashion the modern world. Transistors provided a compact and reliable way to control the flow of electricity, the movement of electrons known as electric current, down a wire. The devices, essentially valves for electricity, enabled miniaturized electronics and the power of contemporary computers. To do anything, whether in the form of a phone playing a video or a government supercomputer simulating a nuclear blast, computers must read out and manipulate digital information, encoded in binary, or strings of 1s and 0s. To represent those two digits requires a switch—the transistor.

The functional part of the ur-transistor in New Jersey was about one centimetre tall. The one-centimetre square processor inside the laptop these words were drafted on has transistors one million times smaller, in a tightly packed array of more than one billion. The digitization of society over the past seventy years is inseparable from that miniaturization and densification. Bell Labs' modernist sculpture has been flattened, shrunk, and multiplied by the billions. Each successive, denser, generation has enabled more powerful and compact computers, propelling society from the 1950s and 60s, when computers were bulky boxes many times larger than a person, to today, when a much more powerful machine can fit on your wrist. Tracing the evolution of the computer chips behind that process—and its latest stage—shows how the computer revolution is as much about topography and geometry as electronics.

Today, Bell Labs is a shadow of its former self in part because that revolution mostly took place thousands of miles to the west. William Shockley, who built that first transistor, set up shop in Mountain View, California in 1956 to commercialize the device. By then the germanium in the original transistor had been replaced by silicon, a brittle blue-grey material with a natural capacity to vary how easily it conducts electricity and one of Earth's most abundant elements. Shockley's company didn't last long. But it put the silicon in Silicon Valley, by seeding the community of physicists and engineers who started the shrinking that grew transistors' power.

It took only a few short years for the gawky handmade transistor from New Jersey to be transformed into a very differently shaped, primarily Californian product that could be manufactured at scale. One of the most crucial early changes was topographic.

In 1959, Swiss physicist Jean Hoerni invented a manufacturing style known as the planar process that flattened the transistor and still defines the industry.

Hoerni's insight was to abstract the protruding 3D components of the day's devices into two-dimensional layers. Transistor manufacturing became more like printing or photography, using masks, photo negatives, and etching to make devices from strata of silicon and metal interlocked by cut-outs, grooves, and ridges. As the printing press did for the written word, the planar process transformed transistors into something that could be churned out en masse. Electronics had previously been assembled from individual components, but now complex devices could be fabricated on a single piece of silicon in the form of an integrated circuit, or chip. More functionality and capacity could be fitted into the same, or even smaller, spaces, and transistors made this way were also more reliable. These advantages helped convince NASA to rely on silicon chips in the control systems for the Apollo space programme, which landed the first humans on the moon in 1969. Ironically, Bell Labs commemorated the success of the transistor in 1961 by building an eighteen-metre replica of its original, bulky shape to function as a water tower on the site of its second, more striking research campus in Holmdel, New Jersey, designed by Eero Saarinen.

In the 1960s, integrated circuits became more complex at astonishing speed. Between 1960 and 1965 the record for the fastest powered flight increased 36 percent. The number of transistors that could be fit onto a single integrated circuit, or chip, increased more than three thousand, and the trend was accelerating. In 1965, an influential young engineer named Gordon Moore was inspired to write a technical article called 'Cramming More Components Onto Integrated Circuits'. He noted that the number of transistors that could be fit into a single chip had doubled every year for the past six years–meaning the performance of those chips was increasing at a similarly dizzying rate. Then he confidently made a prediction that turned the pursuit of densification into the heartbeat of the computer industry for the next six decades. 'Over the short term this rate can be expected to continue', he wrote. 'There is no reason to believe it will not remain nearly constant for at least ten years.' Moore had flipped an observation into a prediction—or perhaps more accurately a wish.

Moore's wish came true. Transistors kept their basic shape: flat and made in the layered planar process. But they shrank and shrank over and over, making computer chips much more powerful. 'Wonders' that Moore predicted in his 1965 paper that denser transistors would deliver, such as home computers, electronic wristwatches, and portable communications devices, became real. In the 1970s, chips began to include tens of thousands of transistors. They were zoned into neighbourhoods to support different specialized functions, each having its own distinct layouts and internal connectivity. Chip designs became more complex and grand—even in name. They called it chip architecture.

The fact that Moore recalibrated his law in 1975 to state that doubling of density would occur at the slower pace of every two years underlines that it had been his invention and not a discovery. Moore's Law was literally that–a precept Moore stipulated on his own authority. It was consequential because others chose to believe it, and to let the concept guide their work. That Moore co-founded Intel three years later, a company that rapidly grew to dominate the chip industry, helped spread and cement his ideas. The identity of the industry and the people in it was built around the constant need to cram smaller transistors together more tightly. Engineers introduced expensive new equipment capable of carving features at smaller sizes. Businesses counted on the densification process to let them lure customers with ever more powerful chips. Successive generations of the chip became known by their scale. The 10-micron (millionths of a metre) generation of 1970 was followed by the 8-, 7-, 6-, and 5-micron generations. Intel's 8088 chip, launched in

1979 and from the 3-micron generation, was powerful and cheap enough to usher in the first mass market personal computers. In the late 1980s the industry dipped into transistors measured in nanometres—a billionth of a metre, slimmer than a bacterium.

Silicon remained king, but engineers had to make constant changes to sustain the procession of denser generations. They invented new ways to 'dope' silicon with other atoms to subtly tune how it modulated the flow of electricity, and reworked the other materials used on chips.

In the mid-1990s, the path ahead stopped looking so clear. The industry was on the 250-nanometre generation of transistors. But they didn't look capable of getting smaller at the pace stipulated by Moore. As they were shrunk, these devices that exist to control the flow of electricity like a valve became too leaky, undermining their primary function and wasting energy (previously smaller generations had generally become more power efficient). DARPA, the United States Department of Defense's research agency, set up a programme intended to spur the invention of a solution, asking for ideas that could make transistors one thousand times smaller, with features as small as 25 nanometres, within ten years.

The military intervention worked. It prompted researchers at the University of California Berkeley to invent a new generation of smaller transistors by reimagining the shape of the devices—just as the industry had got started after Jean Hoerni's invention to flatten what had been protruding 3D devices into stacks of 2D layers.

This time the topographic shift was in the opposite direction. To make transistors that could be reliable, non-leaky electricity valves, researchers from the University of California Berkeley, fourty miles north of Silicon Valley, made them less two-dimensional. They added nanometre scale 'fins' extending upwards from the device, improving its performance by increasing the contact area between different parts. The new transistor leaked less, and could switch faster.

Those 3D transistors, or finFETs, are now the industry standard. Their improved power and efficiency helped bring about the age of the smartphone. The latest chips, like the ones in Apple's latest iPhones, pack together transistors from the 7-nanometre generation. But the devices now appear to be approaching their own size limit—causing another densification crisis because the industry needs to find a new way to keep offering devices with more power and capacity. Once again, the solution appears to be rethinking the form and topography of existing technology, this time even more radically than before.

Instead of just reconfiguring the geometry of the transistors on chips, leading companies are exploring to shatter the concept of the chip altogether. They are experimenting with making them out of mosaics of smaller modules known as 'chiplets' instead of as single, integrated structures. Each chiplet contains just a part of what is needed to make a whole chip.

Notably, that approach has support from the US military, which is again taking an interest in keeping the chip industry to its six-decade promise of ever denser and more capable silicon chips. Now that other superpowers have nuclear warheads and precision-guided weapons, the Pentagon's primary strategy to stay ahead of Russia and China, known as the Third Offset, is to make its forces more capable than their adversaries through technology, mostly more powerful computers and software.

Recombining modular 'chiplets' is supposed to make the process of creating new, more powerful chip designs faster and easier. Established technology and new ideas can be mixed and matched like Lego blocks into novel combinations. Even corporate boundaries can be erased. In 2018, Intel announced a processor for laptops that includes a graphics module from long-time, ferocious competitor AMD.

The chiplet model is also supposed to provide a route for the industry to keep making chips—or at least parts of them—more densely packed with transistors. If the next generations of smaller transistors are used only on some of the chiplets that make up a chip—not across the whole structure—

their costs and technical challenges may be smaller. Chiplets may be stacked vertically as well as tiled horizontally, creating denser, 3D structures equivalent to folding a conventional flat chip back upon itself. New geometry may once again sustain the old obsession.

Veteran chip architect Jim Keller of Intel recently reflected on the psychology of his industry to *WIRED* magazine. 'Moore's law is a collective delusion', he said–a comment not intended to be disparaging. For decades, some of the world's top engineers have oriented their work and multibilliondollar industry around maintaining the reputation of a prophecy from 1965. But that faith, or delusion, has brought us all so much.

# New geometry may once again sustain the old obsession.

P-213 Tom Simonite

# DESIGNING RELATIONAL DENSITY

Momoyo Kaijima

Momoyo Kaijima is an architect and co-founder of the Tokyo-based Atelier Bow-Wow. She is also a professor in Architectural Behaviorology at ETH Zurich and has been visiting professor of Rice University, Delft University, Columbia University and Harvard GSD. Kaijima was the curator of the Japan pavilion at the 2018 Venice Architecture Biennale. Viewing density—in terms of time, space, and use—as opportunity is one of the characteristics of the work done by Atelier Bow-Wow. Like urban detectives they demonstrated—in their publication *Made in Tokyo*—how shortage of space in a city can result in a surprising stacking of functions in buildings and a mix of users, like the Super Car School whereby a supermarket is combined with a driving school on the roof. *Pet Architecture* showed the quality of intensity in a treatment of the special architecture of mini-buildings that are squeezed into gaps between larger buildings, or on miniscule plots. The discoveries they made at the time still inspire their work today. Shortage of space is always translated into a wealth of relations between people and use. JO

In our practice, we use Architectural Behaviorology as a means of perceiving architectural design as an ecosystem, thinking from the perspective of the various relations within an environment. To give some examples of the ecosystem that surrounds architecture (buildings and such), one should consider water or light, and problems such as heat, the people or things that use them and also industries or organizational systems that put pressure from outside and force buildings into certain shapes. To look at this in an integrated manner we are used to drawing up an actor-network map of the architecture's environment so we can share the insights with others. In addition, by further imagining that actor-network map, which was made to improve the circumstances of the environment in question, we can design architecture that is born from these ideas. MK

The origin of this design method is the book *Made in Tokyo*, in which we collected Tokyo-specific hybrid buildings built during the post-war period of rapid growth. In the book, we proposed the 'environmental unit', being a more loosely fitting category than 'architecture', in order to grasp the totality of the ecosystem that surrounds architecture. The analytical model we used for this purpose is the method of spatial composition, as often used in architectural design to describe the ingredients of a landscape. However, we do not utilize this in a normative manner, but rather focus on the architecture that is actively used and embodies the Tokyo-specific, vibrant everyday life. As a result, we started looking beyond the specific plot, at other elements in a building's environment to which it connects, such as infrastructure or manufactured components. That is to say, the architecture is liberated from its interiority, and exists as just one element within a larger urban ecosystem.

All of this takes place in the context of Tokyo's high density; land prices are high, so limited space and adjacency challenges lead to the birth of hybrid types of architecture, bringing about a variety of lifestyles as well as economic effects. Here, the seeds of diversity can sprout. The resulting interconnectivity and organic urbanism create the possibility of freedom with architectural design and space that is not often found elsewhere.

We have since applied the hypothesis from *Made in Tokyo* to various cities. In terms of planning, we tested out the relations of spatial density by combining our own house with our studio. In modern architecture, the residential and the office had become split but we followed the tradition of the *machiya*—or traditional wooden townhouses—which have always been built in Japanese cities as places where living and working come together. In order to demonstrate that the city can become a space for creative living, and not only a place of consumption, we proposed the concept of '24 Hour Architecture' in which we distinguished 'time density' from 'usage density': where in the afternoon a space would be an office, at night it could become a domestic living space. At the same time, it is a hybrid space that uses and co-opts the narrow openings between and structures of the builds around it. We designed the windows as to incorporate the space separating our studio-home from the adjoining buildings, and so we were able to create an open space in the middle, one that does not end with any one construction. As for the thermal environment, we were able to achieve climate control not only through natural light or airflow, but also by using groundwater from forty metres deep to make a heat source for convection heating and cooling panels. By considering architecture though these types of behaviours we could make the various relations that surround architecture apparent, one after the other.

Later, we went on to test our views on forms of density as posed in *Made in Tokyo*, in the countryside. Here, spatial density may be low or non-existent but the density in terms of relations and connections is far richer than within an urban setting. For example, Japan's territory is made up of eighty percent mountains. Its farmer community has developed itself by utilizing water from the mountains on their flatlands, making paddy fields or farms and cultivating rice –thereby making a living and sustaining themselves. The traditional country houses (*minka*) have been built by cutting down the trees in the mountains behind the houses and using the straw that remains after rice cultivation to make its roofs and floors. In other words, within the countryside, architecture embodies a hybrid of mountains, fields, and sceneries as such. If one is to change their occupation, the architecture will also change. Here, as the waves of industrialization and depopulation continue to surge, the architecture and the landscape are changing. While the countryside has a higher relational density than the city, it is today no longer self-sufficient in and of itself but rather inextricably linked to urban space, causing various environmental changes.

We became even more conscious of this relational density during the reconstruction aid activities in response to the 2011 Great East Japan Earthquake. In a village damaged terribly by the impact of the tsunami, an attempt was made to rebuild and restore houses that had been built with traditional and regionally-specific practices. However, this took more time than expected. These practices are founded on the idea that one builds a house using trees cut from one's own mountain, replanting those trees and nurturing the mountain forest for the coming generations. The house was part of the ecosystem's cycle. From a rich and lively mountain filled with healthily developed shrubbery and trees, water filled with minerals and plankton flows to the ocean, in turn making it abundant as well, nurturing the seaweed and oysters along the shores, improving and cultivating various other aspects of the aquaculture. However, even before the earthquake, young people were moving to the city from the fishing village, perpetuating the depopulation, which meant new buildings were not being built. As a result, the forestry and construction industries weakened, and because of the industrialization of the fishing industry fishermen did not have enough time to be concerned about the mountains. Because of all of this, the resources that used to be provided by the mountains and the ocean, and the symbiosis that existed between them had already been completely forgotten. During the reconstruction efforts, many rescue and support staff from the cities were called to the region to bring their talent and materials from the outside and reconstruction activities proceeded at a quick pace. Unfortunately, this meant that many concerns remain unsolved, for example regarding the use of local resources and the application of the principles of adjacency and organic growth. Is it possible to address these issues through architectural design? There is no clear answer, but if architecture is able to materialize the various relations through design, it should be effective to some degree.

The Architectural Behaviorology actor-network map I spoke about at the outset is a framework for this very purpose. Regardless of whether it is the city or the countryside, one must grasp the relations that surround a piece of architecture and should consequently design that density as architecture. The hope is that by re-energizing our life-style and personal environment in such ways, the necessary vitality can be produced to make society sustainable.

… within the countryside, architecture embodies a hybrid of mountains, fields, and sceneries as such.

P-217 Momoyo Kaijima

**DENSIFYING SPACE, TIME AND USE** To avoid many hours of travelling between home and work in Tokyo, the architects decide to combine their new home with their studio. The small plot is surrounded by other buildings on four sides and a narrow path connects it to the street. The limitations of the location, such as its small footprint and bevelled building envelope are translated into spatial qualities for the interior with its shifted stacking of functions. The house of 109 m² is like a big open staircase, with the steps as floors. On the lower steps are the work spaces, and higher up the level of private and living functions increases. Working and living are not deliberately separated here, but are connected, making the small building a large office in the daytime, but also a large home at night.

Atelier Bow-Wow
House & Atelier,
Tokyo, Japan
Atelier Bow-Wow (2005)

Exterior

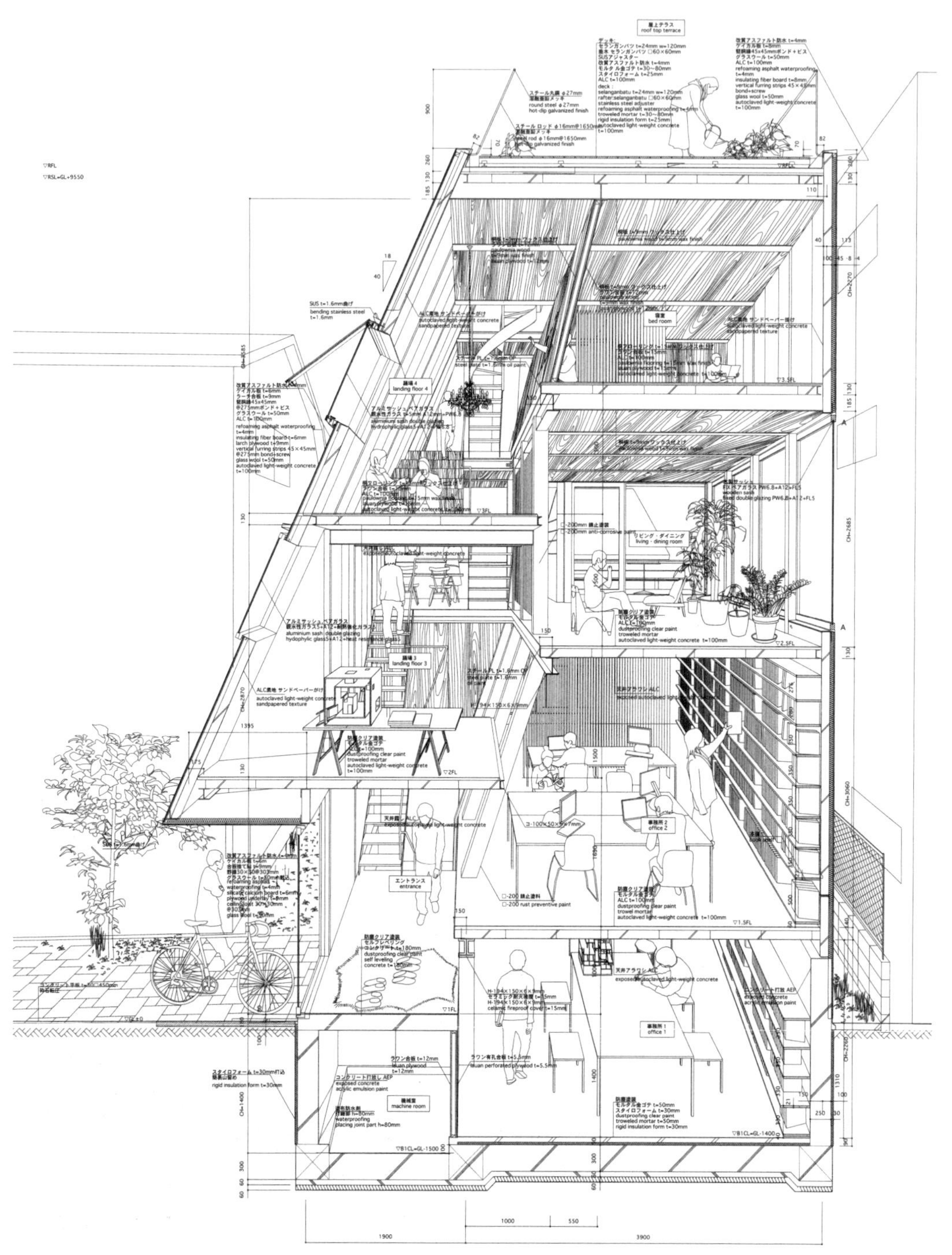


Section

220 DENSIFY

Atelier Bow-Wow House &
Atelier, Tokyo, JP

MvI

## DINING IN AN ABANDONED GARAGE

World of Food is a three thousand square metres international food court housed in a former car park in the Bijlmermeer. This neighbourhood is part of the larger borough of Amsterdam Zuidoost (South East), which was developed after the Second World War as a modern, functional 'town of the future', before becoming subject to large-scale urban renewal. For a long time, the old car park under the Develstein block was left abandoned, before being turned into a multicultural (street)food market, where dozens of entrepreneurs sell their signature dishes from all over the world. The small stalls are surrounded by larger restaurants, which helps to generate more traffic and keeps the rents of the smaller units affordable. To create room for the various new functions, the space was subdivided and upgraded while preserving and reusing certain characteristic elements: the old guardrail serves as a balustrade and glass and steel from other, identical and demolished car parks were used. The result is a complex and interconnected environment that reflects and celebrates the diversity of the 180 nationalities living together in the Bijlmermeer.

World of Food,
Amsterdam Zuidoost,
the Netherlands
Ted Schulten & Harvey
Otten (2015)

**A CITY IN A HOUSE** In 1764, the Scot Robert Adam was excavating in the city of Split and discovered that the remains of a Roman palace had been preserved in the city's centre, or rather, that the city centre itself was the Roman palace. This rectangular palace, measuring 215 by 180 metres, was built in the year 305 as a retirement residence for Emperor Diocletian. Its design followed the principles of a *castrum*, a Roman army base, with two streets crossing each other, forming four quadrants. After the Romans had abandoned the Palace it stood empty, until people from the area sought protection against looters behind its walls, in the seventh century. Slowly but surely, the dwelling was transformed into a city of 4000 inhabitants in its heyday. A couple of important buildings and the walls of the palace have remained unchanged, but inside them a densification process of many centuries has taken place with each generation, style, and culture still legible. A radical form of urbanization, not by expanding but by *im*panding.

Diocletian's Palace,
Split, Croatia
(fourth century AD –)

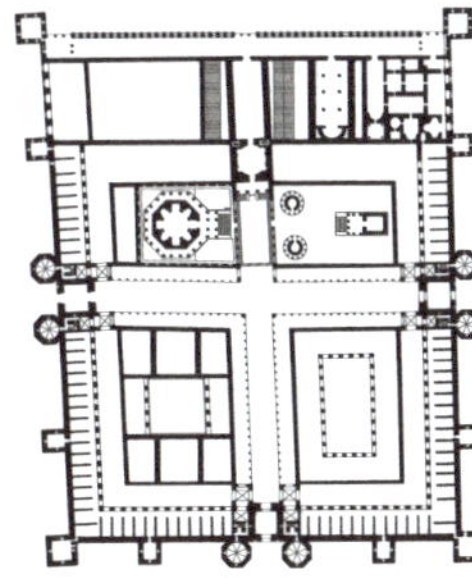

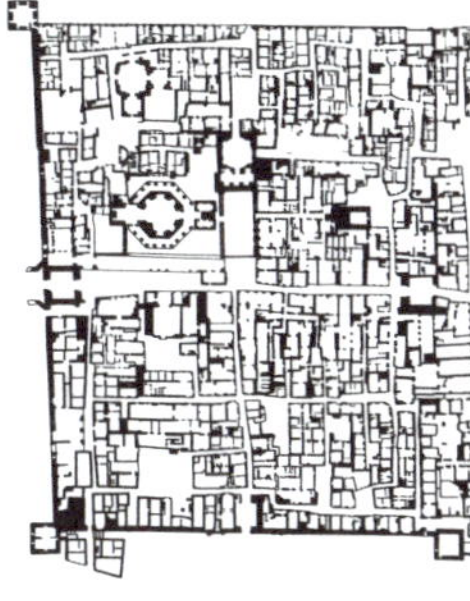

Floor plans of the situation in Roman times and of the situation today

Diocletian's Palace,
Split, HR

**LIVELY ALLEYWAYS** In recent years, the Cairo Lab for Urban Studies, Training and Environmental Research, or CLUSTER, has done extensive research into the network of passageways, back alleys, side streets, and interspaces in Downtown Cairo. Partially modelled after European cities of the late nineteenth century, the area shows a rich diversity of interstitial urban spaces. Their use ranges from food places and coffee shops to sites for trade and retail, as well as galleries and art spaces and small prayer corners. The largely overlooked network of spaces provides an alternative framework for the revitalization of the area and has the potential to accommodate more artistic, cultural, and recreational programmes. CLUSTER has identified dozens of passageways and re-designed and upgraded two of them. The alleyways form a welcome alternative to the busy main roads, where traffic is heavy and rents are high. Over time, these interspaces have gained popularity and have become the inverse of the surrounding buildings, which are now mostly abandoned due to disinvestment and ownership disputes. With their facades stuck in time, collecting dust from the desert, the plinth and backside of the buildings are full of life.

Cairo Downtown
Passageways, Egypt
A project by
CLUSTER, ongoing

Main streets versus
Passageway network

Kodak Passageway
before redesign

Kodak Passageway
after implementation

MvI

PROVIDING A NEW PERSPECTIVE In 2010 artist Krijn de Koning was asked to make a temporary installation to mark the Nieuwe Kerk's 600th anniversary. In his work De Koning often combines sculpture, painting, and architecture to create colourful spatial interventions that let people look at their environment from a new perspective. For the Nieuwe Kerk, one of Amsterdam's oldest churches and most important buildings, he installed a viewing and performance platform of eight hundred square meters largely occupying the entire nave and transept, and incorporating columns and the roof of a sculpted pulpit from the seventeenth century. After climbing up a set of stairs to a height of five metres, visitors could walk around freely and would find themselves surrounded, at eye level, by beautiful stained-glass windows and other details that normally would not be visible, including Johannes Lutma's gilded choir screen from 1654. In the centre of the platform people could descend another pair of stairs, ending up in a sunken structure consisting of interconnected and more introverted rooms where one could sense the silence. By adding a simple structure in an already densely decorated and intensely used space, De Koning managed to literally lift people out of their daily lives and bring them closer to the church building and each other.

Church Warden, Nieuwe Kerk, Amsterdam, the Netherlands
Krijn de Koning (2010)

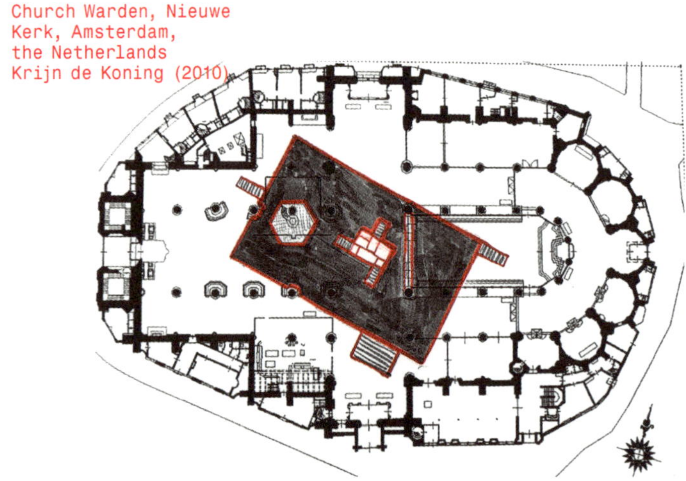

Drawing of installation on floor plan

Detail of installation: sunken interior
↓ Overview of the installation
→ The church at eye-level

Krijn de Koning
Kerkgestel / Church
[illegible], Nieuwe Kerk,
Amsterdam, NL

THE FORWARD FLIGHT A modernist city district in the town of Cagliari on the Mediterranean island of Sardinia is built according to CIAM principles, with an elevated pedestrian level connecting the buildings via bridges. Seen from above, it's all quite idyllic, but the district has developed into an extremely dangerous neighbourhood where the drugs and arms trade of Sardinia is concentrated and where many residents no longer bother to pay any rent. As a last resort, the government considered tearing down the entire neighbourhood. In OMA's plan, however, the solution is sought in densifying the neighbourhood, using the original urban structure as the base from which to realize the original, but since lost ideals after all. Densification is a tool for adding qualities such as liveability and safety.

Sant'Elia,
Cagliari, Italy
OMA / Rem Koolhaas,
Floris Alkemade
Partners (2008)

Existing

Second phase

CITY IN A CITY Before its demolition, Kowloon Walled City was an informal, densely populated settlement. Originally a Chinese military fort, the Walled City became a residential enclave after Britain obtained a 99-year lease of Hong Kong in 1898. Following the Japanese occupation during the Second World War, the population increased dramatically. By the 1990s, an estimated 50,000 people were living in the massive complex of three hundred interconnected and haphazardly constructed buildings that took up an entire city block. This organic 'city in a city' was a hotbed of illegal activity, and a hiding place for numerous brothels and opium dens, but also boasted a wide array of specialized shops and small industry. The only regulation enforced was the height of buildings. Because of the nearby (and now demolished) Kai Tak Airport, buildings were not allowed to betaller than thirteen or fourteen storeys. Covering 2.6 hectare, the Walled City became one of the most crowded places on earth with a population density of 3.2 million people per square mile. To compare: this number is only 66,940 for Manhattan. After a long and heated eviction process, demolition began in 1993 and was completed in the following year.

Kowloon Walled City,
Hong Kong
No (known) architect
(1898–1993)

Walled City,
Hong Kong, 1989

Playground in front
of the walled city

Kowloon Walled City,
Hong Kong, HK

HOUSE IN A HOUSE First pioneered in Beijing, the Plugin Houses are small-scale modular living units that can be embedded in an existing urban environment. Using a modular building system of prefabricated panels, the houses can be customized to fit a particular site and can be built by unskilled labour in less than a day. They leave the original structure untouched while a new home with modern amenities—such as a private bathroom—is woven into the existing urban fabric. In Shangwei Village, a rural community engulfed by nearby Shenzhen, the Huang Family's new home fits into a tiny fifteen square metres space. Because part of the original roof still remains, the 'house in house' insertion acts as structural reinforcement of the original house. To add space, the bedroom is placed on a mezzanine level that cantilevers over a collapsed wall. The Fang Family Plugin House is slightly larger at twenty square metres. Both Plugin Houses demonstrate the possibilities of smaller, customized and more affordable living in dense and fragile urban landscapes.

Shangwei Village Plugin Houses, Shenzhen, China
People's Architecture Office (2018)

Fang Family exterior

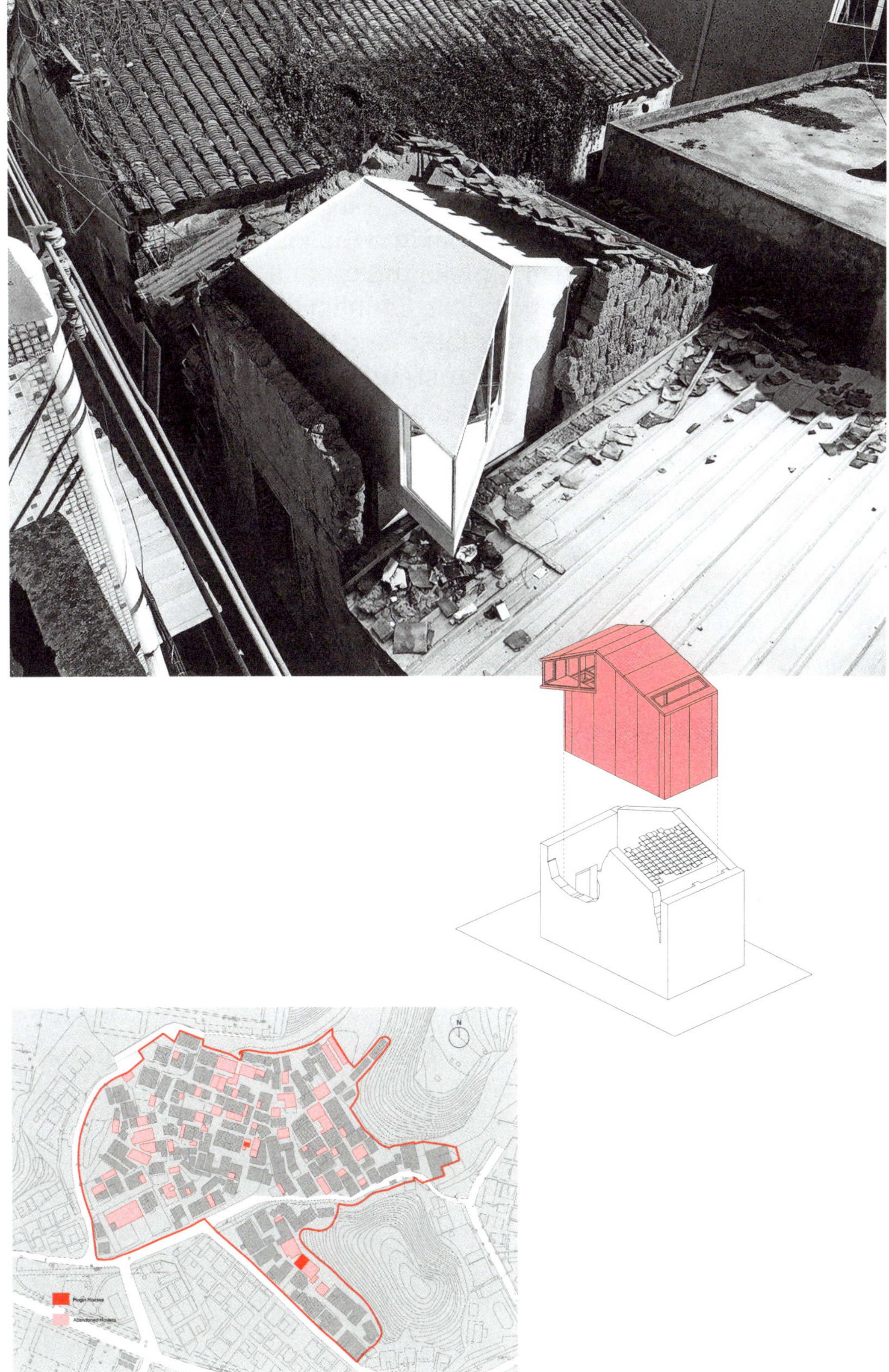


Huang Family bird view

Diagram

Abandoned houses and plugin houses

**FRAMING A SPACE** A Michelin-star chef wants to welcome guests for dining in his restaurant kitchen. Translucent plastic strips, which are normally used in freezer rooms, are hung around a table already there to create a dining space within the kitchen space. The strips blur the less representative and hectic elements of the kitchen during a busy evening and ensure that sounds are muffled and odours are kept out. The strips create 'windows' in the translucent 'walls' and frame specific views from the dining table into the kitchen, and vice versa. Mirrored panels in the ceiling make the room appear twice as high as the kitchen, further enhancing the contrast between the spatial experience of the candle-lit 'Chef's Table' and the fluorescent-lit kitchen. The two worlds of kitchen and restaurant that are functionally so connected but often spatially so separated merge into one.

Chef's Table, Amsterdam,
the Netherlands
HOH Architecten (2018)

Chef's Table,
Amsterdam, NL

J0

## 3D ALLEY

This project studies the urban transformation of one of the oldest parts of the city with the aid of one of the most modern technologies. With smart phones, digital maps, and augmented reality, previously invisible places and functions can now be discovered by anyone. This makes a block of buildings lose its traditional front- and backside, and hidden locations suddenly become interesting spaces for densification. This strategy is tested with precision and care by densifying the Keizerrijk alley with studios, shops, and twenty apartments. The alley itself is given a third dimension, which transforms it into a public route along its various functions. In terms of design and materialization the project builds on the criss-cross maze-like nature of the location, thereby making a spatial experience of something that often remains hidden for many people.

A Frontside for the Backside, Amsterdam, the Netherlands
Ivar van der Zwan, graduation project (2014)

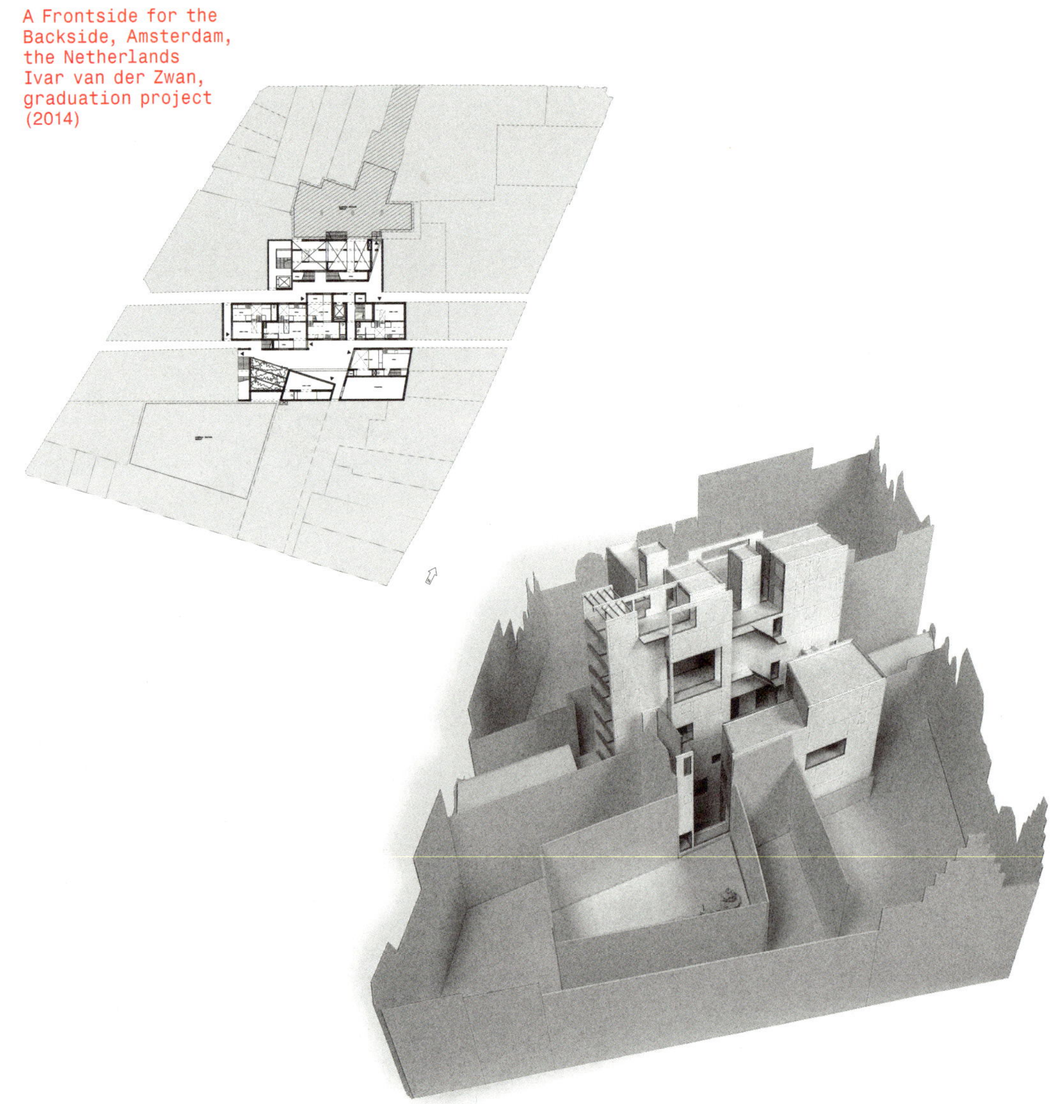

Ground floor plan

# COPY—BUILDING ON BLUE-PRINTS

3

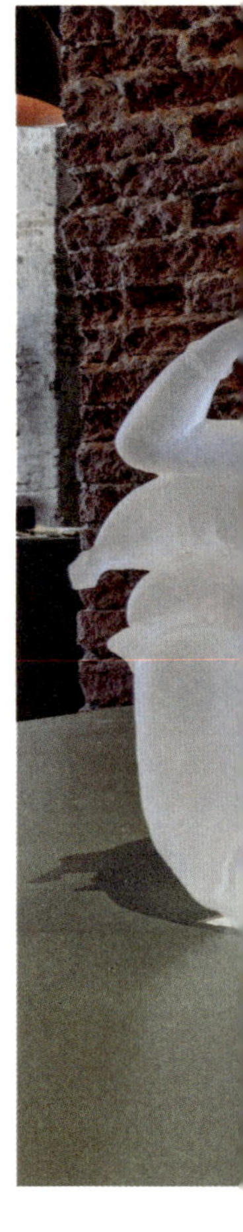

4

3 *The Great Wave Off Kanagawa* by Katsushika Hokusai. The original wood-block print was conceived between 1829 and 1833 and likely produced around 5,000 copies.

4 Cyndi Lauper's 1983 *Girls Just Want to Have Fun* was a cover version of a song that was written and first recorded in 1979 by Robert Hazard.

5 Three copies of Pauline Bonaparte as *Venus Victrix* by Antonio Canova (1805–1808) as part of the Victoria and Albert Museum exhibition 'A World of Fragile Parts' at the 2016 Venice Architecture Biennale

6 Embroidered copies of Johannes Vermeer's *The Milkmaid*, collected and displayed by artist Rob Scholte

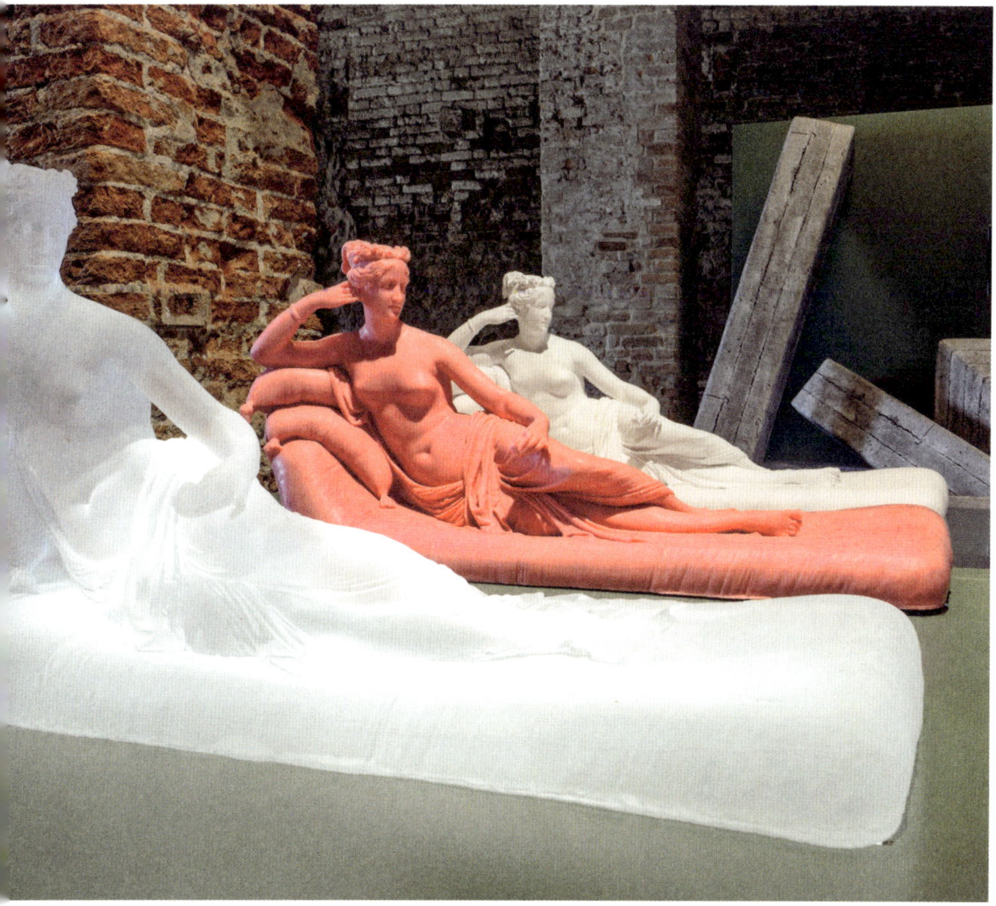

5

6

7

8

7 Copy of the Gutenberg Bible, 1454–1456. It is named after Johannes Gutenberg, the inventor of the printing press which allowed the mass (re)production of books for the first time. Before Gutenberg, every book—Asia excepted, here some printed books had been produced much earlier—had to be copied by hand. Now it was possible to speed up the process without sacrificing quality.

8 High-fashion imitations on West Nanjing Road in Shanghai

# COPYING FETISH

Tamar Shafrir

Tamar Shafrir is a design writer and curator. She was acting co-head of the Design Curating & Writing Master's programme at Design Academy Eindhoven and also teaches theory at the Gerrit Rietveld Academie Amsterdam and London College of Communication. Her research applies the themes of agency, process, value, and meaning to a broad spectrum of topics, from cave paintings and object taxonomies to Missy Elliott videos and machine learning. She is currently working on CTRL V—a project on copying, copyright, and creativity. In this essay, Shafrir unravels Western culture's paradoxical moral problems with copying. MM

Copying is a bit like sex. It's one of the fundamental mechanisms of the continuation of life on Earth. But it is also something that most people raised in Western cultural contexts are taught to think of, beyond a certain age, as bad, wrong, and shameful (if tempting nonetheless)–unless done in a precisely approved way. Early on in life, we begin to view the act of copying as an ethical dilemma: we copy incessantly, consciously or unconsciously, as a matter of survival, cultural practice, and artistic and intellectual study, but we defend these kinds of copying as instinct, identity, and fair use, respectively. At times, though, the act of copying seems to cross some invisible line, even if we can't explain it rationally, and so we attempt to backtrack or hide our tracks for fear of social, professional, or legal punishment. TS

Again, much like sex. In Jacobellis vs. Ohio, a 1964 U.S. Supreme Court trial on obscenity, Justice Potter Stewart explained his criteria for hard-core pornography: 'I know it when I see it.' In modern Western contexts, when something seems ambiguous from a theoretical perspective but intuitively wrong from a moral perspective, two explanations are commonly at play. The first is capitalism, and the second is Abrahamic religion (including Judaism, Christianity, and Islam, as well as smaller branches such as Bahá'í, Druze, and more). What both ideologies share is a slithery meritocracy that makes you personally responsible for your own strife in order to discourage you from challenging the injustices of those above you in the socioeconomic hierarchy–to say nothing of challenging the hierarchy itself.

As the Genovese singer-songwriter Fabrizio De André said, 'It is a crime *not* to steal bread when you are hungry.' Today, we might continue, 'It is a crime *not* to download a copy of a paywalled journal article when you are curious'–not least because the authors themselves see no share of the fee, and it costs the publisher virtually nothing if we download a digital file. Without the capitalist and religious sanctification of property, condemnation of stealing, and erasure of inequality and desperation, would Aaron Swartz have faced time in federal prison for downloading JSTOR files? Would Jonah Lehrer have lost his job at *The New Yorker* for self-plagiarizing from his columns for the *Wall Street Journal*? Would the estate of Marvin Gaye get $5 million from Robin Thicke and Pharrell Williams for copying a dead man's 'vibe'? Would Vitra and PP Møbler destroy perfectly functional chairs because they look like the chairs they licensed from dead men? Would we feel guilty for pirating an e-book when Verso publishers sell the hardback-ebook combi-pack for less than the hardback alone? Would Diet Prada, the Instagram account that exposes fashion knock-offs, even exist?

Together, capitalism and Abrahamic religion form a foundation, riddled with paradoxes and inconsistencies, for the suppression of copying through an ethically-inflected understanding of value–one that is miraculously adaptive in the face of accelerating technological change. As copying becomes easier and cheaper, and as the owner or maker experiences less labour and material costs as a result, we might expect the moral implications of copying to dwindle or disappear. (In other words, photocopying a printed book equates to one less sale of a book made of paper, glue, and ink and transported physically from printer to shop; downloading a PDF equates to one less sale of a digital file made only of computer code generated by software and transported through network infrastructure.) In fact, the opposite is true: the same technological changes make it easier to identify, allege, and penalize copying. They also progressively locate ownership in digital files rather than physical objects, making the act of copying more about conceptual transgression than loss.

One caveat: the Bible does not condemn copying outright. On the contrary–the Old Testament is full of copying, copiers, and copies: as God says (twice), 'be fruitful and multiply' (Genesis 1:22). Adam is a copy of God's image (Genesis 1:27). Moses copies the tablets of the ten commandments after he breaks the first set (Exodus 34:1). And when his copying skills fall short, God imbues the craftsman Bezalel with his own spirit, perfecting his workmanship to enable him to carry out his extremely specific instructions. Bezalel copies a pattern given by God to build the tabernacle, with golden statues in the form of cherubim for the Ark of the Covenant, a candlestick that imitates branches with almond blossoms, priestly robes decorated with pomegranates made of purple wool, and anointing oil and incense made according to God's recipes.

It may seem contradictory, then, that God later declares: 'Thou shalt not make unto thee a graven image, nor any manner of likeness, of any thing that is in heaven above, or that is in the earth beneath, or that is in the water under the earth.' And there are countless graven and molten images (statues) made by nonbelievers, the most egregious being a large copy of a phallus made by Queen Maacah and destroyed by her son Asa. With regards to the anointing oil and incense used in the holy rites of the sanctuary, he is even more specific: 'Whosoever compounds any like it ... shall be cut off from his people.'

In the Old Testament, copying is one of the most reliable ways to get yourself killed.

How are we to reconcile these contradictions? Why is it allowed to make golden copies of cherubim but idolatrous to make a golden copy of a calf? More importantly, how does today's secular post-industrial capitalism preserve, relatively intact, the distinction between tolerable and forbidden forms of copying found in pre-industrial religious societies? In order to answer these questions, it is necessary to untangle the word itself. Copying is a composite phenomenon involving three elements–the human copier, the material copy, and its immaterial content–that are largely independent of one another. The morality of the act of copying is determined by the nuanced interactions between these elements, and thus each one must be interrogated in its own right.

Let us begin with the human copier–the only element which has sentience, intent, and culpability. The copier is not merely someone who copies but someone who copies something in a forbidden manner. Therefore, the work of Bezalel, and of his assistant Oholiab, is permitted because the right to copy the tabernacle's pattern is transmitted from God via Moses through the act of delegation. By its very nature, delegation is not an equal relation among peers but a hierarchy between individuals of different stature, where one person's work is completed by another through force or for pay. Bezalel has the right to copy the pattern for the tabernacle or the cherubim for the ark because God orders him to do so, and God's legitimacy is sacrosanct. In modern copyright law, this also manifests as the 'work made for hire' principle, which grants to employers the authorship rights over the original creations of their employees. According to the Compendium of U.S. Copyright Office Practices, an architectural firm would be considered the author of a design for a building made by one of its employees but not the author of a design for a website made by an independent contractor. Legal employment is the critical factor, not the creative process.

Here we encounter a paradox. In order to copy something in service to a higher power, patriarch, or boss, the worker must possess the necessary knowledge, skills, and prowess; however, these assets destabilize the power structure that forces them to work for another's gain. If a worker is allowed to copy at another's behest, how can they be discouraged from copying for themselves? Take the assistants of Damien Hirst, who made the vast majority of his spot paintings —why wouldn't they make an extra one and sell it on the side, or even at auction? It cannot be called inauthentic. Punitive measures prove inadequate because they can only target objects that no one is allowed to copy ('graven images' or idols in the Bible, currency or passports or atomic weapons or drugs in reality), and even then they are mainly implemented after the act. The only effective way to prevent copying is to make copiers believe that it is inherently wrong *unless* it is done for someone or something more powerful (Ecclesiastes 2:26).

The Ten Commandments say that it is wrong not only to steal but also to desire the possessions of another. But the vilification of the copier permeates through the allegories and prophecies with even greater nuance. In his vision of Jerusalem's day of judgment, Isaiah condemns man as an idolater—'to the work of his hands he prostrates himself, to that which his fingers made'—and imagines God's indignation: 'Shall the axe boast over the one who hews with it, or shall the saw hold itself greater than he who wields it?' In reducing the craftsman from a free agent to a tool controlled by its operator, he denies them any claim to their creations. This echoes the medieval prohibition on guild members from removing tools from the workshops, in order that they could not produce personal commissions outside of the collective system.

Copiers are both vain and inferior; 'their eyes are bedaubed from seeing, their hearts from understanding.' To make an identical copy—whether by repeating a tweeted joke verbatim, by making an impressively skilful forgery of an old painting, or by performing an eerily accurate imitation of a famous song—is to demonstrate a lack of taste, originality, and independent thinking, to act duplicitously for personal gain and recognition. But to make a bad copy—when Zara copies Prada's designs straight from the runway or when furniture manufacturers make Thonet knockoffs—is to expose one's ignorance and inferiority, to denigrate the original idea by remaking it using cheaper materials, details, or processes.

Yet these critiques contradict one another. When technical skill is dissociated from conceptual knowledge and ethical judgment, the incriminating act of transgression becomes harder to identify. The copier is simultaneously decadent and deficient: on one hand, their craftiness deceives the naive observer, and on the other, their fundamental ineptitude is betrayed by their haphazard mimicry. This dichotomy needs to be displaced from the person to the copied object, and divided between the physical object and its immaterial essence. God compares the duplicitous maker's copies to illegitimate children, harlots, vanities, and false gods to force an ethical surrender: like unfaithful women, the craftsman's illicit reproductions are worthless and degenerate forgeries of the perfect, virtuous originals He placed in the world. 'Every man is brutish without knowledge; every smith is put to shame by his graven image, for his molten images are false, without spirit in them.' (Jeremiah 10:14)

Here we find the rather tortuous, aforementioned link between Abrahamic and capitalist ideology in relation to the copy. In 1951, the Biblical scholar Yehezkel Kaufmann put forward an argument that the Bible does not actually ban the creation of an image of God nor of any gods worshipped by other people. 'What is forbidden is the "making" of gods, the worship of one's own handiwork.... These laws, then, ban the making of an image of visible, material objects —organic and inorganic—and forbid serving them as gods.' This forbidden act of religious fetishism corresponds precisely to commodity fetishism: neither the Bible nor capitalism can tolerate a personal engagement with a physical object in its concrete, material presence, much less taking pleasure in making a copy and suffering no sense of guilt as a consequence. On the contrary, we must believe that the object is more than its matter, that it contains the immaterial values and relations of a society that cannot be replicated. As Marx says in *Capital*, 'to find an analogy [for the relation between things], we must have recourse to the mist-enveloped regions of the religious world ... the productions of the human brain appear as independent beings endowed with life'. We would no more copy an object than clone a human without a deep moral reckoning.

To find value in copying, it is necessary to question not only the morality of the act, in an ethical lineage from Abrahamic religion to capitalism, but equally the act as labour itself. Copying, more than any other action today, provides the thrill of having cheated the game, of having given into the temptation of subjectless, blissful ease. Rather than taking these sensations as the precursors to guilt, we should recognize them as a momentary escape from the hierarchical onus of our religio-economic condition. The reproduction by another person will still be a new experience for that person. And not only for that person. If we really want to do something valuable for the creator of the object of our admiration; if we want to offer them respite, amplify their voice, and democratize their work, then we must copy them–to spare them the drudgery of having to copy themselves.

# Copying is a bit like sex.

P-243 Tamar Shafrir

# THE GOOD COPY

Sam Jacob

Sam Jacob is an architect and founder of Sam Jacob Studio. He is Professor of Architecture at UIC and Visiting Professor at Yale School of Architecture. He was co-curator of the British Pavilion at the Architecture Biennale in Venice (2014) and writes for *Dezeen*, *Art Review*, *Icon* and other media. Previously, he was co-founder and principal of FAT Architecture. The copy has been a recurring topic in his research, exhibition work and architectural projects. Long considered a taboo in architecture, where authenticity and unicity are considered virtuous, Jacob wonders how replication and repetition can be of value. Instead of seeing copying as forgery, could architecture decriminalize the productive copy? MM

There is a story—most likely apocryphal—of a customs officer at the Hong Kong border. He stops someone entering from mainland China, opens the suitcase and finds an array of Rolex watches. Investigating further, he opens up one of them and finds the complete complex geared workings all ticking away, as expected. But unexpectedly, made from intricately carved bamboo. There's another story (this one definitely true) of a Chinese development themed around the image of an English village. If you see it now, it's nothing remarkable—red brick, black slate roof and so on. But you should have seen it before the cladding was applied: the form of a quaint cottage, its pitched roof, eaves details, window frames and lintels all cast in in situ concrete. Like a brutalist's bad dream where the logic of one kind of construction assembling different materials, trades, skills, and traditions is obliterated by a monolithic material singularity. A vernacular rooted in a specific place, time and culture made unheimlich through an entirely other form of production, dislocation and decontextualization. SJ

There's a moral, in some sense, to these tales. That the act of copying is first of all really difficult: reproducing the outer appearance and inner workings of something is a challenge when materials and techniques have changed from when the original was made. To produce a copy often requires immense ingenuity, with all of that originality then skinned with a veneer of normality that conceals the weirdness beneath.

Speaking personally, the only Rolex I would wear would be a bamboo powered one, and I'd enjoy it even more holed up in a concrete cottage. Why? Because these, despite being classified as copies, have a kind of contemporary authenticity. An authenticity that resonates with the complexity, contradiction, doubt, anxiety, confusion, and ambiguities of our time.

Here we find ourselves amongst the contradictory intricacies of the copy. And if the copy is a difficult cultural issue, for architecture it seems extra hard. There are several reasons for this.

First, that the dominant idea since Modernism's break with the Beaux-Arts tradition of repeating historical forms is of a certain kind of originality, often associated with a single iconoclastic author rejecting history and reference, imagining instead the plane of production as a tabula rasa. Paradoxically, the Modernists dreamt of a different kind of repetition. The new blank slate would be filled with the replication of standardization and mass production that characterized the epoch of industrialization. Not copies, but serially produced architecture.

Second, the legal protections that exist to protect the original. The act of designing automatically generates intellectual property rights. These rights are both cultural and economic: they are the outcome of a particular idea of authorship, and express creative activity as an economic entity. They serve a specific formulation of the act of creation within capitalist economies. This is evidenced by the patent system, mobilized during the industrial revolution and designed to stimulate innovation with the reward of a (time-limited) market monopoly providing a period of unchallenged economic exploitation.

Third, the condition of architecture itself is different from so many other forms of cultural production that allow (or indeed are born out of) reproducibility. The medium of architecture in the form of a building is always different (in terms of site, environmental conditions, context, use, and so on). Sites, unlike pages, canvases, screens, stages and so on, are fundamentally different, making the resulting reproduction unlikely to be of the same quality as the original.

Fourth, the moral sentiment against the copy. The reputation of the copy is often characterized as a low resolution, inauthentic, debased version of the original, something from which the original meaning has been drained. In contrast to the authenticity of the original, the copy stands accused of pastiche and fakery.

Yet it is possible to construct arguments in favour of the copy—even of sameness. At its most primeval, we learn language through copying. As Barbara Kruger writes in her 1994 book *Remote Control: Power, Cultures, and the World of Appearances*, applied to an image of a baby at her mother breast: 'We are obliged to steal language.' She suggests that language (and with it identity, culture, behaviour, and all of the other things that make us socialized humans) is voraciously, almost aggressively, acquired. This is also true of architecture, one of whose roles is to construct the shared common ground of the city. The city, it should be remembered, is a synthetic construction, the sum product of human culture, or even culture *as* habitat. And like all culture, it is produced collectively.

Architectural culture is a commons, a public body of knowledge. Copying from one culture to another, from one architect to another and from one time to another is an act that actually manufactures architectural culture. Think of the Greeks copying the Egyptians, the Romans copying the Greeks, the Renaissance copying Antiquity. In each case, the act of copying produced a radically new, totally contemporary architectural form. More recently, Modernist elevation of industrial building forms also presents a case for copying as a fertile ground for producing radical breaks. It's not what you steal, it's the way that you steal it. Architecture, one might speculate, is produced in the transmission of itself from project to project, site to site, city to city.

Historically, forms of copying have been means of establishing collective languages. Palladio's *The Four Books of Architecture* (1570), for example, turned Palladio into Palladianism, transformed his own body of work into a shared style. His books were nothing less than an invitation to copy, produced to transmit and share an architectural language. The copies of Palladio's books begat architectural copies. Printing (itself a means of reproduction), publishing and distributing became intrinsic to the production of architecture. Palladianism, then, was not only a style of building but a new kind of architecture made possible by multiple kinds of reproduction.

Of course, Palladio himself was remaking an architectural language found in antique Roman architecture. And his remaking was so radical that it produced not a copy but what one might refer to (sympathetically) as a 'Frankenstein monster'—entirely new forms of life assembled from the parts of corpses.

The process of multiplication through duplication, reference, and remaking turns an individual exception into something more collective: a lone shriek becomes a participative conversation.

The copy is intrinsically social in its formation. It is made in reference to something that pre-existed both materially and in its accrued values and meanings. The copy's own physical body is an assemblage of the knowledge of the original, projected into a different circumstance. Because of its engaged relationship with the world, the copy is an act of socialized creation.

The copy does not only reproduce the past, it also creates alternative presents and new possibilities for the future. As it emerges into the world, it takes on, absorbs, or creates its own meanings. This was the premise for Architectural Doppelgangers, a research cluster at the Architectural Association School of Architecture run by myself and Ines Weisman. Its interest was in the status of the architectural copy and a series of studies of examples explored the unexpected ways they perform (or perhaps more accurately re-perform) in the world.

For example, the Basilica of Our Lady of Peace in Yamoussoukro in the Ivory Coast is–give or take a detail here and a proportion there–a replica of St. Peter's Basilica in Rome beamed down onto the flat African landscape. Presented as a 'gift' from President Félix Houphouët-Boigny to Pope John Paul II, it was also part of his project to relocate the capital to the town of his birthplace. On September 10, 1990, the Pope came to Yamoussoukro to consecrate the church. Our Lady of Peace may seem just another post-colonial genuflection to European culture but perhaps this concealed a sophisticated sleight of hand. Opposition to Houphouët-Boigny had been organized by local Catholic Bishops. While the construction of Our Lady of Peace appeared to be a benefaction to Rome, it really served to mobilize the power of the Vatican to endorse the president's position and repress local Catholic opposition. The doubling of St. Peter's redirected the iconographic power of the original against those who it seemed to honour.

Another example. On 15 April 2012, a recreation of the Austrian alpine village Hallstatt opened in Huizhou, an area of mountains and lakes in the southern Chinese province of Guangdong. 'Hallstatt Villa Zone' opened with two product types: Townhouse and Larry Villa. 110 of 134 villas for sale were sold that day. While the replica was dubbed the 'only genuinely Austrian town in the whole of China' others argued that it was an act of theft, the work of 'spies' who secretly prepared blueprints of European cities and villages. No permission had been sought to produce the copy, and Austrian villagers and intellectual property lawyers alike began to debate the legality of copying an entire village.

The original village is a major tourist attraction and a UNESCO World Heritage Site. This title is bestowed because of a site's historical and cultural uniqueness. A WHS is a mechanism used to preserve those unique qualities. If Hallstatt II threatens that singularity, should UNESCO intervene? Or conversely, is doubling a way of protecting its uniqueness? Copying the originality that belongs to someone else and pretending that it is your own is termed 'passing off' by intellectual property law. We often think of it as morally wrong, as a debased form of creativity. But the mayor of Austrian Hallstatt Alexander Scheutz looked at it differently as he proclaimed 'nothing is wrong'. Seeing that almost nine thousand Chinese tourists came to visit the 'original' in 2011, he declared that his village is now 'proud to see there is another Austrian-style town on the other side of the world'. Here the replica performs as a kind of international diplomacy.

These architectural doppelgängers suggest, by acknowledging the past and referring to shared languages and images, that the copy creates trajectories that escape the limits of the original. These forms of copying rewire fixed cultural arguments over authenticity, becoming alternatives that unlock new possibilities for architecture by reusing the past with imagination.

The copy–a good copy, that is–has a heightened interest in the world around us. Not as the Modernist dream of the tabula rasa nor as the reconstruction of a nostalgic past that never existed. Its very existence depends upon its relationship to the world (and the thing that it is replicating). This awareness of the material and cultural qualities of the subject means that the copy is already in productive dialogue with its contexts. And like the bamboo Rolex (or the shuttering required to pour a concrete cottage), the technical production of a copy requires ingenuity and precision of one kind or another. These, in a roundabout way, are means of engaging with core disciplinary issues of both context and tectonics. It is precisely that long journey, ingeniously and skilfully routed through wide maps of culture, that can make the copy so powerful.

The etymological root of the word copy is *cornucopia*, from its Latin root *cornu copiae* in turn derived from the mythical horn of the goat Amalthea that nurtured the infant Zeus. This root meaning figures the copy as a form of boundless plenty, a source of endless nourishment. The copy here is not a static object but a flow.

If we recognize the copy as a central part of the production of culture, as the mechanism of architectural production and even as an intrinsic quality of the city itself, we would perhaps release ourselves into that *cornucopic* state of abundance. If we recognize the ways in which repetition and replication provide us not only with pre-existing solutions and models but also as a way to express difference, even novelty. Overthrowing the tyranny of originality in its simplistic formal sense could mean redirecting all that energy and effort into other forms of innovation.

# It’s not what you steal, it’s the way you steal it.

P-251 Sam Jacob

**OVERCOMING ORIGINALITY** This makeshift monument revived Austrian Modernist architect Adolf Loos' 1921 design for a mausoleum for art historian Max Dvořák. Though never built, this proposal has inspired many artists and architects. In his book *Adolf Loos: The Art of Architecture*, writer Joseph Masheck draws parallels between Loos' mausoleum and the work of several post-war artists and architects, including the brick installations of Carl Andre, the 'grey prisms' of Robert Morris, the sculptures of Tony Smith, and the work of I. M. Pei. Following in their footsteps, Jacob (re)created the mausoleum at a 1:1 scale, using a lightweight timber frame and scaffold to resemble the heavy dark and masonic form of the original design. In addition to his work as an architect, Loos was also an influential and provocative theorist of modern architecture. In his 1913 essay 'Ornament and Crime', he (in)famously argued that 'the development of culture is concurrent with the removal of ornaments from objects of daily use'. With this translucent re-enactment of a Loos' unrealized architectural project, Jacob seems to suggest that originality—like ornamentation —is something to be overcome for the sake of cultural progress.

A Very Small Part of Architecture, Highgate Cemetery, London, United Kingdom
Sam Jacob Studio (2016)

Original design by Adolf Loos, 1921

↓ The installation in Highgate Cemetery, London

Sam Jacob Studio
A Very Small Part of
Architecture, Highgate
Cemetery, London, GB

THE CONTEXT OF THE COPY In 1952 the first *Unité d'habitation* was completed: a social housing project for 1600 residents with 23 types of apartments, varying from one-room apartments to homes for families with four children. The building's design does not take the surroundings into account and this is one of the reasons why it is raised on pilotis, allowing the landscape to continue underneath the building. The only condition for the location was that the building must have a North-South orientation so that the apartments that were accessed via an interior street would all enjoy both morning and evening sunlight. The building is designed as a small town with many collective amenities: a small shopping centre, a laundromat, hairdresser's, post office, restaurant, a kindergarten/crèche, and a gym/dance hall on the roof. The architect was convinced that society would change for the better through industrial thinking. 'Mass production demands a search for standards. Standards lead to perfection.' In that spirit, five more Unités were built. With each reproduction, more and more of the original qualities were lost, as with an old photocopier. The original pilotis, which because of the post-war shortage of steel were made extra massive, became more and more minimal, losing their tactile quality. The variety in apartments, and therefore in residents, was severely limited and the collective programme was minimized or even banned. The differences between original and reproduction demonstrate how technological progress does not necessarily lead to architectural progress and that good commissioning—determining and safeguarding the right programme—is affected by the times and may vary per culture. The big surplus value of the reproductions is that they, more so than with unique buildings, show us the qualities of the original in retrospect, as a lesson for any future reproductions.

Unité d'habitation,
Marseille (1952),
Nantes-Rezé (1955),
Briey (1963), Firminy-
Vert (1965), France and
Berlin (1975), Germany
Le Corbusier

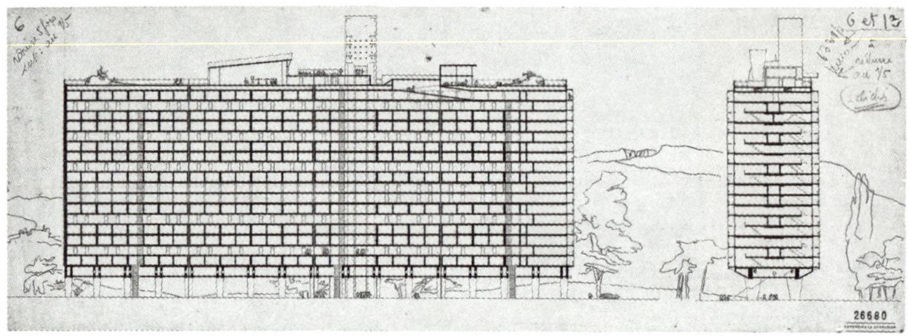


Section

→ Unité Marseille,
1945–1953
Pilotis, Marseille

Unité d'Habitation,
Marseille, Nantes-Rezé,
Briey, Firminy-Vert, FR
and Berlin, DE

Unité Nantes-Rezé, 1953–1955

Pilotis, Nantes-Rezé

Unité Berlin,
1956–1959

Pilotis, Firminy

Unité Firminy,
1965–1973

Le Corbusier
Unité d'Habitation, Marseille,
Nantes-Rezé, Briey, Firminy-
Vert, FR and Berlin, DE

MvI

**THE GOOD COPY** Built in the last open space of Trafalgar Square in the heart of London, the Sainsbury Wing houses the collections of early Italian and Northern Renaissance paintings of the National Gallery. The Wing was designed to connect to and stylistically mirror the already existing main building of the museum, which was designed by William Wilkins and opened in 1838. The architects' playful appropriation of stylistic elements is best illustrated by the 'echo facade', which starts by repeating the rhythms and forms of the main Gallery building, before the space between columns gradually increases until fading to a plain wall as it moves further away from the classical source. Robert Venturi once said: 'It is better to be good than to be original. You have to have something basic that you either build on or evolve from or revolt against. You have to have something there in the first place and the only way to get it is to copy, in a good sense of the word.' This idea of the 'good copy' lies at the heart of the many stylistic citations in these architects' own work and still resonates strongly with those who agree, with Denise Scott Brown, that it's terrible when architects consider a sheet of white paper as the ideal context of their creations.

Sainsbury Wing,
National Gallery,
London, United Kingdom
Venturi, Scott
Brown and Associates
(1989–1991)

Echo facade

ETERNAL ISE The Naikü shrine is part of the Isu Jingü, a complex of Shinto shrines, and since the year 630 it is rebuilt every twenty years, out of a belief that transience and renewal are inextricably linked. Twenty years is also the average time between two generations, the renewal of life itself. The carpenter who helped build the last shrine can pass on his ancient craftsmanship to a new generation. This tradition not only preserves the shrine but, even more important, the ability of building the shrine itself. For the rebuilding, the location of the shrine is divided into two identical plots, one of which holds the present shrine while the other is empty. The empty plot was the location of the shrine before the present one and will be the location of the new one. When it's time to rebuild the shrine, the old one serves as the model for the new one. In 2013, the shrine was copied for the 62nd time. At the moment that the new temple is finished and the old one not yet demolished, there are two identical buildings standing side-by-side. Both originals and both copies, together demonstrating transience and the passing of time.

Ise Shrine, Ise, Japan
(630 AD–)

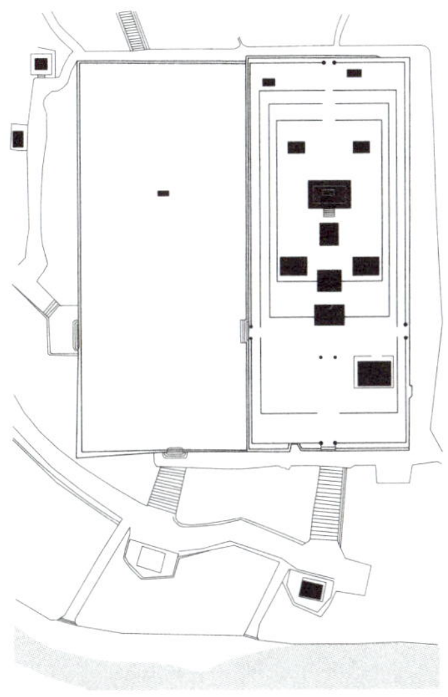

↑ Site plan, 1953
Aerial view of the site

↓ Before the dismant-ling, the original and the copy coexist like here in 2013

Ise Shrine, Ise, JP

MvI

## REPLICABLE CRISIS RESPONSE

For a little over three decades, Shigeru Ban, the Japanese architect responsible for such iconic designs as the Centre Pompidou-Metz, has devoted a lot of his time and resources to constructing high-quality, low-cost and easily replicable shelters for victims of disasters across the world, from Japan, Sri Lanka and India to Rwanda, Haiti, Kenya, and more. Through his paid, commercial commissions he has gained extensive knowledge of recyclable materials, particularly paper and cardboard, which he applies in his non-profit work. He founded his own NGO, Voluntary Architects Network (VAN), which focuses on the design and distribution of shelters for which no or little technical supervision is required. For the actual construction VAN uses building techniques and materials that are locally available, affordable, and sustainable, allowing inhabitants to do the maintenance and future upgrades themselves. In Nepal, for example, people used salvaged rubble bricks to construct new quake-proof walls. Whenever possible, the VAN team involves people in the construction of their own homes. On several occasions Ban has expressed his hope that people will copy the designs, waiving his own copyrights and making the designs available for others to build upon and share legally.

Post-disaster shelters,
various locations
Shigeru Ban / Voluntary
Architects Network

Construction of the timber framework of a prototype house.

Prototype houses in Kalobeyei Settlement in Kenya

Paper Log House,
India, 2001

Kirinda House, Tsunami
Reconstruction Project,
Sri Lanka, 2007

Post-disaster shelters,
various locations

J0 COPYING A CATHEDRAL After a period of post-war industrial growth, the shipyards in the northern French harbour town of Dunkirk all closed down in the 1980s. The AP2 building, nicknamed 'The Cathedral', where sailboats and warships were built, was one of the few that was not demolished. A competition was held for the reuse of the building as a FRAC, a regional institute for contemporary art. The new programme would fill up the entire hall, which would mean that the huge open space (the very quality that gave the building its nickname) would be lost. It was decided to duplicate the existing building in a transparent version, as an annex to the AP2 and with a view of the sea. The transparent volume contains the climate-controlled spaces for exhibitions, workshops, and offices. The existing 'cathedral' remains empty and can be used for events and for exhibiting large works of art. Duplicating, not for the sake of creating a new version, but in order to preserve the original.

FRAC, Dunkirk, France
Lacaton & Vassal (2013)

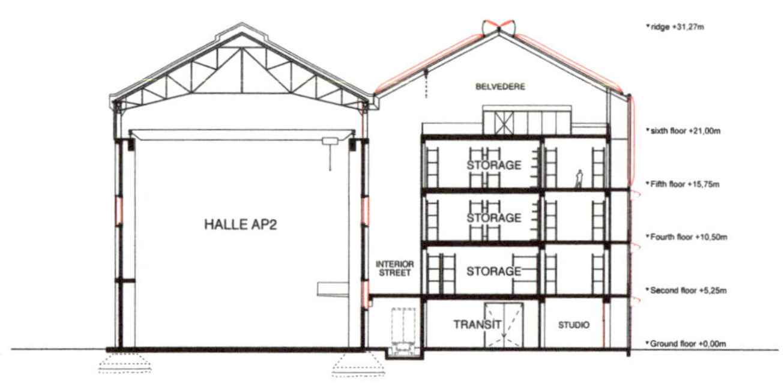

Connection between old and new

Interior AP2

**THE FAIRY-TALE CASTLE** Not having a historical layer is like an incurable trauma for this new town. Copying an old inner city's appeal by imitating history in new buildings is untruthful and never quite credible. Still, at some point the town of Almere was unable to choose between historicizing and modern architecture and decided to adopt both approaches. Opposite the radically modern town centre a copy of Château Jemeppe, an old castle in the Walloon provinces of Belgium, was built at the same time. In a strange kind of schizophrenia, they sought a combination of the power of a modern centre and the charm of a historical-looking castle that could serve as the location for weddings and conferences. The construction of the castle was started a bit brashly. When the concrete shell was finished, the underlying financial plan fell through and construction was halted. Since then, ten years have passed in which nothing has happened and thus the schizophrenia has been resolved splendidly: instead of a fake castle, the town now has a genuine ruin.

The Castle of Almere,
Almere, the Netherlands
Penta Architecten
(1999–)

Château Jemeppe,
Hargimont, Belgium

The Castle of
Almere, 2014

# OVERLAY— SYMBIOTIC SPACES

3

**Merriam-Webster**
@MerriamWebster

A fact is a piece of information presented as having objective reality. merriam-webster.com/news-trend-wat…

**Trending: Conway: 'Alternative Facts'**
Lookups for 'fact' spiked after Kellyanne Conway described false statements as 'alternative facts'
merriam-webster.com

58.1K 7:32 PM - Jan 22, 2017

46.1K people are talking about this

4

6

3 Line marking for different sports games on a wooden floor
4 Merriam-Webster Dictionary tweeted the definition of a fact just hours after President Trump's adviser Kellyanne Conway referred to false statements from White House press secretary Sean Spicer as 'alternative facts'.
5 Room in a *kommunalka*, a multiple-family communal apartment in St. Petersburg
6 Keiichi Matsuda, HYPER-REALITY, 2016
7 Gert Jan Kocken, *Depictions of Amsterdam 1940–1945*, 2009–2019

7

8

9

8 Milton Bradley Company, Twister, 1966
9 Richard Long, *Walking a Line in Peru*, 1972

# THE LIQUID CITY

Keiichi Matsuda

Keiichi Matsuda is an interaction designer and filmmaker. He began working with video as a critical tool to propose new perspectives on the city during his Master's of Architecture at the Bartlett School in London. His ground-breaking work shows and questions the impact of emerging technologies on human perception and the built environment, and the many ways in which media shape everyday life. In his 2016 short film HYPER-REALITY, he presented a provocative and immersive vision of a possible future. Shot on location in Medellín, Colombia, the short film speculates on how technologies such as virtual and augmented reality, wearables, and the internet of things eventually will inundate the city with data. As a viewer you are put in the position of a person who is trying to navigate the Colombian capital, which has become a mesmerizing mixed-reality where buildings are drenched in layers of information and citizens need to earn credits to survive. In this essay, Matsuda reflects on the deeper implications of this troubling scenario and explores what will happen when physical and virtual realities coalesce, architecture becomes augmented, and physical space is perceived through mediating filters. MvI

Technology has become a major driving force in defining our relationships with each other. Now, technology is starting to redefine our relationship with space. KM

New interfaces are emerging: we can talk to virtual assistants through smart speakers in our homes, everyday objects become enchanted through the internet of things, and we can immerse ourselves in media with augmented and virtual reality. Technology is now worn on the body, embedded in our environments. After decades of staring at our TVs, computers, and phones, our attention is slowly being refocused on the objects and environments around us. Media is escaping from our screens, and our world is becoming interlaced with a new dimension.

This is the Liquid City, where physical and virtual collide.

Augmented and Virtual Reality (AR/VR) headsets render software as architectural space. They allow code to appear in front of us, as virtual objects, animated characters, or new skins on our environment. Software is now something you can sit in, move around in. You can interact using your voice, your hands, your eyes. The Liquid City will respond to the movement of your body, even to the signals coming from your brain. This embodied interaction changes our relationship to technology; rather than devices that you control with a keyboard or touchscreen, technology is framed more as an extension of one's own abilities. It can be seen as a new sense or a set of supernatural powers that extend your awareness and agency in the physical world around you.

AR and VR headsets can give each individual a different, subjective view of the world. Two people may experience totally different realities, even when they inhabit the same physical space. Those realities could also be customized to suit the individual tastes and preferences of each user. The first generations of these technologies were characterized by this solipsistic escapism. We are each given an enhanced view of the world, but become isolated from each other.

The future of AR and VR lies in intersubjectivity: a consensual hallucination, where we dream the same dream. Virtual objects placed in the world become visible to passers-by and, over time, accepted as part of 'reality'. The physical city becomes immersed in a persistent virtual substrate that connects the humans and machines that live inside it. Our relationship with technology is no longer inward-looking, but defined by and comprised of our interactions with others.

The Liquid City is inhabited by both physically and virtually present people. In factories, machinery is animated by teleoperators using virtual interfaces. Remote advisors staff help desks and guide surgical procedures, fully immersed but still corporeally present in a distant darkened room or passenger seat.

Avatars allow us a ghostly embodiment over great distances. Business meetings and family get-togethers become liquid spaces, where physically and virtually present people are able to interact naturally with each other. The once-passive observers of media events also become embodied. A pack of ghosts witnessing live rolling news coverage, sporting events, music festivals, and natural disasters, floating above the crowds who are physically present. We are turning into liquid citizens, effortlessly slipping between realities.

Not all ghosts have human souls. Walking amongst the corporeal and ghostly citizens are animate spirits. Some are virtual assistants, obediently taking instruction. Some provide services, such as banking or navigation. Some may haunt a particular location, offering guidance or local knowledge. Brands become characters, on the fringes of your social circle, trying to gain your favour. Technology becomes a portal into this world of ghosts and spirits, and our interaction with computers becomes social and spatial.

Space itself becomes a form of digital media. With this come the effects of digitization: interactivity, democratization and eventual colonization. In the Liquid City, the production of space is no longer the reserve of architects, planners, and property developers; it can now be shaped by private individuals, technology platforms, and advertisers. It may be directly authored, built by software engineers, or assembled on the fly by artificial intelligence. The politics of space are opened for disruption.

This new generation of 'spatial' computing represents the most comprehensive set of surveillance technologies ever conceived. Devices worn on the body and embedded in our environments are packed with sophisticated sensing technologies that track your every move, listen to every conversation, deduce your preferences from the beating of the pulse or a movement and dilation of the eye. These technologies act as a mediating filter between you and everything around you. They respond to your commands, while also shaping your perception of reality. Fact and fiction become blurred. This is spatial computing's great power as well as its great danger.

The technology that enables the Liquid City is easily weaponized. Oppressive regimes may use it for indoctrination, suppression, and manipulation of the truth. Corporations may exploit this personal information to alter our behaviour to better fit their business models. Economic models based on attention and surveillance quickly take root.

As the physical world is mapped, captured, digitized, rendered, it is also commodified. The early builders of the Liquid City are corporations, but we should not take the assumed role of mindless consumer. Digital media also brings the potential of democratization, allowing each individual to impact the space around them.

Through decentralized public channels, citizens may start to build and share their own augmented creations: ornaments and decoration, graffiti and other marks of identity. Over time these become collaborative. Collectives form and build new thematic virtual layers to the city. Start-ups flourish in its streets and alleyways, new impossible architectures are seeded in the parks and public spaces. We could imagine the Liquid City as a new civic space, owned and operated by the citizens that live and work in it.

The organization of space is always political, and the way we design its governing principles could yield widely different outcomes. Different approaches can turn the city into anything from a democratic, expressive, and collaborative Fun Palace, to an enhanced theme-park shopping-mall, to an all-out surveillance hyper-capitalist dystopia.

Building the Liquid City is the creation of an extremely sophisticated illusion, a perceptual filter that shapes behaviour and identity. Its design is therefore entangled with the design of society, governance, justice, and belief. As more of our interactions become technologically mediated, the design of this mediating filter becomes the design of human experience.

Don’t avoid the complexity of reality, let it take you beyond your personal and professional comfort zone.

P-25 Anonymous student

# ENRICHING CHAOS—AN INTERVIEW WITH XAVEER DE GEYTER

Floris Alkemade, Mark Minkjan, Jarrik Ouburg

Xaveer De Geyter is a Belgian architect and founder of XDGA (Xaveer De Geyter Architects). The firm's architectural body of work covers all scales, from individual residences, public buildings, and master plans to regional studies. Their projects distinguish themselves in how they manage to translate complex and contradictory requirements of locations and clients into crystal clear answers in which that same complexity and contradiction turn out to be positive qualities. In addition to realized work, competitions are an important way for the firm to test and demonstrate their daring and critical attitude with regard to the built environment. We meet with De Geyter to discuss a project that was the result of one of the competitions they won: the restructuring of Place Rogier in Brussels. The interview takes place in XDGA's new offices, an old building in the centre of Brussels, structured around a courtyard and with one conspicuous element: an aluminium floor. JO

This aluminium floor seems to be the ultimate abstraction. Is that a contradiction when we talk about how to deal with complexity or is it rather a condition for allowing complexity? FA

XDG We felt the space was already so perfect that we limited the renovation to 15 cm of floor. We only removed all the interior walls. All the cables are integrated in a floor package that follows the structure of the existing building. So yes, it is sort of an extremely minimal intervention in a space that doesn't really need anything. The complexity is in fact underneath the tables.

That quite literally illustrates the theme of 'overlay'. Adding layers to allow for order within the separate layers and also showing that order. At the same time, it is a physical horizon; where the heads are, above the desks, there is quiet. How does that relate to your work, in which you often embrace complexity? FA

XDG Working with layers that are already there is something we have already been doing in many ways for quite some time. For example, the project After-Sprawl was about the Flemish context. It is part reading of what is there and part projection. We felt that there had been enough talking about all the things that go wrong in the fragmented and urbanized landscape of Flanders. We therefore embraced chaos as an interesting, complex order on which you can build in order to produce a nature-city constellation that is still interesting.

FA So, you are not reading the chaotic sprawl of Flanders in the same way as the cables you want to hide under the floor. Once you let go of the idea that things ought to be harmonious and in tune with each other it provides a freedom that suddenly makes many things possible. In the case of Belgium, I always have the feeling of the 'cadavre exquis', the form of poetry in which everyone adds a word without bothering about previous words. What always strikes me is this subtle sense of absurdism, allowing one to deal with things that are insufferable to others. Is that a correct view of Belgium?

XDG I think so, yes. And it's certainly true for Brussels, in a much denser form.

JO Part of the architectural profession is to not limit oneself to the surface, not to work only 'skin deep', but to also think in terms of the cross-section of the space. You are describing the floor in your firm not as an aluminium surface, but as a concealed double floor that allows you to work. Was the double floor of Brussels also a reason for you to establish your firm here, with sites like the 'Europe Square' and the complexity one finds here?

XDG The main reason for me was not so much the complexity, but rather the un-organizedness. I have been long convinced that in Belgium, and in Brussels, one can do projects that wouldn't be possible anywhere else. There is this light form of anarchism that allows for that.

To the average tourist, Brussels is not an interesting city. They are better off going to Paris, which is comfortably orderly, united, and elitist. In Brussels many things have gone wrong according to prevailing standards, but that is exactly what makes a city interesting: that it is not planned orderly and is full of contradictions. It's a type of urbanity that suits us.

FA This contradiction of Brussels is also upheld in a peculiar manner. Everywhere we see how historical inner cities are becoming prohibitively expensive to live in. Just look at Paris, London, or Amsterdam. In Brussels, however, there is a type of lower class living right in the heart of the city, isn't there?

XDG Absolutely. Housing is still cheap here and the affluent classes don't want to live here, precisely for the reasons I just explained.

FA If you accept complexity and contradiction as a starting point, what then is the next step? Just go on without wanting cohesion or ordering? Or do you think that there will still be interventions in which you—partly like you did with Place Rogier—will show the cross-section as a sort of Troy where each generation builds a city on top of the old one? Is this a form of ordering or of freedom?

XDG My feeling is that you must always at least thoroughly understand the layers in the existing situation before you can do anything at all. However, it's not deterministic in the sense that it should always lead to the same kind of projects or proposals. I can imagine at least two ways. It's perfectly feasible to do something that builds on and accommodates what is there. Still, in specific cases, you can say 'okay, I've got it, the history and all those layers, and so on' and then completely ignore all that as a form of over-awareness.

Maybe exactly because that is also part of that history? MM

Yes. In the past, in the 1960s but also at other times, the reasoning wasn't 'we have to completely adapt to what is there' either. XDG

So, it's like saying, from an historic awareness: 'Forget about it'. JO

If we zoom in on the Place Rogier project... What exactly was the question there? FA

It was an absolute mess. It was mainly a square that functioned as a roundabout for cars. It is situated on the inner ring with five, six streets joining it. Amidst all these traffic flows there were a few clumsily arranged spots of grass. The question was how to restructure it as a public space. XDG

It mainly looks like an enormous roof over a square, but there's more to it, isn't there? FA

In terms of money and energy, 75 percent is underground. We have completely rebuilt the surface and in fact extended the brief. There aren't many possibilities there for making a good public space, as there are many high-rise buildings. There are always strong winds, which are no incentive for installing sidewalk cafés. On the other hand, one can realize an agreeable area on the north side of the ring. Aboveground, much comes down to constructing surface. The most visible element is that canopy, but that is something of an outgrowth of what has been done underground. XDG

So, it is mostly organizing movement? FA

Yes, along two lines. At one time, the Place Rogier was quite efficient, as it was the public space of what used to be the North railway station. That is why many hotels were built here over time. Then the North-South link was built, an underground railway. It took fifty years–partly because of two world wars–and was only completed in the 1950s. Because the trains had to go underground, much length was needed for them to resurface. That is why the North railway station was moved five hundred metres to the north and subsequently the Place Rogier sort of lost its raison d'être. That's when it became this chaos of cars. We were asked to create a public space in relation to everything going on underground. Because meanwhile we have metro lines, including a metro line hub, underground trams, and a great number of buses: XDG three come by every minute. So, the natural relationship that used to exist between the railway station and the square–a tram going around it and pedestrian flows–was transformed by us from a horizontal one to a vertical one. The most important intervention to achieve this is a kind of light well. In fact, we just cut out the space of a patio, thereby connecting especially the various layers of public transport but also the large car park and a former exhibition space that will be given a new function.

FA So, it is also a project in which the cross-section is developed like a kind of floor plan and where each layer is constructed from a completely different logic.

XDG Yes, we simply put the horizontal flux upright.

MM So, it's about the relation between these layers that are on top of each other, but I think that by this intervention you have also altered the relation in the public space aboveground.

XDG That is the intention, indeed. There used to be the space of the smaller ring, a wide boulevard, part of which we made into a pedestrian area. On the other side is the square, closed in by these walls of construction. The canopy covers half of the square and half of the boulevard. The buses drive underneath it and if you're driving a car you are almost underneath it.

FA It does feel as if you're passing underneath it.

XDG It is also a gesture to unite those torn-apart neighbourhoods. The Place Rogier is part of the North Quarter, one of the most drastic urban planning interventions Brussels has ever seen, realized in the 1970s.

MM You can already see the canopy from North station.

FA It's actually more conspicuous than the high-rises.

XDG A whole series of streets join the Place Rogier. Some part of the awning is always visible.

JO It's nice how the canopy re-establishes the link with the railway station, even though it was moved 500 metres further north. Can you tell us something about how the awning is positioned in the square itself?

XDG For some reason or other we really wanted to have the canopy in the middle of the square, to create order. However, there was already a load-bearing structure with a grid of columns for the metro line, so that determined the place where we could make a foundation. As this did not coincide with the central axis of the square, we started from four columns from where the foot of the awning changes from quadrangular to hexagonal in an oblique upwards line. Just to arrive at the centre.

And you're not only doing this at street level, but also vertically, three-dimensional. At first sight it seems as if certain functions are hidden and traffic flows are separated, but at Place Rogier you explicitly show and connect them by taking away all the earth that kept everything together. About the rectangle cut out from the ground, did you see a sort of x-ray in which you discovered: 'Here is just have enough space to...'? JO

Yes, that patio was also partly determined by the line of the metro. Still, the possible relations were also limited because all of the underground construction is structurally linked to some of the high-rise buildings around the square. If we had situated that patio in the other direction, it would have had implications for the tower standing next to it. Not that it would have been impossible, but it would have required an enormous additional structure. XDG

Did you uncover any unexpected layers, literally or figuratively? MM

At Place Rogier all underground traffic was in fact flux, because there's also a tunnel to a shopping centre on the other side. All these things had in fact been completely ignored until now. There was a police station three floors underground, once intended to guard the metro. The underground spaces are not unlike the space underneath our aluminium floor. Chaos is quite acceptable and even enriching as long as you provide the right context. XDG

# Chaos is quite acceptable and even enriching as long as you provide the right context.

P-285 Xaveer De Geyter

**SPACE AS A CONNECTION** Place Rogier is the square in front of the North Station in Brussels, so historically it has always been shaped by infrastructure. When the train station was moved in the 1950s, the square was left orphaned, a windy void among anonymous high-rise buildings. The interventions made to transform the square into a high-quality public space again manifest themselves at various levels. Above the square, a round canopy with a diameter of 64 metres is the new gravitational point, providing shelter from wind and rain. At the level of the square itself a green promenade connects it to its immediate surroundings. A large patio, covered by the canopy, connects the complex layers of infrastructure (cars, trains, metro) and the flow of people. The patio not only brings daylight into the subterranean world of artificial light, but especially restores the relation between the square and its infrastructure, both horizontally and vertically.

Place Rogier,
Brussels, Belgium
Xaveer De Geyter
Architects (2006–2018)

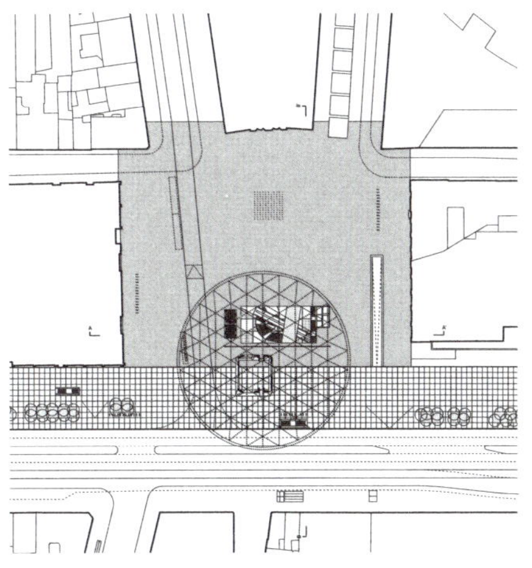

Site

Promenade

Place Rogier,
Brussels, BE

SHERATON

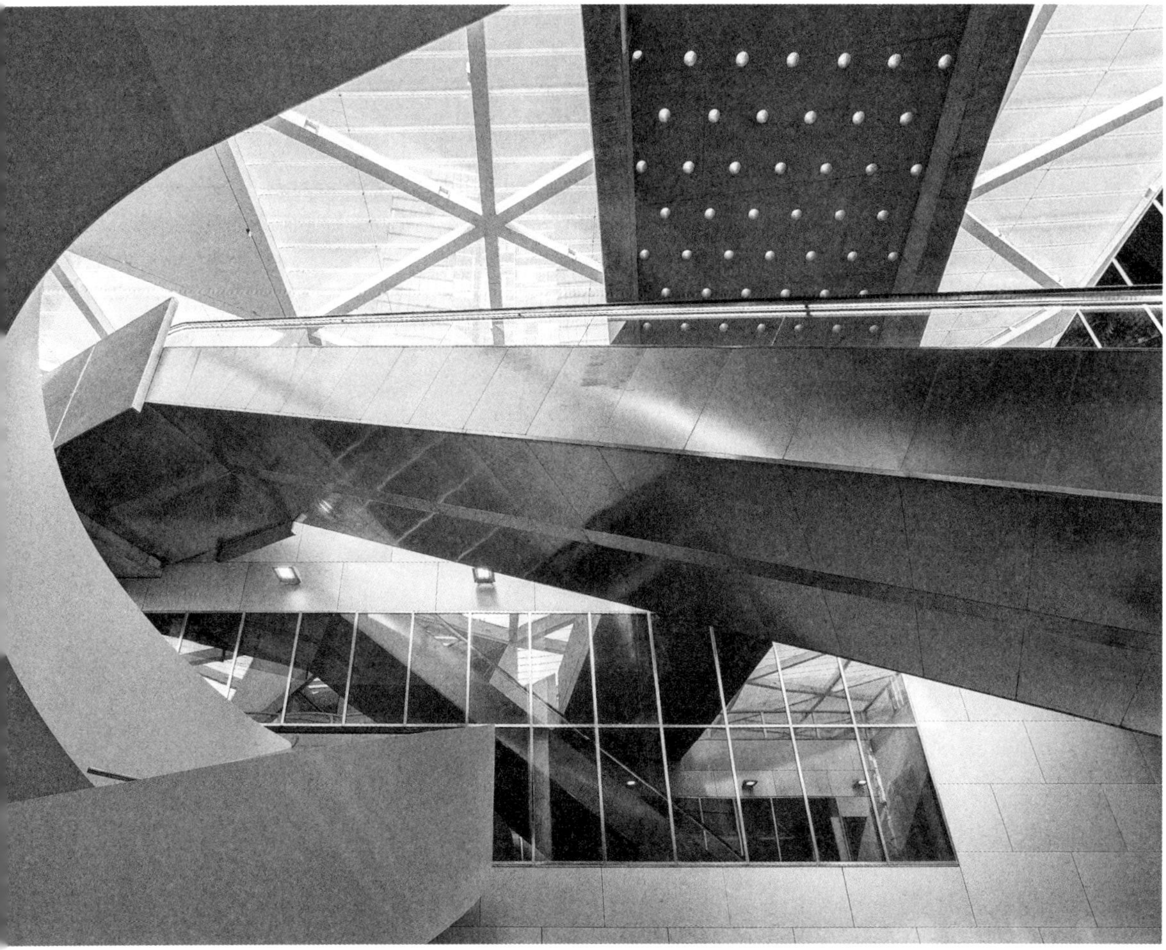

Xaveer De Geyter
Architects
Place Rogier,
Brussels, BE

↑ Section
Canopy, promenade,
square and
surroundings

→ Patio

**BUILDING WITHOUT CUTTING** A 180 m² house is built on a stretch of sand dunes along the Arcachon Bay. Twelve columns raise the volume of the house above the ground in order to let the residents benefit from the splendid views and to leave the existing lower vegetation of the arbutuses and mimosas untouched. All the higher pine trees are preserved too, including the ones located within the volume of the house, which are integrated through special holders to adapt their swinging and growth. The result is a surreal interior whereby the view, the trees, and the columns blend into one.

House Cap Ferret, Cap Ferret, France
Lacaton & Vassal Architectes (1998)

Section

**THE CABLE CAR THAT CHANGED THE CITY** In the early 2000s, the only way for the residents of the hillside neighbourhoods to visit downtown Medellín was to walk, or catch one of the infrequent, unreliable buses. At the same time, the Colombian capital had the reputation of being an exceptionally violent and dangerous place. In response, the city introduced the Metrocable, a cable car that connected the barrios on the hills with the city centre in the valley below. There are currently three aerial cable car lines in operation, serving hundreds of thousands of inhabitants on a daily basis. The Metrocable has cut the average travel time from the barrios to the centre in half, from roughly two hours to one. The area around the first cable car line in some of the poorest parts of the city, became the site for social interventions and investments in public space and services. The success of Medellín's Metrocable inspired other Latin American cities with a similar topography and socioeconomic situation to implement a cable car system.

Metrocable Medellín,
Colombia
Metro de Medellín
(2004–)

JO

## ORDER ABOVE CHAOS

'Tokyo is hopeless... I am leaving everything below thirty metres to others. If they think they can unravel the mess in this city, let them try.' A new city is built in the air. On huge columns that contain the vertical circulation it lands on empty plots. A utopian plan with a high degree of realism, as Tokyo is a city where almost all plots are privately owned and large developments across multiple plots are all but impossible. When in 1964, two years after this plan was published, Tokyo hosted the Olympic Games it was one of the reasons to construct new expressways on large columns above the rivers, as the rivers are city property. Reality has since overtaken the utopian plan and nowadays one recognizes a river in Tokyo by the expressway floating above it.

City in the Air,
Tokyo, Japan
Arata Isozaki (1962)

Site plan

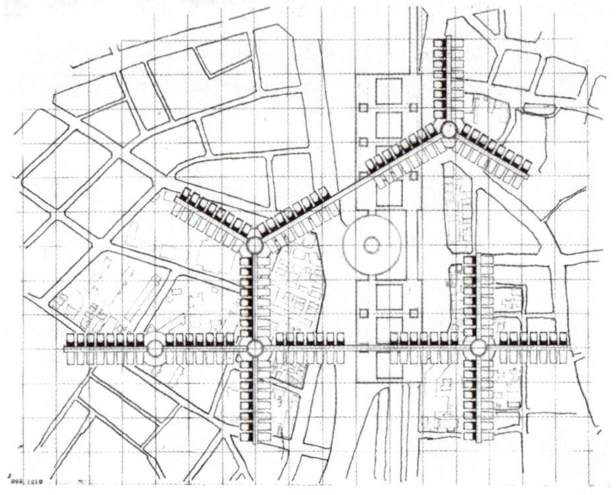

Urban implementation

UN-United Nations
Headquarters, the
'Island' of Crimea

**LAYERED AGRI-TECTURE** The critically acclaimed and hugely popular High Line is a 1.5-mile (or 2.5 km) long public park built on an abandoned elevated railroad stretching from the Meatpacking District to the Hudson Rail Yards, in New York City. During the first phase of the construction existing layers were removed from the structure, including the rail tracks, gravel, soil and plantings, debris, and a thin layer of concrete. During the execution of the design, many of the elements were returned to their original locations and integrated into the landscape design. The original steel structure was intended to carry freight loads, and while its structural strength was more than sufficient to carry the weight of a public park, it only provided, on average, eighteen inches (or approximately 45 cm) of space in which designers had to fit planking, tree planters, soil, and mechanical, electrical, and drainage systems. As a manifestation of what the designers call 'agri-tecture', this thin layer is exactly enough to turn the space from a domain of freight trains into an enjoyable habitat where people and plants can coexist.

High Line, New York City, United States
James Corner Field Operations, Diller Scofidio + Renfro, Piet Oudolf (2003–)

Section showing the relationships between people and plants

Elevated park

High Line,
New York City, US

FA

**AGREE TO DISAGREE** The project explores different domains that occur in the interlocking field of politics and architecture in the aftermath of the annexation of Crimea by the Russian Federation. By creating a setting in which opposing political interpretations can live next to each other within a context of disagreement, architecture can play a role in sorting out how this conflict can be absorbed in a now suddenly more than ever divided society. The project mirrors the well-known institute of the United Nations by erecting a Headquarter for the Un-United Nations. The urban setting of the building is well thought-over and carefully links to the historical grid that characterizes the archaeological site. The building is extreme in every sense, the corridor as the only remaining credible architectural typology in times of conflict.

UN-United Nations Headquarters, the 'Island' of Crimea
Lesia Topolnyk, graduation project (2018)

Interior

Site plan

MvI

SQUARE IN THE SKY With this temporary installation, aptly titled *The Garden Which is the Nearest to God*, Japanese artist Taturo Atzu created an observation deck and gathering space on top of Amsterdam's oldest monument and still active church. Using only scaffolding, white painted wood, and simple tiles, the abstract shape appeared to be hovering above the building. Wrapped around the weathervane and roof turret of the church, and only accessible by a steep staircase snaking its way up the building, visitors were given a unique opportunity to see architectural details that are normally hidden from view. More importantly, it negated the physical dominance of the church, which occupies a vast space in Amsterdam's medieval urban core. By creating a 'square in the sky', the artist created an otherworldly public space above the dense urban fabric, elevating people's daily life and allowing for dramatic views of the city below.

The Garden Which is
the Nearest to God,
Oude Kerk, Amsterdam,
the Netherlands
Taturo Atzu (2014)

Staircase

The installation
on top of Amsterdam's
Old Church
↓ A new public space

The Garden Which is
the Nearest to God, Oude
Kerk, Amsterdam, NL

Taturo Atzu
The Garden Which is the Nearest to God, Oude Kerk, Amsterdam, NL

MvI

**RISING FROM A ROCK** Fallingwater, the famous house designed by architect Frank Lloyd Wright as a weekend home for the Kaufmann family in rural Pennsylvania, has become an early icon of site-specific and nature-sensitive design. It is situated on a rock formation and partly built over a mountain stream. Especially during the spring, when the snow is melting, the sound of water can be heard all throughout the house. Sandstone for the walls was acquired from a nearby quarry. Some parts of the house seem to literally rise from the rocks. The stone formations visible on the floor in the living room are said to be boulders which were on the site, left in place intentionally to link the outside with the inside and keep the house cool on hot summer days. The architect had initially intended that the ledge be cut flush with the floor, but he came to understand that this boulder was Kaufmann's favourite spot for lying in the sun and listening to the falls. According to Wright this natural element is the starting point for the home, determining the height of the main floor and the dimensions of the surrounding structure.

Fallingwater, Mill Run, United States
Frank Lloyd Wright
(1936–1939)

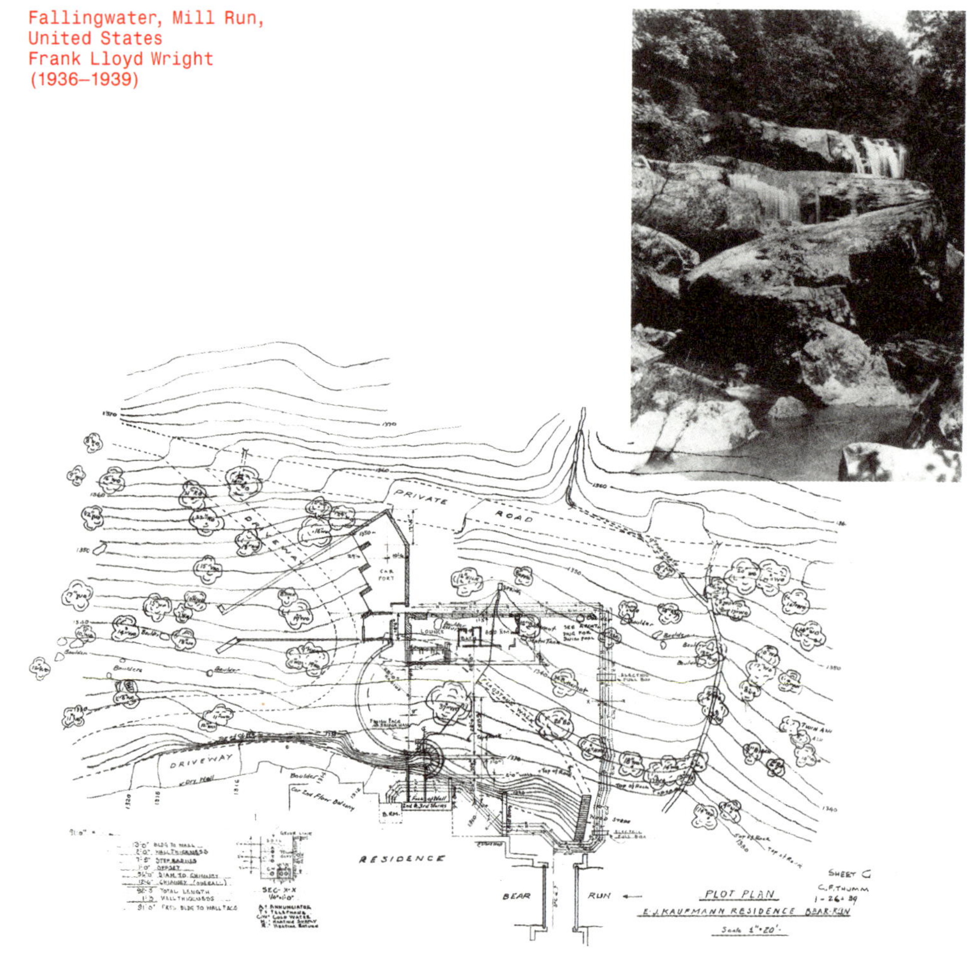


Original site

Plot plan

Living room, natural rock formations emerging from the floor

Fallingwater, Mill Run, US

**THE BEAUTY AND THE BEAST** The historical centre of Paris has become increasingly less flexible in appearance as a result of its stunning beauty. Yet, there are a few places where continuous change still occurs—places that structurally seem to trigger aversion and are therefore rethought, time and again. The Halles, right in the centre of the city where food used to be brought in, were regarded as a disgrace to Paris. On this site, Le Corbusier came up with the infamous Plan Voisin, the ultimate tabula rasa. After the Halles were finally torn down in the 1960s, a large underground node of Metro and RER lines was constructed, along with an immense multi-layered underground shopping centre. The culture that came with it, combined with the paltry park above, soon also led to a similar aversion. A competition was organized. OMA proposed to break up the strict separation between the above- and below-ground worlds by connecting the separate layers both spatially and visually. A 'built' therapy to heal the city by breaking the schizophrenia of the layered structure and make the city whole again.

Les Halles, Paris, France
OMA / Rem Koolhaas, Floris Alkemade Partners (2003)

Model

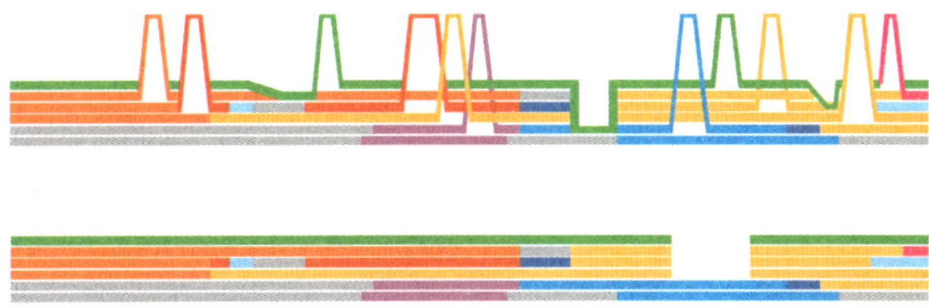

→ Section
Schematic drawing

Les Halles, Paris, FR

OVERLAY 303

JO

# A PEDESTAL FOR THE EXISTING

The client is one of the world's largest manufacturers of fragrances and flavours. The existing headquarters, built in the 1970s, is characterized by its typical floor plan and orange-coloured facade that mirrors the rich green vegetation of the site. The half sunken first floor of the building is expanded into a large rectangular plateau to house new offices and labs. The new building works like an architectural pedestal for the iconic existing building. Overlaying by underlaying. Patios provide daylight to the work places and give employees the opportunity to get some fresh air without leaving the secured environment of the building. Because of the half-sunken condition all work places are in touch with the sky, plants, and trees of the surroundings; the inspiration and ingredients of the company.

Landscape Laboratory,
Hilversum,
the Netherlands
HOH Architecten (2016–)

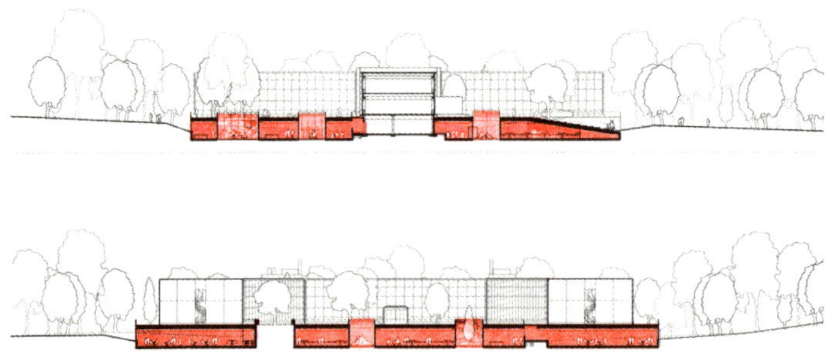

Section

New plateau under existing building

# REIMAGINE —LOOK AGAIN

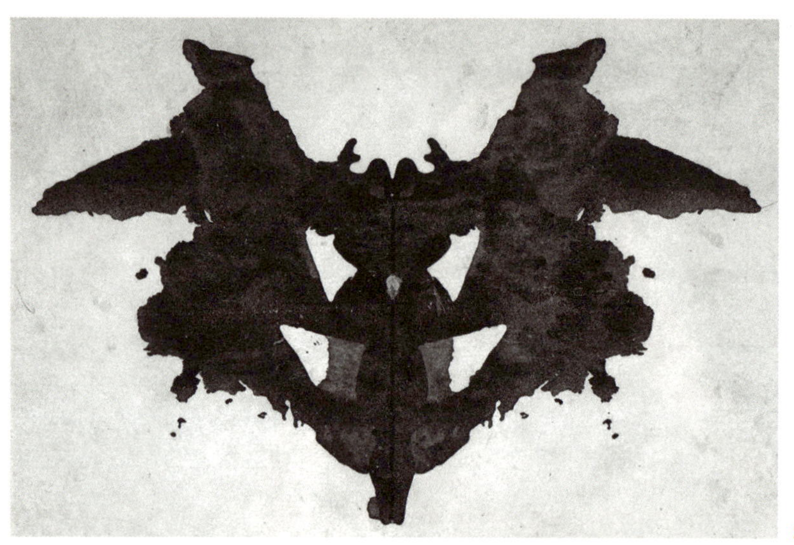

2

3

4

2 Hermann Rorschach, The first blot of the Rorschach ink-blot test, 1921

3 In Robert Mugge's documentary *Sun Ra: A Joyful Noise*, the legendary jazz musician is interviewed in front of the White House and wonders about the absence of a 'Black House'.

4 NASA, William Sanders, *Earthrise*, 1968. This image—the first full-colour view of planet Earth from space—helped to launch the environmental movement.

5

6

5 *The Thinker*, female version
6 A Russian grave in Moscow, husband (1935†) and wive (2002†)

# PREDICTIONS, ERRORS, AND SPACE—AN INTERVIEW WITH JIM VAN OS

Mark Minkjan, Jarrik Ouburg

Jim van Os is Professor of Psychiatric Epidemiology and Public Mental Health at Utrecht University Medical Centre, the Netherlands, and Fellow at King's College London. He was elected 'best psychiatrist' in the Netherlands several times by his peers and has been a member of the Royal Netherlands Academy of Arts and Sciences (KNAW) since 2011. From the very start, Jim van Os has been involved in the Tabula Scripta research and within this context has given several lectures at the Academy, always succeeding in providing insight into abstract neuro-scientific knowledge, making it quite personal, and accessible. We interviewed Van Os about how people perceive space and how spatial design can contribute to their wellbeing. JO

How does our brain process the interaction between us and our environment? MM

Neuroscience has in fact joined the old philosophical debate between realists and constructivists. It is physically impossible to take in your entire environment; through the senses, the brain can process about five percent of the stimuli it receives. So, we experience only five percent of reality. The rest is constructed into a representation of the world around us. Based on that representation we generate emotional signals, because we have to respond–flee, perhaps, or enter into a relationship with it. We also learn from these signals, as we construct this representation in turn on the basis of all previous environments we have experienced. We remember them also because they once generated a certain emotional signal. This explains the difference in perceiving the environment and experiencing meaning, because all interactions with the environment result in different emotional signals with different people. JvO

You are saying that how we experience a space is for five percent based on the objective space and for 95 percent it is projection, emotion, interpretation, memory. It is subjective, different for each individual... JO

Partly individual, yes, but we also learn together in a certain context. You could call it culture. We learn to assign meaning from the generation before us and in the contacts we have and this generates a collective JvO understanding of the environment. There are also universal spatial elements that have a certain effect on their users. The human scale, for example. If that is absent, people no longer meet each other, which may lead to a sense of displacement. There is evidence for this in various disciplines. Urban planners are very well aware that if you create a small park with benches and footpaths, people can meet each other.

JO What is the interaction between that five and 95 percent?

JvO The brain is continually predicting what the environment will do. You can only be consciously in a space if you project yourself in the future of that space, anticipate what is going to happen. Consciousness probably is literally linked to the fact that you move within the space and to everything involved in surviving. If suddenly something occurs that is incompatible with your prediction, you get a prediction error. This presents itself as an attention disruption that is often accompanied by a negative emotion. You then have to process this and figure out whether to fight or accept it.

MM And what is then the value or result of this prediction error?

JvO A prediction error can be useful, as it focuses your attention. You can't deal with everything at the same time in a diffuse manner. The prediction error helps you to focus on just a couple of the millions of stimuli coming at you. However, when an environment bombards you with many prediction errors, you may become lost.

Especially growing up in urban environments may lead you to assign too much meaning to interactions with people and environments: the hyper-meaning syndrome. Urban environments have a high incidence of madness.

Also, when confronted by too many prediction errors, people may protect themselves by withdrawing into apathy, or hypo-meaning. This may lead to a wish to flee the city.

MM This reminds me of what the philosopher Georg Simmel already stated around 1900 in The Metropolis and Mental Life: that there are so many stimuli in the city that people start to behave jaded.

JvO There have been further studies into this. In cities, human interactions are different. They are less easily established and feel less familiar than in the countryside. Both quality and quantity of urban interaction contribute less, on average, to health resilience. We need meaningful interaction with other people especially during our development as children or adolescents.

You're saying that urban interactions are not always optimal for our health. Is that purely mental? MM

No, it is physical as well. In all aspects of health, you are worse off in cities: cardiovascular, musculoskeletal, oncological. JvO

Then why are you living in the centre of a big city yourself? JO

It works for me. Also because I can retreat if I want to. That is much harder to do if you are exposed to the noise of other people on a daily basis and do not have the means to go and live elsewhere. JvO

I grew up in the countryside but it never felt as my natural habitat. In the city everyone comes together. It provides a wealth which of course also means pressure but you could also see it as a kind of white noise. There is so much sound that it produces a kind of silence at the same time. JO

It may seem as if there is a huge diversity in cities, but if you look at with whom people associate in networks there is much stratification. In a city like Amsterdam highly educated people associate with other highly educated people. In the countryside people mix more, in that sense. For example, through church, a symbol with universal values that unites all. There are less and less of such symbols, especially in large cities. JvO

There used to be the square, the church, and the pub. Straightforward typologies with clear functions, which also provide cultural identity within the community. Now that all these values are changing, and with them the meaning of the square, how do we deal with this? JO

In spatial interventions a local dialogue about values with specific groups living there is important. You will never totally agree with each other, but in such a dialogue you can create co-ownership. In this co-creation people take ownership of their surroundings and this makes it a more pleasant place for them. Social capital then grows, the extent to which people work together to make something of a public environment and defend it. When this dialogue is conducted properly you can create something of which many people will think 'this is us'. I think that that is where the real challenge lies. Co-creation really means that you are one step ahead of the prediction error. People can help shape JvO the thing they will eventually experience. They become involved beforehand, how it works is explained to them, and perhaps there is also room for some changes.

MM Can you give a successful example of this?

JvO Healing environments such as hospitals are interesting because there one has a much more shared experience of the environment. All users are going through a similar, very existential process: you are ill, you can no longer take your life for granted and you have to reinvent yourself. In such an environment you do not need to engage in value dialogue with each person individually because there are many common needs. As the architect or maker of public space in such circumstances you can therefore have quite a lot of influence.

By holding a value dialogue people can find each other and generate new meaning. In medicine, if you have a brain tumour you may decide, for example, not to have an operation but instead give meaning to the six months you have left. The environment you need should therefore not be cold or clinically focused on 'fixing', but rather on 'healing and dealing', which is more something that the patients involved must do themselves.

MM How can a physical environment contribute to this?

JvO At the Radboud Hospital in Nijmegen, the Netherlands, they purposefully consulted architects in order to create a healing environment. They have a lot of psychiatric patients there. In various spaces, also in the Intensive Care Unit, there are lines on the floor to mark what 'your space' is. Even if you are quite psychotic and everyone thinks you're dangerous, no one may cross that line without asking. This turns out to have quite an important effect on people. Patients also control how much light there is and they are involved in furnishing and decorating spaces. So not everything is arranged to accommodate the work of nurses and doctors. Patients have choices too. This appears to be quite healing for people and makes them take responsibility for their own vulnerability and health management, as it's called, much quicker. The famous 'Three Hospitals Study' of already half a century ago showed how psychiatric patients who are given a toothbrush and their own small closet to hang their clothes, suddenly start to take more responsibility for themselves. It really is about the question of allowing this person some space. This can be done in several ways, not just physically.

JO The Sick Building Syndrome—probably the opposite of the 'healing environment'—occurs when everything in a space is being controlled for you. The climate control is precisely calibrated and doesn't allow for windows to be opened. The air becomes oppressive and people become ill.

In how you describe the healing environment it seems as if our bodies are actually the first space. Not an object in a space, but a space in itself. The first space. Only then come the room, the building, and so on. If you make that first space more controllable to begin with, do you then create ownership which is perhaps also better expressed in the next spaces? I mean, if you already lose control in the first space...

JvO Yes, then you become sort of a passive consumer. The challenge is to have an existential discussion with the persons that will be using your space. This means, for example, that you can have a conversation about suffering. Instead of taking action to relieve the suffering, you must also be able to ask what that suffering means exactly, whether perhaps it has meaning, and what autonomy exactly means. To do this, you have to give up your technical attitude and just talk to some one and also reveal something of yourself, and acknowledge the uniqueness of the other person. This goes for doctors as well as for architects or urban planners. Such conversations must succeed in order to make negotiation possible. But it is the hardest thing to do, especially in technical professions that may impact other people. But I say, give up your technical attitude and try to understand the other person for whom you are creating something.

… give up your technical attitude and try to understand the other person for whom you are creating something.

P-315 Jim van Os

# ARCHITECTURAL SYMBOLS FOR A SHARED FUTURE

Arna Mačkić

Arna Mačkić is an architect and founder of Studio L A. She was head of Architectural Design at Gerrit Rietveld Academie Amsterdam and author of the book *Mortal Cities & Forgotten Monuments*. Much of the work of Studio L A revolves around the investigation of societal issues through architecture and the design of inclusive spaces that foster encounter and collectivity. Mačkić has researched architecture as a means of visualizing alternative narratives for segregated and post-conflict cities, taking her personal history as a refugee from Bosnia in the 1990s as a starting point. In this essay, she discusses the architectural politics of exclusion and inclusion, followed by an exploration of languages and spatial rituals that can help reimagine the city as a shared experience. MM

Architecture does not consist of just cold stone and concrete, but also of stories and memories that are linked to places that people identify with. When these places are about to change because of social, economic, or political influences, this identification by the current residents or users is at stake. This is the case, for example, when destroyed cities are rebuilt or when neighbourhoods change rapidly as a result of large-scale property development and gentrification. This process of change always involves creating future images and narratives for the place in question. The space is redistributed and groups of people are included, whereas other groups are excluded. In such situations, symbols are often deployed which suppress or overwrite existing meanings, including architecture. In shaping these narratives architecture can also be deployed as a language for giving users the space to achieve ownership of places. When these narratives are layered and different people feel represented in them, architecture can bring together people of various backgrounds. AM

My hometown Mostar in Bosnia-Herzegovina lends itself well to illustrate the including and excluding mechanisms of architecture and the role of imagination.

In 1993, the Old Bridge in Mostar was destroyed by Croat military forces during the

Croat-Bosniak War. Before the war, Mostar, named after the bridge that was originally built in 1566, was the city with the most mixed marriages in what was then Yugoslavia; a city where people of various ethnic and religious backgrounds lived together and no one cared about your family name or your religion. In addition to being a historic and architecturally important site, the bridge was also a public meeting space for residents on both sides of the river. It was also the place where for centuries a diving ritual was practised by people from various backgrounds. Ever since the bridge was built men and boys dive off it to prove their virility and impress the women, but it is also a ritual for paying homage to the city. All residents, regardless of their religion or ethical background, identified with the Old Bridge. The diving champions–whatever their background is–are still regarded as important role models by all the residents.

The bombing of the Old Bridge was part of a broader war strategy in which destruction of public and cultural buildings was used to eradicate a certain culture and identity. This made it an attack on the residents of Mostar as well. To destroy a people, you first have to destroy everything they identify with.

After the war there was little left of the mixed city of Mostar. Seventy percent of the city was in ruins and the competition for space during and after the war resulted in the division of Mostar. On one side of the front line we now have people from a predominantly Islamic background–although most Islamic Bosnians are not religious people–and on the other side people from a predominantly Catholic-Croat background. Each population has its own schools, books, football clubs, cultural centres, fire brigade, and telephone network.

And both populations also have their own way of rebuilding. During the reconstruction choices had to be made about what stories would be told and which groups would be given room in the stories. Each restoration or new building project became a political statement. The past was retold and emphasized in competing ways by symbolic and politically charged architectural interventions. In 2004 the Old Bridge and the old town were completely restored to their original state–with European financial backing and support from politicians–as the symbol of a reunited Mostar. In reality, the New Old Bridge became primarily a tourist attraction while in the rest of the city symbols and monuments of division were erected. Streets were given new, often 'nationalist' names, and ethnically and politically coloured institutions were given prominent places in the city. In West Mostar, most of this has served to erase the communist past and refer to the motherland of Croatia. Own space was expanded instead of shared.

The Bosnian reconstruction process has given me a new look on the architectural profession. Architecture cannot solve the conflict in Mostar but it can most certainly either reinforce or mitigate it. Through the imagination, architects can tell an inclusive story. Meeting places for diverse groups can be realized when various groups feel represented in the process, design, and programming.

One example of architecture that produces collective places also lies in the history of the former Yugoslavia. After the Second World War Josip Broz, aka Tito, became the leader of the newly formed nation. To deal with the nationalist tendencies in the region, he introduced a strict socialist regime. While this regime squashed any public nationalist and religious outings (which arguably only fuelled the violent outbursts of the 1990s) it also emphasized the similarities and mutual dependencies between the different ethnic groups of the six republics that together formed Yugoslavia. The country became a laboratory for making different ethnicities and religions live side by side via education, media, theatre, film, and architecture.

Between 1960 and 1980, Tito had architects and artists design over a hundred monuments in memory of the victims of fascism during the Second World War. These were not designed only to commemorate horrendous events; they also had to become public meeting places that told a new narrative of the shared future of citizens of Yugoslavia. In order to appeal to all citizens –regardless of their religion or ethnic background–a new visual language was developed without any religious, political, ideological, or nationalistic symbols. Most artists and architects designed abstract and futuristic looking monuments that radiated power and grandeur, often made of one material and with little detail or ornamentation.

One exception was the architect and urban planner Bogdan Bogdanović (1922–2010) from Belgrade. For Bogdanović, cities were living beings with a distinct soul that only becomes truly evident after the city has acquired a particular historical character. This character, he believed, can be detected in the city's buildings. The monuments he designed complied with the set rules, but Bogdanović also sought to insert elements referring to the city's history. Symbolic elements proved to be crucial for this. During Tito's regime, he designed numerous monuments and public spaces, none of which contained explicitly religious or ethno-nationalistic symbols.

Bogdanović attempted to create places that offered new perspectives on both history and the future. An important aspect of his method was using recognizable and widely used local symbols and materials belonging to what he considered the 'soul' of a place, rather than to any specific community or religion. These ranged from particular rock types to the techniques employed during construction, or the experiences and activities of the inhabitants' everyday lives. As such, the familiar, recognizable and everyday connected past and future. These elements were then combined with metaphysical and cosmological symbols, demonstrating that humans are also part of a much larger universe.

> I often sought inspiration in archaeological materials; I ventured deeper into the world of archaic images; I was looking for ancient imaginative matrices. I wanted, in terms of the universal human, the presumed 'anthropological memories' to represent war and death, the conqueror, the conquered, and above all the indestructible joy of life.
> –Bogdan Bogdanović

One of Bogdanović's exemplary works in this regard is the Partisan Necropolis in Mostar, completed in 1966. Apart from being a memorial site dedicated to 810 Mostar partisans who fought against fascists during the Second World War, it also became a place where Mostar's inhabitants spent their free time walking, playing, and picnicking. Bogdanović described the monument as an 'acro-necropolis': a microcosm of the city of Mostar where 'the city of the dead mirrors the city of the living'. To Bogdanović it was a small-scale replica of the city in its ideal form, a diagram of Mostar.

On the way up to the monument, you can hear the water running down from the monument's total of five terraces into a basin with a ribbed surface, causing the running water to sound almost like an organ. Water was an essential element of the design, demonstrating the city's dependence on the Neretva River. Furthermore, the monument features the cobblestones, alleys, and gates that are so characteristic of Mostar. The limestone was sourced from nearby mountains. Stones and rocks were recuperated from destroyed or otherwise damaged houses and donated by the inhabitants, showing traces of their previous usage. Reaching the top of the monument, you encounter a fountain paired with the central architectural element of the monument: a cosmological sundial.

The local elements used refer to the city's continuity from the past into the future. Bogdanović pointed out that the ways in which communities relate to and interact with one another are only temporary. This transitory nature–symbolized by the running water–contrasts with the longue durée of the material and the physical, even geological, qualities of Mostar. This way, the everyday becomes part of 'something bigger' to which different communities and religions can relate. Bogdanović's site-specific design makes it seem as if the Partisan Necropolis has always been there, and that it will continue to be; the megalomaniac scale, the monumentality of the construction, and the near-mythical impression of indestructibility also add to this impression. Finally, the cosmological sundial conveys the feeling that the monument has found its proper place in the universe, and connects Mostar to the cosmos.

Despite Bogdanović's attempt to make the monument accessible to all Mostar residents, nowadays it is no longer appreciated by a large part of the Catholic-Croat community because of its connection with the Second World War and Tito's ideology. They no longer wish to identify themselves with the monument that is a symbol of a fight they have not yet come to terms with and which is for them still unfinished. During the Second World War, Croatia was an ally of Nazi Germany and tens of thousands of Roma, Jews, Serbians, and participants were murdered in extermination camps. In both Bosnia-Herzegovina and Croatia this historical period is now being glorified, and the extreme right is on the rise. It is as if the communist and Yugoslav history is being erased.

As an architect critically examining exclusionary practices that value the history of one ethnic group over the access to public space of another, I have drawn from the visual language that Bogdan Bogdanović used to create a more inclusive public space in the divided city of Mostar. My design proposal Jump takes the still functioning ritual of diving off the bridge as its starting point. The act of jumping has remained as one of the few shared traditions amongst all residents. Jump is a monument dedicated to diving and a structure where citizens can learn, step by step, to dive from great heights, and prepare for the plunge from the New Old Bridge as the final step. It is located in the city centre where the two sides of the city meet, just across from the segregated high school where a Croatian-Catholic and a Bosnian school share the roof but do not communicate. The design offers an urban ritual for all inhabitants of the city, regardless of their nationality, religion, gender, or age. The monument's proximity to the high school should invite boys and girls from different backgrounds to collectively practice this physical activity.

Jumping from the bridge can be seen as a sign of being a Mostarac or Mostarka, and not just a member of some district. Jumping off the bridge is an individual activity, but one that connects all Mostarians, as equals, through the courage to do so. The three-second jump towards the water provides a feeling of weightlessness and freedom where one becomes detached from everything around oneself, including one's entanglement in the struggles of Mostar. Individual, physical, and emotional activities that require courage and trust can foster the feeling of belonging to a place and a community. They can help people to reclaim and reimagine the city and its architecture for a moment, and dive into the future with a new version of the old in mind.

… change always involves creating future images and narratives for the place in question.

P-317 Arna Mačkić

DIVING FROM A MONUMENT Jumping off the Old Bridge in Mostar used to bring young men together: Muslims from the east bank and Christians from the West Bank. For centuries, it made this bridge from the Ottoman period the symbol of religious harmony until it was destroyed during the Yugoslavian war, in 1993. The bridge has since been rebuilt, in the physical sense, but the Mostar residents are living more separate from each other than ever before. A new building focuses fully on the tradition of the jump and on a new generation of children, boys and girls, Muslim and Christian; it is a 'diving school'. In the square in the 'neutral zone' of Mostar it seems to rise from the ground in large steps. With each step of fifty centimetres high children increasingly overcome their fear and eventually they reach a height of eighteen metres, preparing them for a jump off the Old Bridge. As of old, the bridge can then again be the place for encouraging friendship among a generation who have met at the 'diving school'. The structure's design does not include any references to religion, nationality, or ethnicity— it only refers to the act of jumping and is therefore open to a new meaning, as a symbol for a new perspective.

Jump, Mostar,
Bosnia-Herzegovina
Arna Mačkić (2016)

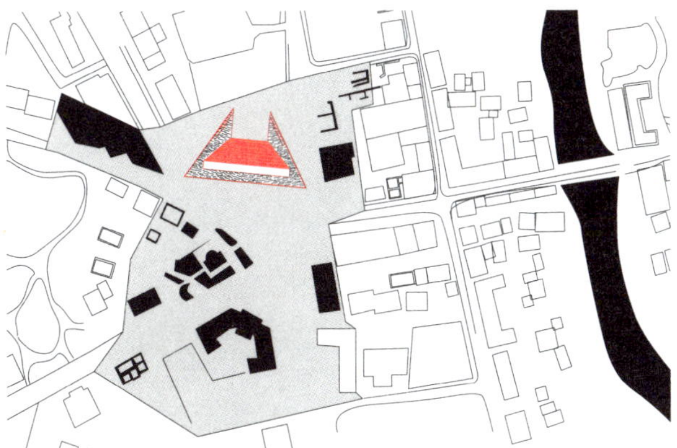

Context

Backside
↓ Facing the square

Arna Mačkić
Jump, Mostar, BA

**SPACE OF FLOWS** Skateboarding changes your perspective on a city and the potential of urban spaces. It offers (young) people a way to re-define their own environment and invent new ways of interacting with it. The so-called Undercroft, an undefined space underneath the Southbank Centre in London, which is considered to be the birthplace of the British skateboarding scene, provides powerful proof of this potential. It was first appropriated in 1973 and quickly developed into one of the most important skateboarding spots in the world. With the intention of a temporary closure, part of the Undercroft was boarded up in 2004 and remained inaccessible for almost a decade. The Long Live Southbank! grassroots initiative, which brought together skaters, architects, and many others, successfully defeated the other proposals, managed to save the space, and gained a legal guarantee for its long-term future. In 2013, a crowdfunding campaign kick-started the restoration and redesign of the space, seamlessly merging the 1960s design with the current skate function. Apart from rehabilitating the 'little banks' and timber ledges, used by skaters to do their tricks, the restoration helped to reconstitute the Undercroft as a place of collective creativity.

Southbank Undercroft,
London, United Kingdom
Feilden Clegg Bradley
Studios (2019–)

Southbank Undercroft after the restoration

**CONNECTING MIND, BODY, AND SOUL** Heritage, art, and, on Sundays, churchgoers all come together in Amsterdam's oldest building (since 1306). After careful restoration, the monumental church building was reopened to the public in 2013, with a new programme centring on contemporary art. Various artists present site-specific art installations in the church space. Aptly named Come Closer, an ongoing public programme wants to bring visitors closer to these art works, to the building, and to each other. Developed by cultural collective Non-fiction, the programme offers a new approach and collaboration every year. In 2014, artists Amie Dicke and Rafe Copeland developed a scripted tour of the church that invited visitors to look at architectural details from unexpected perspectives, for example by laying on the floor or by leaning against a staircase. In 2017, in collaboration with Bureau LADA and in response to a solo show with works by artist Marinus Boezem, visitors could engage in various exercises to literally get a feel for the building. Wearing a blindfold, they had to navigate the space with their other senses. In all iterations of Come Closer, visitors establish a personal connection with the space, going beyond what's visible and connecting mind, body, and soul.

MvI

Come Closer,
Oude Kerk, Amsterdam,
the Netherlands
Non-fiction in collaboration with Amie Dicke, Rafe Copeland, Bureau LADA, and others (2015–ongoing)

Exploring the paintings on the ceiling (part of *Come Closer: Scattered Stories*)

Guided tour with blindfolds (part of *Come Closer: Scattered Stories*)

MvI

**A BUILDING FOR BECOMING** Occupying a full city block in the heart of Hollywood, the campus stands as a beacon of hope and pride for the LGBT+ community in Los Angeles. Since 1969, the LGBT Center has offered a safe space for lesbian, gay, bisexual, transgender, and other individuals across the spectrums of sexuality and gender who have historically faced discrimination, violence, and marginalization. The new campus includes diverse affordable housing programmes, as well as a hundred beds for homeless youth, a youth academy, administrative areas, and a retail space. The multifaceted design expresses the idea of queerness (from 'queer', an umbrella term for sexual and gender minorities who are not heterosexual or whose sense of personal identity and gender does not correspond with their birth sex). The architects define queerness as a state of fluidity, or a process of continual becoming. This idea is expressed in their design through the fragmented facade, reflecting surfaces and other visual elements that suggest a multiplicity of identities. While walking, or driving, around the campus, forms start to collide, overlap, and align.

LGBT Center Anita
May Rosenstein
Campus, Los Angeles,
United States
Leong Leong + Killefer
Flammang Architects
(2019)

Fragmented facade

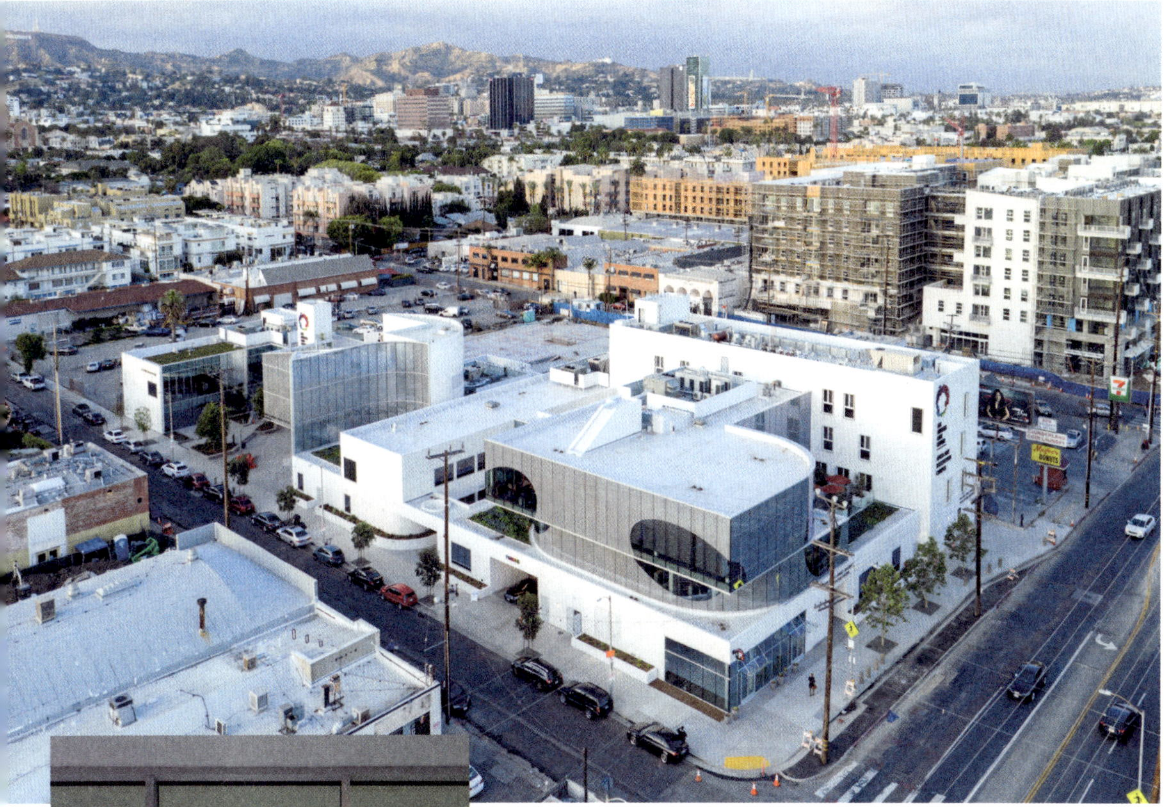

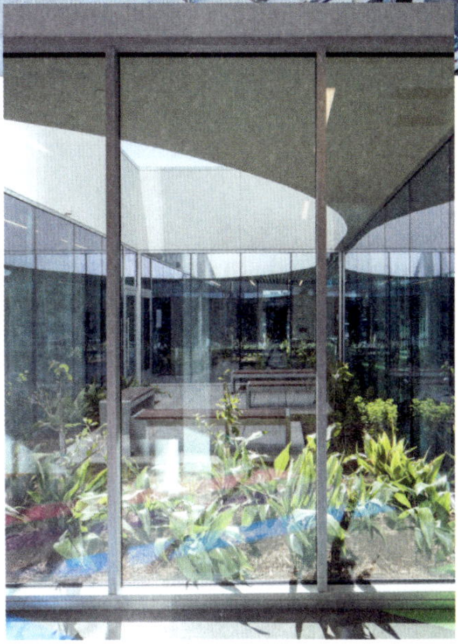

→ Aerial view with Los Angeles skyline
Interior with reflecting surfaces

Ground floor plan

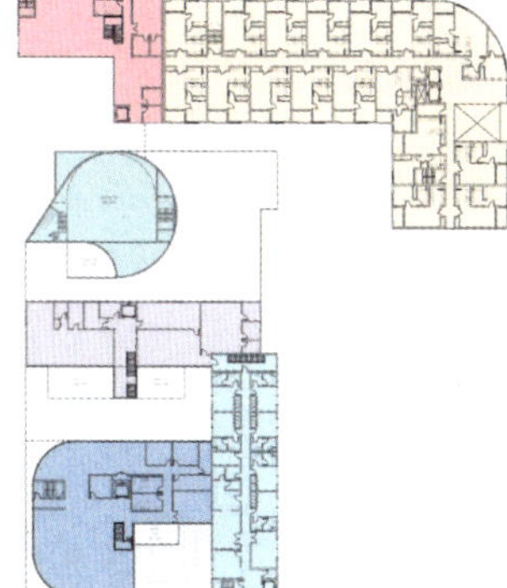

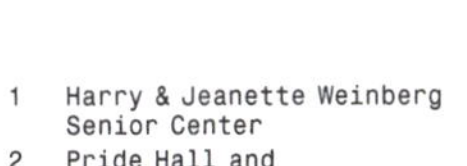

1 Harry & Jeanette Weinberg Senior Center
2 Pride Hall and Administrative Offices
5 The Ariadne Getty Foundation Youth Academy
7 Transitional Living Program
8 Administrative Offices
10 Senior Affordable Housing (to be completed 2020)
11 Youth Micro-Unit Housing (to be completed 2020)

LGBT Center Anita May Rosenstein Campus, Los Angeles, US

## ADDING MISSING LINKS

Homeless often see their neighbourhood as their home, in which living room, kitchen, and bedroom are connected like a network of amenities. The number of homeless people in Amsterdam is growing, which means that sometimes there is no place in the kitchen or the bed is already occupied. This causes much unrest and stress. Without the security of bed, bath, and bread, people cannot work on developing themselves and are always busy with simply surviving.    To fill in the missing links in this fragile network, the project made use of waste materials, residual flows and residual spaces that society leaves everywhere. On the Dapper Market in Amsterdam a kitchen was built for homeless people, to cook meals with left-over food from the market stalls. In an unused alley in the Jordaan neighbourhood a place to sleep was made from cardboard: the bed-alley, where a homeless person could stay for one night when there was no more room in the shelter. The project shows that if the problems of homeless people are not being solved within the domain of politics and on the level of the state, they must be solved within the domain of architecture and on the level of the street.

A Sense of Home,
Amsterdam,
the Netherlands
Patrick Roegiers,
graduation
project (2019)

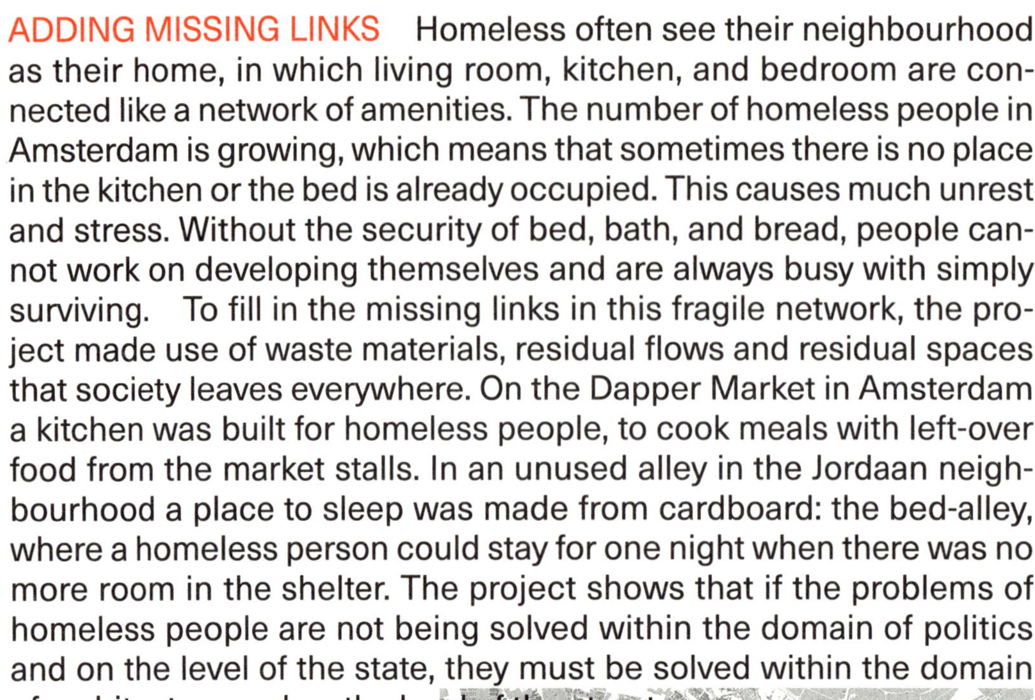

Homeless network of Amsterdam

Bed-alley exterior and interior

EMPOWERING IMPEDIMENT For those who end up in a wheelchair, the world changes, leaving only the horizontal plane as manoeuvring space. This villa in Bordeaux provides an environment in which not this limitation but becoming free of it is taken as the starting point. The key to this is a central room that moves between the floors, like an elevator. When the wheelchair user reaches a certain floor, his arrival adds a room to the floor plan, thereby changing the house. All thanks to the imaginative power that doesn't accept a limitation and adds a third dimension to it, changing a restriction into an enrichment.

Maison à Bordeaux,
Bordeaux, France
OMA / Rem Koolhaas
partner (1995–1998)

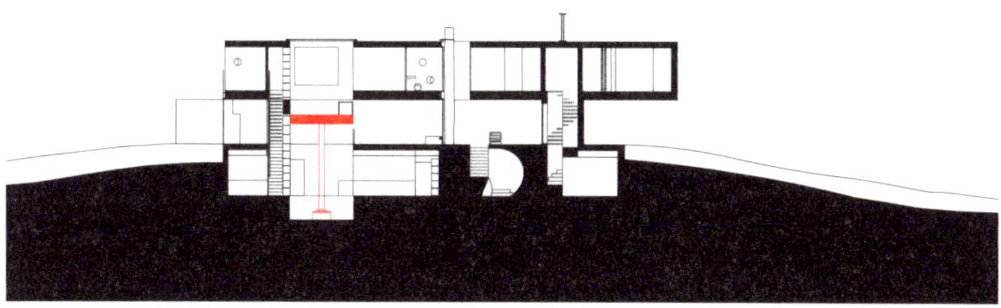

The villa on a hill

The 3 × 3.5 m
elevator platform

Maison à Bordeaux,
Bordeaux, FR

MvI

**CAN A BUILDING HEAL?** The Butaro District Hospital opened in 2011 in a joint effort to bring high-quality healthcare to one of the country's poorest regions, a half a day's drive from Rwanda's capital city of Kigali. The 150-bed hospital and cancer centre form a patient-centred campus of buildings on a terraced hillside, developed around an old *umuvumu*, or indigenous Ficus tree. Thousands of local community members were employed during construction of the hospital and whenever possible, local materials were used. The visible presence of vegetation and gardens has proven to reduce the stress levels and pain perception of patients, as well as retain nurses within health care facilities. Additionally, shaded seating areas were created all across the campus to encourage patients to spend more time outdoors, which greatly reduces the transmission of airborne disease. In the same spirit, a children's play area was placed in the central courtyard. Located on an adjacent site to the Butaro Hospital, the Butaro Doctors' Housing is designed to attract and retain skilled physicians at the new hospital as part of a community where the idea of health is reimagined and boundaries between patients and other people are blurred.

Butaro District Hospital, Burera, Rwanda
MASS Design Group in cooperation with the Rwandan Ministry of Health and Partners in Health (2011)

Aerial view

Hospital ward (exterior)
↓ Hospital ward (interior)

Butaro District
Hospital, Burera, RW

J0

## THE CITY OF THE CHILD

After the Second World War, Amsterdam was expanded with new neighbourhoods for young families. The building sites with their piles of bricks and mounds of sand served as informal playgrounds for children. When the neighbourhoods were completed, the children had to play between the cars that were parked along the streets. Jakoba Mulder, an urban planner for the municipality, observed that the public space had not been designed from the children's perspective and she commissioned architect Aldo van Eyck to design playgrounds that would harmonize with the existing public space. More than seven hundred playgrounds were designed using standard elements that were characterized by an abstract form language and materials that could previously be found on the building sites: steel, concrete, and sand. Where nowadays garish plastic play equipment often contrasts with the surroundings and is designed monofunctionally, these play elements seamlessly fitted in with the urban landscape, stimulating children (and grown-ups alike) to explore the possibilities of the elements themselves. A dome-shaped climbing frame became a high bar and a house at the same time; the wide edge of the sandpit was a great place to build your sandcastle and it also served as a bench and meeting place for the parents in the neighbourhood.

Playgrounds, Amsterdam, the Netherlands
Aldo van Eyck (1947–1978)

Situation after the urban plan was realized

Situation after the playground was added

Cas Oorthuys,
*The Iglo*, 1963

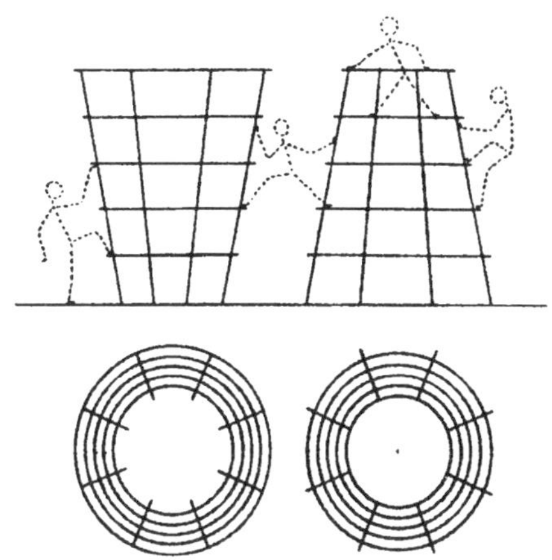

Climbing funnels plans
and elevations

J0

**DON'T SOLVE, DESIGN** Public space should be the place where the collective intelligence in the fields of policy, design, and craftsmanship coincide in a Gesamtkunstwerk to the greater honour and glory of a city's residents. The opposite is often the case and the lack of integration of disciplines is evident from the impromptu solutions applied in the place where it affects people most. The BXL 100 study presents interventions in public space that demonstrate how minimal means can achieve a maximum improvement, from the perspective of the daily social world of residents. These examples go beyond damage control or repair work. They show the surplus value of good design for the daily lives and everyday happiness of the inhabitants of the city, which is, in a way, the essence of the discipline.

BXL 100, Brussels, Belgium
URA, Yves Malysse, Kiki Verbeeck, Topotronic (2008)

Before

After

MvI

**AFROFUTURIST CAPITAL** The imaginary Golden City is the thriving Afrofuturist capital of Wakanda, a fictional nation appearing in comic books published by Marvel Comics. Both first appeared in the Fantastic Four #52 comic book in 1966, and gained global fame after the release of the 2018 blockbuster movie *Black Panther*. Wakanda is situated somewhere in Africa and challenges dominant assumptions about the continent. It has never been colonized or conquered because it's sitting on a mass of valuable Vibranium, a magical metal that transformed the nation into a technological wonder, allowing it to remain invisible to the outside world. Combining elements from African and African American (diaspora) culture with advanced technology, the movie mixes tradition with the latest advancements in the fields of design, communication, and transportation. Taking inspiration from the histories and creativity of black communities from across Africa and the United States, from the landscapes and townships of South Africa to the streets of Oakland, California, the design team created a city that exists before, above and beyond existing realities; a place where African (American) identity is carefully reconsidered and celebrated.

The Golden City, Wakanda,
somewhere in Africa
Hannah Beachler
(Production Designer)
(2018)

Blyde River Canyon

Sites that served as inspiration for the Wakanda landscape and the Golden City

**NAVIGATING WITH THE SENSES** Situated to the south of Glasgow, the Hazelwood School caters for students, aged three to eighteen years, with a combination of severe visual, hearing, mobility or cognitive impairments and highly complex needs. The school meanders through a parkland site, forming gentle curves around the existing mature trees and allowing daylight and other natural elements to enter the building. The design focused on creating a safe, stimulating environment that can be navigated easily and independently. Visual and tactile aids, such as contrasting colours and materials, were incorporated. Signage throughout the school is in braille, in pictures, and in moon (a system made up of lines and curves including some ordinary letters in simplified form). The curved 'Trail Rail', stretching the length of the entire complex, guides the pupils gently down the main corridor. Clad in cork, the wall has warmth and tactile qualities and provides signifiers or messages along the route to confirm the children's location within the school.

Hazelwood School,
Glasgow, Scotland,
United Kingdom
Alan Dunlop Architect
Limited (2007)

Curving around existing trees

Trail Rail

# (RE)START —OVER AND OVER AND OVER

3

Fortnite
@FortniteGame
...
LIVE 17.3K viewers
Fortnite @FortniteGame
....
1:56 PM · Oct 13, 2019 · Twitter Media Studio
123.9K Retweets 317.9K Likes

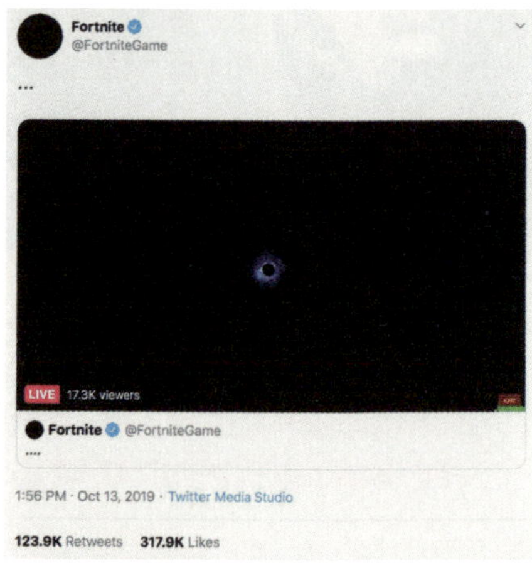

4

5

6

3 Nelson Mandela spent 27 years in prison before becoming president of South Africa, after the country's first democratic and multiracial general elections in 1994.

4 On 13 October 2019, the immensely popular game Fortnite shut down. Its entire playing map was attacked by rockets and the game was sucked into a dark hole, witnessed live by six million people worldwide. This narrative offered the game's developers a moment to launch a highly anticipated new chapter of Fortnite.

5 Fra Angelico, *The Annunciation*, c. 1437–1446. The Annunciation is the Catholic and Eastern Orthodox celebration of the announcement by the Archangel Gabriel to the Blessed Virgin Mary that she would conceive and become the mother of Jesus.

6 Laura McPhee, *Guardians of Solitude*, 2008. After more than 40,000 acres of forest in the White Cloud Mountains of central Idaho burned in a wildfire, the ecosystem quickly restored itself.

7 Jim Carrey's character Joel Barish has the memories of his relationship with Clementine Kruczynski (Kate Winslet) erased in the movie *Eternal Sunshine of the Spotless Mind* from 2004.

7

8

9

8 A palimpsest is a manuscript page, often from animal hide, from which the text has been erased so that the page can be reused for another document. These leaves from an ancient Qur'an were treated with ammonia in the late nineteenth century to enhance the under-writing.

9 A protester calling for a reset of the financial system during legal disputes over the fallen bank Icesave in 2009.

# FROM THE ASHES

Karin Riley

Karin Riley is a research ecologist with the US Forest Service in Missoula, Montana. Dr Riley's interests and job duties range from predicting the spread and extent of active wildfires, to modelling risk from wildfires under different fire suppression and funding policies, to studying how fires might change under climate change. She argues that, despite people's fear for the destructive forces of nature, wildfires are necessary to preserve and strengthen ecosystems. They unlock the life that lies hidden in dormant seeds and clear the way for growth. Through cycles of creative destruction, the forest is regenerated. It shows that a 'scorched-earth' approach can sometimes be a positive force. And it provides a powerful metaphor for thinking about the complex interplay between preservation and how destruction can help regenerate an environment. MvI

The world's societies have likely proved one thing to themselves by now: try as we may, we can't eradicate wildland fircs. And if we could, what would happen to our forests and grasslands? Many ecosystems depend on fire for their health. Destruction of one organism often clears the way for another. Sometimes what appears to be destruction is synthesis, the conversion of one substance to another. The question then, becomes how can humans best live with fire? The answer to this question will likely vary from culture to culture, and from fire regime to fire regime. KR

Fire has played across the earth's surface as long as vegetation has existed, some 420 million years, ignited primarily by lightning. Not long ago (and in fact still in some parts of the world) our ancestors used fire to herd animals while hunting, to cultivate fresh grass for grazing animals, to produce the straightest stems of hazel for basket weaving, to clear ground for planting crops. And yes, of course, fire could also be a foe: for example, used by one tribe to burn the resources of an enemy. But today's societies are likely more at odds with fire than any previously, as the traditional uses of fire have been suppressed and many have become irrelevant in an increasingly urban and technological society.

In many cultures, fire is seen as a hazard, a force that can only destroy, not benefit. Billions of dollars are spent every year to put fires out: firefighters are deployed from fire engines, helicopters, and airplanes, while water and chemical fire retardants are dropped from air tankers. These fire suppression measures meet with varying degrees of success. Under mild weather conditions, fires are likely to be contained. Under extreme weather conditions (hot, dry, and windy) fires are resistant to human control. Some researchers ask, if we are extinguishing fires under mild conditions, are we allowing vegetation to become thicker, making the next fire more difficult to control? Or, conversely, are forest fires necessary if we want to create environments that are resilient, allowing humans and non-humans to co-exist?

While climate change does appear to be exacerbating wildfires in some areas, globally, the area burned by fires has been declining for the past few decades, due mainly to decreases in burning in the African savannas. Yet, the number of tragic stories about fires causing human deaths and destruction of homes is increasing in the news. This is likely because despite fewer fires, we find ourselves more often in the way, as the built environment expands.

Wildfire exhibits a spectrum of moods. It depends on the weather (fiercely hot, dry, and windy, or moist with springtime and still?). It depends on the type of tree and the prevalence of grass. It matters whether the ground is flat or mountainous (fire tends to race up slopes, and slowly down them). At one end of the spectrum is what fire scientists call a high-severity fire regime. Here, fire engulfs the forest, burning all vegetation from the forest floor to the tops of the trees. The flames are often much taller than the forest itself. At the other end of the spectrum is what is called a low-severity fire regime, where surface fires occur. Flames might be only six inches tall, and the fire is often patchy, burning some spots on the forest floor, but not others.

One example of the high-severity regime often used by scientists is the lodgepole pine forest in the western United States (though low-severity fires also occur here from time to time). The lodgepole forest requires fire in order to regenerate. A few months after a stand-replacing fire that engulfs the forest and burns all vegetation from the forest floor to the top of the trees, this is the likely scene: scorched tree trunks stand with branches intact but bare, their needles consumed during the fire. Bare soil and ash comprise the exposed ground, where all plants and the dead leaves they dropped have burned.

After a few months, however, new plants have started to emerge, with their green striking against the black backdrop. Aspen trees re-sprout from their bases. The pink Bicknell's geranium springs from a seed bank that survived the fire stored in the soil. A few years after the fire, lodgepole pine seedlings grow from seeds freed from serotinous pine cones (cones that were glued shut prior to the fire, and open to drop seed only when stand-replacing fire passes).

Many types of birds love the post-fire forest, where insects abound in the dead tree trunks. For instance, the black-backed woodpecker (an endangered species) is found only in areas recently burned at high severity. It's difficult to spot this woodpecker, as its back is camouflaged to match the burned tree trunks, until it commences a noisy tapping. The grizzly bear (another endangered species) finds forage among the grasses and berry bushes in recently burned areas, browsing the bright magenta fireweed that favours recently disturbed areas.

The lodgepole pine forest experiences a cycle of fire, where fire causes widespread mortality of trees and surface vegetation (like bushes and flowers), and then succession through a number of stages. Plants usually sprout rapidly after the fire, and a decade after a fire a carpet of lodgepole pine seedlings so thick as to be impenetrable might be found. Over time, the thick trees thin as some die due to competition for water and nutrients, and perhaps reoccurrence of low-severity fire. As decades pass, the trees grow taller, trunks thicken. After a hundred or more years, another high-severity fire occurs and the cycle restarts.

In low-severity regimes fire may occur as often as every seven years without widespread mortality of the forest. In the western United States, the ponderosa pine forest is often used as an example of this fire regime. Fire is often patchy, burning some spots but not others. Fire is likely to kill many tree seedlings, and a tenth to a quarter of larger trees. Fire maintains wide spacing between trees, and the forest floor is often grassy because the sunlight can reach it. The year after a fire, it may be difficult to tell that a fire happened here.

Ponderosa pines resist fire due to their thick bark, which keeps the heat of the flames from killing them. Other trees in the low-severity regime, such as oaks, can re-sprout from their bases. Because many trees survive most fires here, the forest typically regenerates from surviving trees dropping seed.

In low-severity regimes where fires have been suppressed, many scientists agree it is ecologically appropriate to cut and remove some of the smaller trees (thinning) to keep future fires from getting more intense, and to set small fires under mild weather conditions to restrict the growth of future fires.

Humans tend to cause a lot of impact on these ecosystems, which occur at lower elevations and near many towns. Where logging has occurred, it tends to eliminate the large trees with the thickest bark (those most likely to survive fire); these are often replaced with more smaller trees that are closer together, producing a forest that is more susceptible to death during the next fire. Fire suppression promotes a high density of trees as well as ladder fuels (shrubs and brush that grow in between fires and tend to carry fire up into the treetops), which result in higher tree mortality. Because there is often a home or town nearby, this increases society's desire to suppress fires, exacerbating the outcome of future fires.

The elemental building blocks in the forest are reused over and over. During fire, vegetation is converted into smoke (primarily carbon dioxide that goes into the atmosphere) and ash (minerals) on the forest floor. As the forest regrows, carbon is combed from the atmosphere during photosynthesis.

Where a forest regrows to its pre-fire condition, there is no net flux of carbon into the atmosphere.

But climate change means that a forest may burn at higher severity than it would have in the past, due to longer fire seasons and hotter, drier conditions. Climate change also means that the forest may not regrow with the same species that were there before, because the climate may have changed enough that it is, for example, too hot or dry for the species to thrive. Or, a previously forested area may not regrow as a forest at all, but may change to shrub or grass (in this case, some carbon emitted during the fire remains in the atmosphere, exacerbating climate change, since forests tend to contain more carbon than shrub or grasslands). The new ecosystem may be better adapted to the new climate–but with consequences for animals and people that live here.

In many of the world's ecosystems, fire is necessary for healthy forests. Stasis brings dysfunction. While in the short term, fire brings mortality and disturbance, over the long term, fire maintains the character of the ecosystem.

Fire contributes to diversity at the landscape scale, similar to when architecture experiences a re-set, for example when outdated or even unsafe buildings are retrofitted or completely replaced by something new. When forests and shrublands have a mosaic of vegetation of different ages, they are more resilient to future disturbance, as architecture of different vintages might be. This mosaic presents a variety of habitats for different species, as a diverse architectural setting might provide different functions.

Throughout geologic time, fires and their environment have shaped each other, a dynamic interplay between climate, weather, and vegetation. While some iconic types of forests have proliferated and gone extinct over these hundreds of millions of years, the fire regimes described here appear to have been consistent. As Earth's ecosystems change more rapidly, driven by climate change, we can be sure that flames will be our companion, shaping and re-shaping the environment.

# MOVING, SOWING, GROWING—AN INTERVIEW WITH ELMA VAN BOXEL AND KRISTIAN KOREMAN (ZUS)

Mark Minkjan, Jarrik Ouburg

ZUS [Zones Urbaines Sensibles] is an interdisciplinary design bureau for city and landscape founded by Elma van Boxel and Kristian Koreman. Trained as landscape architects but also doing urban planning and architecture projects, their unsolicited advice and actions have impacted the Schieblock area around their office (and former home) in Rotterdam. They instigated and facilitated various infrastructural, cultural and social projects just east of the city's central train station—the Luchtsingel elevated walkway that re-established previously cut-off pedestrian routes is perhaps best-known. Their incremental restart of a previously neglected area dominated by car infrastructure and office towers has put the urban quarter back on the map as a cultural destination, but also onto the radar of planners and investors. The city's new plans for the area currently present ZUS with the demand for a next restart and the challenge to both retain the area's newfound dynamic and develop 120,000 extra profitable square metres, for which the city has invited a developer. We talk about approaching urban development as landscape architects, strategically planting seeds and letting them take root over time, and how to sustain and revive healthy growth. MM

How do you, as landscape architects, view the theme of tabula scripta, the inscribed page? JO

We are part of that inscribed page. Everyone is philosophizing freely about what we can do with the surface of the Earth because we think we know how it works, but it's really about what you're not seeing and how that plays a role in the project. We see ourselves as 'embedded designers'. We try to acknowledge that we are part of an ecosystem that is many times more powerful than we are. In that sense make-ability is relative, as you have to incorporate so many parameters in your design to steer it in a certain direction. E&K

If we shift that perspective from landscape to architecture and urban planning, how did that work in the case of the Schieblock? MM

In hindsight, we went through a number of episodes, starting with the first eight years we were here, from 2000 to 2008. At the time, we were mainly concerned with the space we needed to live and work. What surprised E&K

us most is how it was possible that at this super central site–Triple A location, right across from City Hall at Coolsingel, on Hofplein square, two of the most expensive streets in Monopoly, and with high-speed railway–there were 100,000 square metres of empty space. It took us a while to figure out how that could be. You can only understand it if you go way back in history. Before the Second World War, this was the city centre; here were the routes through the city where everything came together: culture, economy, traffic, buzz, street life–what Jane Jacobs calls 'weak ties', the foundation of the economy. It was an important entertainment district in Rotterdam: Louis Armstrong has performed here in one of the jazz joints. During the post-war reconstruction of the destroyed city a new plan was overlaid on it –Bam! The railway had been elevated, but was now lowered, which resulted in a kind of Berlin wall that literally cut the urban fabric in two. There are now only two miserly tunnels connecting the parts of the city on the north and south side of the railway. If you look at the ant-like behaviour of humans: they will start looking for ways around it. And if people move more in cars than on foot, it is only logical that at some point nothing feeds an area such as this one anymore, regardless of how centrally located it is.

Economy and history are also a landscape lying underneath this. In that first period we explored all these layers in order to understand how the ground beneath our feet is structured and where the potential lies. By doing this we knew what seeds needed to be planted to be effective. The Luchtsingel, for example, is really just an old line that was already there before the war but was cut off by the planners. We brought it back.

MM Half a century ago, this was supposed to become a huge office area.

E&K For a short while, in the 1980s, this was a multinational strip where big companies had their offices. At the time, the scale of these buildings and that of the economy were very briefly matched. But the economy is volatile and Shell suddenly announced 'we're going to London'. That was a real setback. They spent hardly fifteen years in Hofpoort, that gigantic brutalist tower. Then it stood empty for about twenty years. The choice had been made for big design statements and not to gradually add something to the city. Big statements are very difficult to adapt.

Understanding the spatial, economic, and cultural history has been necessary to be able to do certain interventions that have given the area a restart.

MM Ten, fifteen years ago, the area was indeed in need of such a restart and now it is in full swing. What interventions were made that really made this restart possible?

E&K These interventions really began in 2007, when we went from 'paper' to 'action'. From understanding to intervening, because otherwise the area would have disappeared. A new–but quite old-school–master plan was made that featured a straight arrow from Central Station to the east. Everyone would have to be able to walk on it or ride a bicycle on it; to avoid any bends in the route, many of the existing buildings had to be torn down. This is understandable from the post-war history of Rotterdam, as everything was done with grand gestures. However, we felt that thc timc was ripc to start thinking about other gestures as well. We didn't know yet how to go about it at the time. Then the financial crisis hit, and what role did we actually have to play in the area? We, squatters of someone else's property?

That's when we had our Jane Jacobs moment: let's break open one corner of this sealed-off block as a public space and invite all the cultural institutes of the city there. Then it would no longer be just about us, but there would be multiple voices saying 'hey, this is actually a very interesting spot'. And when the crisis really took hold and both the city and project developers realized as well that they would not be building those planned towers of 240,000 square metres here any time soon, we said: 'Give us four, five years to show that the existing building is still worth something. That was the start of Schieblock. In the scale-model we made at the time we had already included a hole through the building for a future bridge. It went from nothing to nowhere, like in the master plan made by the city, so they were happy about it.

Next, we were able to develop the Luchtsingel. It was literally a Trojan horse that anchored the site in the mental map of everyone to whom this had initially been a blind spot or was only familiar with it as an official zero tolerance zone. The Luchtsingel was always intended to gently stir things. To demonstrate that there was an alternative to large buildings along a six-lane road right through the heart of the city; that even within this context a small-scale, walkable city could be realized. Then came the popular intervention with the Biergarten at the back of the building, in the parking lot. There is lots of sun there and you're next to the railway line so it's okay to make noise; add beer to the mix and a lot of people start hanging out there. It became a huge success. We wanted to reach a wider public than our own circle and have that public tell the story about the qualities of this place. This really put quite some pressure on things.

JO And this seed for the development, was it just the use, the human capital?

E&K We call it 'public capital'. Everybody knows about private capital, but the trick is to generate public capital. A combination of physical interventions and a valuable and fitting programme.

JO The building is then a means to get public capital to operate, by programming it.

MM A sort of a spatial mobilization.

JO I find the metaphor of the Trojan horse interesting. All these people were actually hidden behind a built layer. Only the built layer, the horse, was already there: the Schieblock itself. All you had to do was create a doorway for people to go and stand inside the Trojan horse. The same applies to the buildings across from here.

E&K It's becoming a full Trojan stable now, ha! Our strategy was to rehabilitate the pre-war urban fabric, so that all these places become stronger again, together. So, our explanation was: we wheeled this wooden thing inside, as a temporary bridge with a cosy name. Because it was temporary, it was Trojan, but also something that explodes at the moment it opens up. And now the bridge has become a permanent connection. We never said it out loud, but of course the intention was to reappropriate everything here.

JO You use the term 'permanent temporality', thereby actually creating an opportunity to start things afresh, time and again. When there is 'public capital' you can make the jump to the next temporary thing.

E&K Always. It's a sort of movement, or rebellion. Like the people of Troy rebelled and did so quite cleverly. We try not to be too obvious; the attack should always come from multiple sides. Always know your enemies and try to create energy from their energy, but point it in the opposite direction. We always try to understand energies, for example when the city administration spoke of 'making things green' or sustainability. We thought, let's make a green and public roof and to top it off grow vegetables there. A big fat exclamation mark for what the city administration was already saying, so that they would come and look for themselves and say: 'What you are doing here is actually what we mean.' In that sense it was also a kind of sandwich of strategies. We converted various agendas that were already drawn up at the municipal level but were never implemented and tested them through temporality.

MM How can we sum up this sandwich of strategies?

E&K They are actually five parallel trajectories: writing, place-making, transformation, densification, and local economy. In all these trajectories we have developed projects that we knew would start influencing each other. Schieblock is of course the ultimate node where all these things converge, but in other places in the area we see seeds budding as well, even by cloning. And things we never planned: the nicest example of this is perhaps Operator, a radio station that was founded by a graphic designer, who also created the Schieblock logo and made a success of the Biergarten, together with two guys from the catering industry. All these young DJs, for instance from the Hip Hop House next door, find a place there, as are other DJs that have no platform anywhere else. The local station Radio Rijnmond also began in this area at one time. The aerials were still on the roof and they also had a bar where David Bowie had a drink once.

JO And obviously this kind of original layers of energy appeal to you.

E&K They do. And the more of these layers you stack on top of each other, the stronger the whole thing becomes. History is then made productive again. It was also recognized in cultural-historical publications, but we made them manifest. Then it starts to make sense to a growing number of people who have to tell the story, who are part of the area, why you're doing certain things. The city council then was obliged to include the conservation of the existing built and cultural fabric in the most recent plans for the area.

MM Still, the area also has to produce a profit for the city and property owners.

E&K We have always been aware of the pressure of big capital on this area. It will always be there and we have not been naïve in this. That is why, for three years, we ran the Gentrification Lab at Syracuse University in New York to understand how capital works over there and what can be done against gentrification in the traditional sense. Letting artists flourish in a nicely hipster-ized area and then chased them out again; how can we defend ourselves against that? Our only conclusion was: through ownership. We had to anchor ourselves even deeper in this place economically in order to eventually make that narrative even more permanent. If you have to rent this place from a new project developer who doesn't get it, the rent will go up and the ecosystem will be gone. It is no coincidence that the building designed by the famous Rotterdam architect Hugh Maaskant now houses the Independent School for the City –which he co-founded–and also Crimson Architectural Historians, with Maaskant's biographer. Just try and get rid of them. It's becoming a judo-like hold. That property on the corner and the adjacent row will then not be demolished, but of course the costs have to be recovered. In that area at least 120,000 square metres of new programming must be added to recover the 25 million euros debt that's been weighing on this area for a long time now.

JO The debt to be paid is the economic layer that will eventually determine what will happen here. The cultural layer prevailed for a little while and could set the tone. Is it this tone you wish to preserve now?

E&K Yes, while at the same time it will be capitalized.

JO How can you make sure that the cultural layer, this public capital, will not be literally overshadowed by that other, private capital?

E&K Well, for one thing, fortunately our story has become strong enough to make private capital also want to partly preserve what is here now. The ambition paper of the municipality states that the liveliness, the bustle that is created here, should remain. Of course, that is very open to interpretation. Some would argue that a nice Starbucks also brings liveliness, but we think that everyone understands by now that the solution should be more local. We did oppose the Starbucks that is here now, but because of its presence everyone now understands that the authenticity we still have here is at risk. Big capital understands that as well. Schieblock has had a huge impact. Many big companies have arrived here recently because this super corporate and dull area has also become very cool over the past ten years.

JO That's what makes it such a nice layered place. There are public functions here where you don't really expect them and that is also why these big companies are coming here. That they will eventually move into that tower, is hard to plan.

E&K A big project developer has put in an offer of sixty million euros for the area and is already talking to Rafael Viñoly Architects. This developer has already said that the Biergarten and pop venue Annabel should stay. But what else will they do to support this? Looking at business cases of this kind of development there is certainly a margin to accommodate these things. In the development of the Amsterdam Zuidas this never happened; there, the developers simply took the full profit margin and gave it to their stockholders. Here, though, they understand that it is their ticket to be allowed to develop something here in the first place, but that they will have to use their margin to realize a less profitable but livelier plinth that will eventually attract businesses.

MM Is this to make sure that the restart does not become a full reset?

E&K In the diagram we propose, permanent temporality is a gradual evolution. And of course, an extra 120,000 square metres on top of the 20,000 that are already there has a huge impact, but it's not about the buildings but about what goes on inside them. If you want to keep that whole ecosystem healthy, you must serve the entire spectrum and negotiate to create an inclusory city part where things do not exclude each other. Where millionaires live, but also these guys that are now creating all this crazy stuff here.

JO By being here for a long time, you can see how the ecosystem works. If you look ten years ahead, you can see the promise of how this ecosystem may look in yet another ten years' time. Back then, did you already have the tools to see it as an ecosystem instead of physical expression, with possibly a new tower of two hundred metres high in ten years?

E&K No, that is really an advancing insight. You simply cannot know that, it's impossible.

We have given up our ideals of make-ability as well, the idea that 'if I do this, then that will happen'. It usually doesn't. We've turned that around: we know roughly what may happen. As Rory Hyde says in his essay 'Dancing with Second Order Effects' in our book *City of Permanent Temporality*: you throw a stone into the water and you never know what those ripples will do, but you do know that they will do something. We can now explain quite well how everything was built up over the past eighteen years, but that is advancing insight. Now we have turned that around; if we understand what happened over the past eighteen years, we may roughly imagine how the next eighteen years will be. Just in different proportions and quantities.

JO Your thinking is still very much that of landscape architects. There's not only a lot under the ground, but you also don't know exactly what will come up. You sow all kinds of different things, some come up, some overshoot. The way you look at things is very different from that of an architect or urban planner.

E&K The conditions for growth for that new tower are perfect. And we created them by saying: 'Just chop off a piece of the Schieblock.' The project developer didn't understand that we would be willing to tear down some of the Schieblock. But in ecosystems there are leavers and stayers, and sometimes you have to cut smaller bushes to make room for an oak to grow.

**ROOTING THE TEMPORARY** At the start of the millennium, landscape architects Elma van Boxel and Kristian Koreman moved their home as well as their newly established firm ZUS into a run-down modernist office building. The area surrounding it was a blind spot for many Rotterdammers and a zero-tolerance zone for the police, but at the same time it provided fertile ground for experimentation. After a few years of observing, ZUS began giving unsolicited advice and criticism regarding the area's development. Just after the financial crisis hit and traditional property development halted, they started to activate the building by getting creative entrepreneurs and cultural institutions to set up shop in the Schieblock, while initiating public programming for debating architecture and urbanism on the ground floor. Bars, music venues, and shops followed, culturally rooting the site. ZUS' crowd-sourced and much celebrated elevated 'Luchtsingel' walkway further increased the public capital of the area, while also reconstructing its previously designed-away pedestrian routes, contributing to the sprouting of other cultural as well as more upscale projects in the area. Initially starting out as temporary projects, many grew into permanent local functions. Currently the area's owner demands additional profitable floorspace, challenging ZUS to design a proposal that delivers this while preserving the ecosystem that it created over the past decade.

Schieblock, Rotterdam, the Netherlands
ZUS [Zones Urbaines Sensibles] (2000–)

The new plan with which ZUS are hoping to preserve the current dynamics.

↓ Aerial view of the Luchtsingel elevated walkway

Luchtsingel, Rotterdam, NL

ZUS [Zones Urbaines Sensibles]
Luchtsingel, Rotterdam, NL

MvI

## RISING FROM THE RUBBLE

In order to help residents of Guangming Village, which was badly damaged in an earthquake in 2014, a team of researchers and designers has developed an earthquake-proof house using a traditional rammed-earth construction technique. Inhabitants had turned towards brick and concrete to reconstruct, but these materials became too expensive for them. As most of the village was originally built using rammed earth, a new more earthquake-proof method based on traditional techniques was developed by the design and construction team. The walls are made using rubble, clay, sand, grass, and other locally sourced materials, a choice made for their low cost and weight, but also to improve resistance to seismic activity and to limit the impact of future earthquakes. Steel bars and concrete belts were only added to walls to improve structural integrity and to avoid vertical cracking. The team tested out its plans by building a prototype home for an elderly couple in the village, while applying the so-called '3L' (local technology, local materials, and local labour) strategy. Since the realization of the project in 2016, this anti-seismic earth building system has also been applied to other rural projects in Southwest China.

Post-Earthquake Reconstruction Project, Zhaotong, China
One University One Village project team, collaboration between the Chinese University of Hong Kong & Kunming University of Science and Technology (2016)

Exterior of second anti-seismic rammed earth demonstration house

Interior

Post-Earthquake Reconstruction Project, Zhaotong, CN

**RESTARTING A LOST NEIGHBOURHOOD** On 13 May 2000, a fireworks factory located in the residential neighbourhood Roombeek in the city of Enschede exploded. The historically grown integration of businesses in the heart of large, closed blocks was typical of this neighbourhood, but proved fatal in this case: 23 people lost their lives, almost a thousand were injured, and hundreds of homes were destroyed. The new houses were largely realized under private ownership, which had a positive effect on the bonding among residents in the new neighbourhood. In addition, an intensive participation trajectory was initiated for residents, most of whom wanted to return to the old neighbourhood. From this it transpired that they wanted a neighbourhood with both historical and future value. Therefore, the urban plan took as it starting point strengthening the existing 'beek' (brook)—the name giver of the neighbourhood—and the same layout of streets as before. The large, closed block returns as the basic typology, but this time with various types of apartments at its heart.

Roombeek, Enschede,
the Netherlands
de Architekten Cie.
(2000–2008)

Fireworks disaster,
13 May 2000

Roombeek, 2015

Fireworks monument

**THE IMMACULATE CONCEPTION** The monasterial ideal of the Cistercian order reaches for the utmost purity. Realizing that mankind is sinful in all things, the order looked for sites that had never been touched by man to build their monasteries. An attempt to make this world not be of this world. Reaching for an ideal to leave evil behind and make a new start in all purity.

Cistercian Monastery

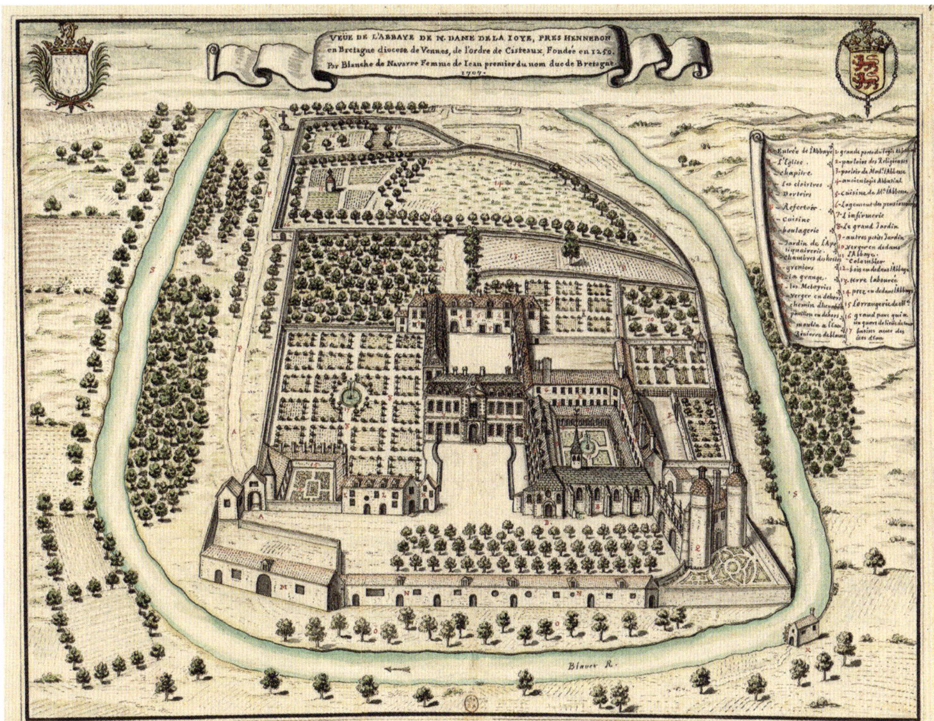


Louis Bodan, *Abbaye Notre-Dame-de-la-Joie, Hennebont*, 1707

THE PICTURE OF DORIAN GRAY – OSCAR WILDE Within a stone's throw from Amsterdam, a new city has risen on what until recently was the bottom of a sea. Lacking the mitigating circumstance of the historical centre that lends its neighbour city its identity, Almere is Amsterdam's opposite in so many ways that it has to go through life as the 'evil twin'. It seems so natural to regard this new city as imperfect that we don't face up to the fact that the severe character of this new town actually reflects the true face of our generation. With this project OMA adds a centre of gravity and urbanity to this fast-growing sea of houses, in an attempt to not accept that we ought to be disappointed in our own times.

Almere Masterplan, the Netherlands
OMA / Rem Koolhaas, Floris Alkemade Partners (1994–2007)

Reclaimed land in Almere, 1988

Aerial view

GIVING BACK TO NATURE Between 1960 and 1962 Club Med built a privative holiday village on the north-eastern tip of the Iberian Peninsula. With the advent of democracy in Spain, and the rise of ecological consciousness, Cap de Creus was declared a Natural Park in 1998. In the period, 2008–2010, the sprawling Club Med was 'deconstructed' and the cape was given back to nature. Landscape architects EMF teamed up with architecture firm Ardèvol to remove the buildings and turn the landscape into a series of meandering pathways and coastal viewpoints. Hundreds of buildings were knocked down, the road surface and cove and beach paving were removed—which in turn meant processing tens of thousands of cubic meters of rubble and thousands of cubic metres of organic earth contaminated by exotic and invasive plant remains before the forces of nature could take over again.

Tudela-Culip Restoration Project,
Cap de Creus, Spain
EMF&Ardèvol (2008–2010)

Cap de Creus before and after the demolition of Club Med

↓ New sculptural elements and re-use of existing paths

EMF&Ardèvol
Tudela-Culip
Restoration Project,
Cap de Creus, ES

JO

**AND ANOTHER NEW START** The client of the house was the architect's grieving sister who, after her husband died, gave him his first commission to design a house for herself and her two young daughters. The concrete house had a distinctive U-shape with windows facing an inner courtyard, rejecting the outside world and making it a place for reflection, healing, and a new start. Twenty-one years after the construction of the house, the daughters were grown-up and the family was ready to face a new phase in life. In the meantime, the house had lost its hard-white concrete exterior and was covered in ivy as if it symbolized the healing process of the family. The plot of land was sold and the house was destroyed under the eyes of the architect, making space for a new house and another new start.

U-house, Tokyo, Japan
Toyo Ito & Associates,
Architects (1976),
demolished (1997)

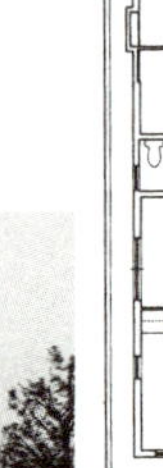

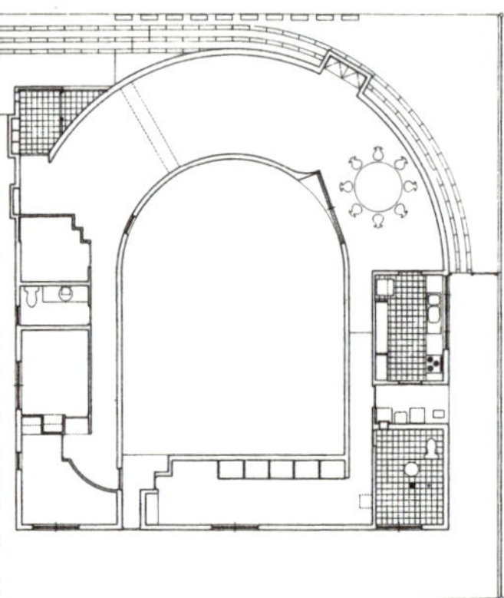

Floor plan

Street facade

Transformation over the years

A CLEAN SLATE Some cities come into being, some are designed. The centre of Amsterdam is a bit of both. With four large urban expansions the historical city sees an explosive growth in the seventeenth century, becoming one of the largest cities in Europe. The fourth expansion, the so-called 'Vierde Uitleg', continues where the third one stopped and is bounded by the fortification plans designed earlier. It is decided to expropriate and demolish the existing housing in the plan area and to not include the existing parcellation in the urban expansion. This is a departure from the third expansion, which partly did so. The city administration wishes to finance the construction of fortifications and canals completely from the revenues of the sale of plots, and therefore a pragmatic and efficient parcellation is called for; the existing one does not fit in this strategy. The new neighbourhood starts with a clean slate and the radial-concentric plan that was already begun in the third expansion is now completed right up to the fortification, resulting in the famous half circle of Amsterdam.

The 'Vierde Uitleg' of Amsterdam, the Netherlands
Attributed to Daniël Stalpaert (1662)

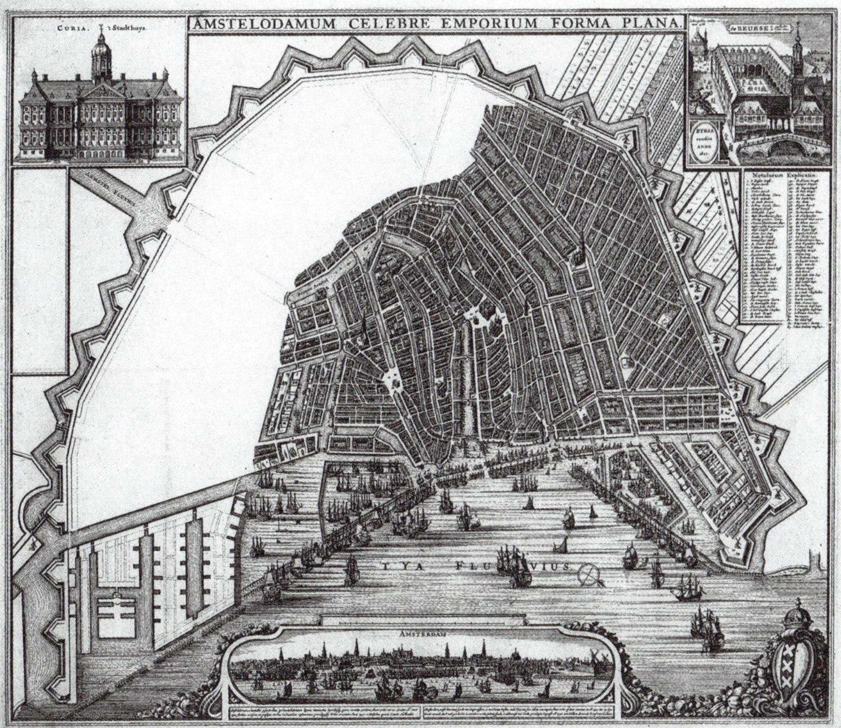


Claes Jansz. Visscher, Map of the 'Vierde Uitleg' ('Fourth Expansion') of Amsterdam, c. 1661

MvI

**CITY ON THE MOVE** To prevent it from imploding, the mining town of Kiruna in Sweden's far north, and many of its 20,000 residents, are slowly being moved to a new and safe location. Being situated atop one of the world's largest iron ore deposits 100 kilometres above the Arctic Circle, the town is literally being undermined by the activities of state-owned mining company LKAB. The Kiruna municipality, in collaboration with the mining company and in consultation with residents, is now working to move the entire city centre to a new location, three kilometres to the east of the current location, at a cost of more than one billion euros. Residents and property owners are compensated for their losses and are provided with new and better homes and public amenities. The relocation also offers the opportunity to turn the sprawling town into a compact and more efficient and liveable city. By densifying the urban core, and integrating residential areas in the surrounding Arctic landscape, residents are never more than a few minutes away from nature. And by re-using materials salvaged from demolished buildings, and incorporating culturally significant architecture, including an old wooden church and elements of the old city hall, Kiruna's past will help to spark a new beginning.

Kiruna, Sweden
White Arkitekter and
Ghilardi + Hellsten
Arkitekter (2013–2033)

Kiruna masterplan: mine (left), site of old city center (middle) and new city (right).

The existing city centre of Kiruna with the LKAB mine in the background

Relocation of a listed building

Artist impression of the new civic square, first phase of the masterplan

MvI

**FRONTIER FANTASIES** Cairo is constantly being re-invented. Throughout its long history, the Egyptian capital has been slowly moving across the map in an eastward shift. With each new iteration, the idea and appearance of the city are re-defined. It started around 3,000 BC as a small settlement along the Nile River under the rule of pharaoh Menes and subsequent rulers and regimes have consistently tried to surpass the architectural legacy of their predecessors and overcome the chaos of the existing city by establishing their own seat of power and aesthetic norms. Over the past centuries, urban life moved from the old Islamic Cairo, to colonial Downtown Cairo, to modern Nasr City and New Cairo. And now, the city is reinventing itself once again with a new development out in the desert. Ordered by Egyptian President el-Sissi, and developed by Emaar Properties from Dubai, the costly and controversial project aims to offer a clean and efficient base for the government and finance industry, as well as homes for at least 6.5 million people. While the foundations of the new villas and shopping malls are slowly emerging from the sand on satellite images, Cairo is slowly closing in on the city of Suez to the East, trading the river Nile for the Red Sea.

Desert Developments,
Cairo, Egypt
Ongoing

New streets in New Cairo

Madinaty area from the air, the province of Cairo, Egypt

# ABSTAIN —ACTIVE PASSIVITY

2

3

4

2 Jenny Holzer, from *Survival* (1983–1985), Times Square, New York City, 1985
3 Johan Cruijff as coach of FC Barcelona in 1996, after just having quit smoking.
4 San Francisco 49ers players Eli Harold, Colin Kaepernick and Eric Reid refused to stand for the United States national anthem, before an NFL football game, in protest of the wrongdoings against African Americans and minorities in the US.

5

5 The seal that secured the doors leading to the third of four nested shrines in Tutankhamun's tomb, Egypt, 1325 BC (photo 1923).

# THREE CITY EXPLO-RATIONS— MUMBAI, CAIRO, AMSTER-DAM

JO Living or working in another city, country, or continent or simply visiting it is an opportunity to learn to understand such places. At the same time, it is an opportunity to take a fresh look at one's own city, country, or continent and wonder about one's own familiar built environment. Especially for students—whose identity as architects is still in the making—these are indeed valuable experiences. Students at the Amsterdam Academy of Architecture combine work and study, which makes it hard for them to study abroad for any considerable length of time. For this reason, we visited various cities with students within the context of the Tabula Scripta research and organized education projects there. The most important objective was for students to experience how various cities and cultures deal with and build on their built past. One of these cities was Mumbai. Why Mumbai? When one of the students took a taxi from the airport to his accommodations and saw where he was to spend the next two weeks, he was so panicked by all the impressions made upon him in just one hour that he immediately wanted to get on the first plane back home. Literally. Then we knew that we had made the right choice.

# THE INDIAN BRAIN—NOTES ON A DAY IN MUMBAI

Jarrik Ouburg

Cities are sometimes characterized as being either a 'cat' or a 'dog' city. A cat city plays hardtoget, does not easily reveal its most interesting and beautiful features, and one must be patient before it will climb onto your lap. A dog city is accessible, contagious; it comes at you happily wagging its tail, anxiously waiting for you to come and play with it. This Sunday morning in February, after a long flight and a short night, Mumbai is barking at my bedside.

We are in the hotel where I have stayed before in vain attempts to get a grip on this city. Some things indeed haven't changed. The hotel owner opens the door in the middle of the night as usual and once again I enter my room in the awkward awareness that I'm in a building full of beds where the entire staff is sleeping on sheets of cardboard in the lobby. The area surrounding the hotel has however changed radically in the two years since my previous visit. The street has been dug up for the construction of the underground, next to the hotel a concrete skeleton of a building is waiting for better days, and the rest of the plot has been dug out to a depth of five metres. The question 'would you like a quiet room?' suddenly makes a lot more sense; we are sleeping on a construction site.

After a quick reorientation I realize why a city like Mumbai is so appealing from a Dutch or European perspective: it's because of this construction site quality. At the level of a building it is the beauty of a wonderful concrete skeleton that clearly reveals the spatiality of a structure before a mirroring facade will conceal this quality. At the urban level it is the promise of things to come and the progressive hope and energy that come with it, unlike the conservative fear and anxiety that what is there may be lost.

From the building site we walk to a place that is always an oasis of space and quiet in this city: Shivaji Park, in the Dadar neighbourhood. With its 22 hectares it is Mumbai's largest park and also a historically important place because of the political rallies that were held there both before and since India's independence in 1947. On this Sunday morning it's busy here. Very busy. Spread out across the park men in colourful outfits, some with cricket bats, are standing or running around. Balls are flying. From a distance the whole thing looks like massive warming up, although it is unclear where the game is to be played. In order to go to the other side of the park we decide not to walk around it but to take the shortest route, straight through it. In the middle of the park we come to a halt to ask ourselves what it is we are actually seeing. Immediately next to us we see men in at least eight different outfits. One man is staring with great concentration in one direction, another one suddenly begins to sprint in the opposite direction, two men are engaged in lively conversation, and still another one squats down while a ball rolls past him, fanatically chased by yet another man. This is no warming up. This is a game in progress. In fact, these are multiple games going on simultaneously, criss-crossing each other.

Shivaji Park, Sunday morning, 4 April 2018

I've always found cricket a mysterious sport. 'Running to stand still' in optima forma, and slightly boring to watch as a match can easily last for up to six hours. Here, however, a performance takes place that I can't get enough of. Probably, all teams would prefer to reserve the park for six hours to play their own match, but then it would take a week for all the matches to finish. And since spare time and spare space are scarce in a city like Mumbai, at least twenty games are played simultaneously in the same space. Some of the pitches are laid out, more or less next to each other with enough space between them, but there are just as many improvised pitches that cross right over them. The result is a colourful ensemble of players walking criss-cross on the field at speeds varying from sprinting to almost sleepwalking. The differently coloured outfits seem chaotic at first, but turn out to be the ordering layer; it makes it easy to see who belong to the same team and which match is played where. Another thing we notice is that some of the players are in full regalia, with impeccable white clothing, helmets and pads, whereas others wear wrinkled T-shirts. Important matches are not treated differently from other matches. The urge to play is simply bigger than the wish to have a pitch of one's own. In Europe, in football or tennis both matches are stopped when a ball from one game ends up in the play area of the other game. Here, both matches simply go on, while four more games are in progress in the same space. This is pure profit in terms of time and space. Shivaji Park demonstrates how if a limited space is to be shared with others it may result in more rather than less space, depending on the flexibility of its users.

Cricket players positioning, regular match

From the park we take a taxi to a stonier oasis of space and quiet in the Malabar Hill neighbourhood. Banganga Tank is a large rectangular water basin with a fresh water source, at less than a hundred metres from the salty Indian Ocean. From all four sides of the basin steps lead from the water to the edges, resulting in a kind of amphitheatre. According to legend, water first sprang up here when Lord Rama, the seventh incarnation of the god Vishnu, shot an arrow into the ground. A large wooden stake in the water marks the spot. The water is considered to be holy because the source is seen as a branch of the river Ganges, which actually flows at a distance of five thousand kilometres.

The serene quiet, the wide, open space, the water, and the stately design of the steps underline the sacredness of this place. But Banganga Tank is more than just that. Children here use the steps to play on and the water to swim in, among the swans. Next to a couple of pilgrims bringing sacrificial gifts, a woman is washing clothes, which she spreads out on the steps to dry. This Banganga Tank too demonstrates the and-and-and mentality in the use of space. No one here denies someone else the right of use. The water is holy *and* cooling *and* cleansing.

Looking up from the steps we see that this also applies to the architecture and urban layout. Here too it is immediately obvious that this is a holy place; around the tank are many small temples that are part of the Walkeshwar temple complex. Some are made of wood, dating back to the eighteenth century, others are made of stone and painted with many colours. Beside the temples there are also regular houses and on the top steps of the tank people are living in improvised huts. Another contrast comes from the luxurious apartment towers that not only define the background of Banganga Tank, but in one case even the foreground, as the tower almost reaches the edge of the water. From a historical perspective, the tank may be in a holy religious place, but today it is also in a holy economic location. Over the years, Malabar Hill has become one of Mumbai's most exclusive neighbourhoods.

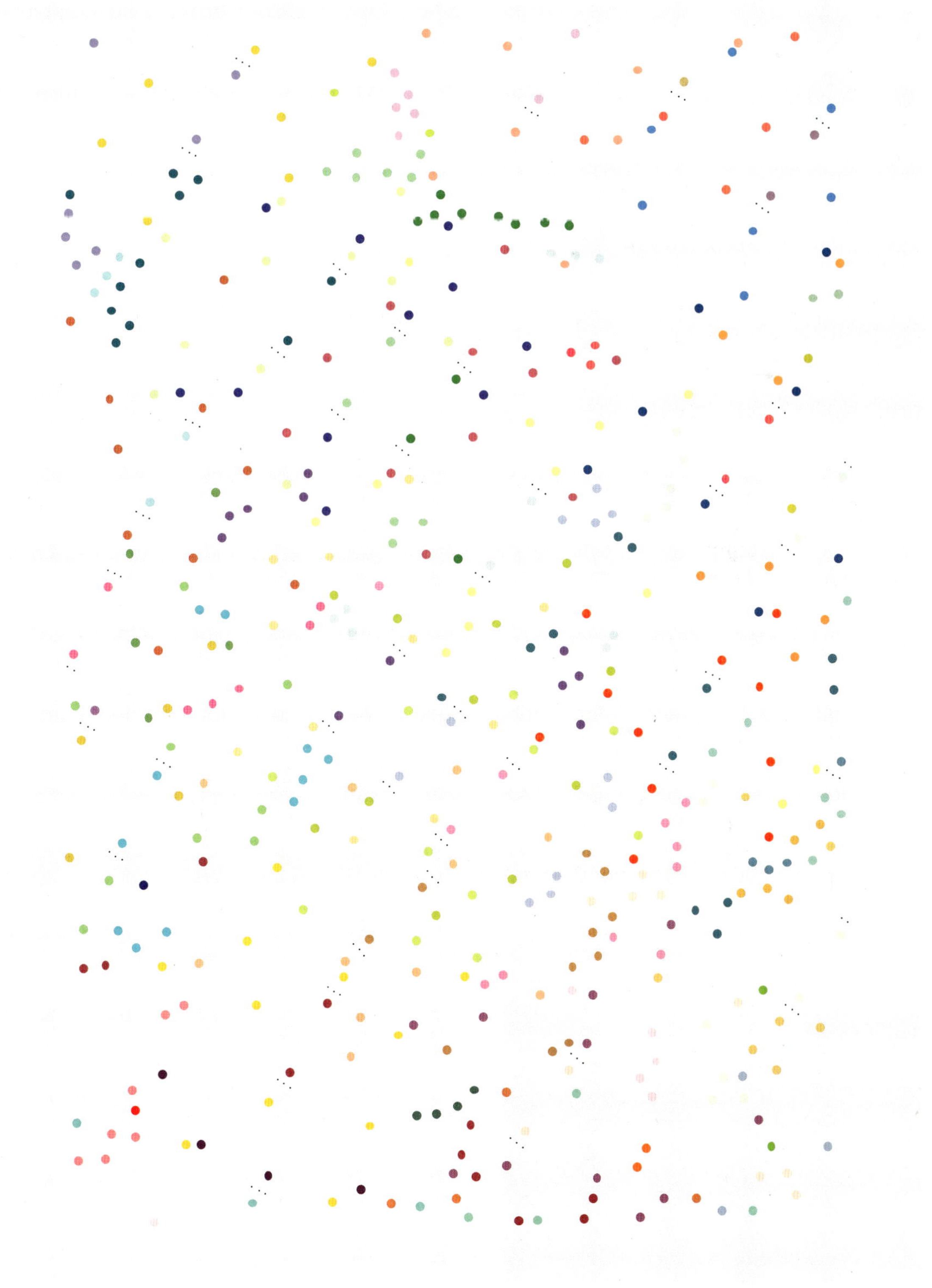

Cricket players positioning, Shivaji Park

# FAHLAWA URBANISM—THE UNPOLISHED INTELLIGENCE OF CAIRO

Michiel van Iersel

There is probably no better place to experience the spirit of the idea of tabula scripta than in Cairo. Egypt's capital is one of the oldest and largest cities on earth and the impressive result of two millennia of continuous habitation. Shaped by a mix of Roman, Christian, Islamic, Ottoman, French, and (other) colonial influences, the city is a multidimensional collage of conflicting styles and ideologies. Now the exploding population is pushing the city to its limits, resulting in a radical form of urbanism. During a series of visits, we, René Boer and some of our Amsterdam Architecture Academy students, traversed this sprawling megalopolis, meeting local spatial practitioners and scratching only the surface of 'The City of a Thousand Minarets' and much more. We got to know it as a restless and ruthless urban environment, for which you need a mix of 'wit and unpolished intelligence' to carve out your own space.

The city and its surroundings already house more than twenty million people, a figure that is projected to rise to forty million by 2050. Greater Cairo has been named 'the world's fastest-growing city', with a population increase of half a million people in 2017 alone.[1] As a consequence, the city expands at an unimaginable pace in all directions, both horizontally and vertically. It spreads like an oil spill, eating up the fertile Nile River valley and invading the desert. Most new-borns or recently arrived residents end up in the so-called *ashwa'iyyat*, or informal areas, which often merely consist of bare concrete tower blocks with red brick infill, often built illegally on agricultural land without sufficient infrastructure and public amenities. Such neighbourhoods house approximately seventy percent of Cairenes. Stuck in traffic on Cairo's ring road you find yourself surrounded by a sea of the same type of buildings, forming an almost monolithic mass with small windows, and narrow streets running through it. At the same time, the elites live in airy gated communities, in the new towns and remote desert cities built on virgin land far beyond the floor area of the Nile: tabula rasa in its most destructive disguise.

Islamic Cairo with pigeon towers

The millions of people living in the city's older neighbourhoods have little space to manoeuvre. Ignoring the building codes and heritage regulations, and often defying the laws of gravity and sanitation, they are forced to build their shops and extra bedrooms in front, between, and on top of existing buildings, everything covered by a thick powdery layer of desert sand. Rising above it like miniature skyscrapers, are the self-built pigeon towers. Used to house the pigeons that compete in contests in which whole neighbourhoods clash to capture each other's pigeons, they symbolize the DIY-mentality and competitiveness of many Cairenes.

## FOREST IN THE DESERT

Dubbed 'Cairo along the Nile' for its grandiose French colonial architecture, the Downtown area lost its allure a long time ago. Now largely abandoned, partly because of decades-long disputes over the ownership and lease of apartments, the few entrepreneurs and residents remaining have added parasitical structures on rooftops and in the many hidden alleyways between the buildings. During Friday Prayer worshippers flood the streets, temporarily occupying sidewalks under manually operated foldable sunscreens, creating a brief moment of order in a chaotic city.

CLUSTER—short for Cairo Lab for Urban Studies, Training and Environmental Research—has done extremely important work to map, understand, and upgrade these spaces and situations in the Downtown Area that were largely overlooked and disregarded. Their projects include the mapping of networks of passageways and rooftops as sites for potential development and a series of self-initiated interventions that have helped to rehabilitate and reactivate the area.

Close by, in the dark and dusty alleys of Historic Islamic Cairo, people live in buildings that are caught halfway between disintegration and reconstruction. Abandoned structures serve as urban quarries, where ancient stones are mined and reassembled in surrounding buildings. Brutal concrete towers and beautifully restored mosques are rubbing shoulders with the ruins. Overlooking 'old' Cairo you witness an endless cycle of entropic degradation and new creation, (re-)using the urban tissue as a compost layer to regenerate the built environment. A city as a self-contained organism, a forest in the desert, where architecture lives, dies, and reincarnates.

As a World Heritage Site, it defies prevailing ideas about the preservation of cultural heritage. In a part of the city where some of the poorest people live, preserving the authenticity and integrity—or the 'wholeness and intactness' of the heritage—has no priority. But despite this destitution, or maybe because of it, people's physical surroundings are often a vital part of their identity. Out of sheer necessity, e.g. to keep the roof from collapsing or create space for their new-born child, people have to actively engage with the built environment. Heritage not as a scripted and static space, but as a dynamic situation that demands active and collective participation. And with the help of an organization like the Built Environment Collective (Megawra), an NGO that tries to reconnect residents with local monuments by linking residents' personal needs and abilities to restoration efforts, one of the oldest and deprived parts of Cairo becomes a place of progress.

Beyond the blueprint: overlooking Imbaba with original buildings (white outline) and additions (the rest)

## BEYOND THE BLUEPRINT

The people of Cairo are masters of improvisation. Cairenes, as the saying goes, can weave and sew with a donkey's leg (in the absence of a needle). Despite the lack of formal urban planning, their ingenuity and 'swagger' help them to live in the face of mounting demographic pressures and political turmoil.

Egypt's population growth first took off in the 1960s due to rising birth rates as well as rural-urban migration to the city. This created an urgent need to provide housing for the growing population of Cairo. Massive public housing projects were carried out in the poor and densely populated districts of the city, based on then president Nasser's vision of social redistribution. Providing affordable housing, these projects became laboratories for an organic urbanism.

Cottage style home covered with self-build apartments on top of it

Family tree: example of a growing family home in Imbaba with the original stone building in black and additions in full colour

Transformer: original building typology in black with examples of additions in full colour

The Workers' City in Imbaba, a working-class neighbourhood with about one thousand dwelling units situated west of the Nile in Giza, was the first of these public housing projects. The original houses were built in cottage-style, resembling British or French vernacular stone-clad architecture. The project started as public housing for the workers of the nearby state-owned cement factories. Construction began before the 1952 revolution, a coup d'état by a group of army officers (including future president Gamal Abdel Nasser), but subsequent developments put the original design under pressure. Due to the severely austere design of the building typologies, with minimal square footage that disregarded the demographic reality of family structures and generational growth, the residents themselves soon started adding rooms or entire floors.

As noted by ETH's André Perronnet and Thomas Rodemeier,[2] residents altered the volumetric and structural composition of the housing projects. By adding multiple new layers of informality to the original two- and three-storey buildings, the homes could now accommodate growing families and future generations. Still mostly occupied by the original residents and their (grand)children, the topped-up and upgraded houses now function as an inhabitable family tree. When a child marries and 'leaves' the house, a new room or floor is simply added to the open structure. When the newly-wed couple have their first child, they add another (baby) room. Even when some siblings are forced to live elsewhere, due to spatial and financial constraints, they keep visiting the family home for special gatherings or use it as a pied-a-terre for those who live out of town. This way the organically grown family (tree) house is kept alive, sometimes even long after the grandparents have passed away, thus nurturing intergenerational communities.

Transformer: building in its current state

## UNPOLISHED INTELLIGENCE

These situations in Cairo might be best characterized by the Egyptian concept of *fahlawa*.[3] This term was first introduced to us by Prof. Abbas M el Zafarany of Cairo University, who used it to characterize the development of his neighbourhood in Nasr City, which transformed from a well-planned low-rise residential district to a mishmash of tower blocks and illegal infills. The family home of his childhood, where he still lives and which was brand new when they moved there in the 1960s, was built in an open space surrounded by sand and smaller buildings.

Half a century, and many political and social upheavals, later, the freestanding house is now entrapped by concrete tower blocks. They were built without permission, or by bending the rules, and cast their shadow over the back garden—or what practically has become a courtyard—of Prof. El Zafarany's house. In the place where his children and he himself used to play on green grass, there only remains a dried-up lawn, which withered and died when the house became outgrown and overshadowed by the surrounding buildings. Staring at the sad scene, and mourning the loss of his own oasis, the professor hesitantly admitted that the attitude that caused the silent takeover of private property, is also the reason why his neighbours can live next door and why Nasser City and Cairo can absorb the millions of people who arrived after him.

Writer Nael M. Shama described *fahlawa* as 'a slang term referring to a combination of wit and unpolished intelligence, and to the ability to use them to accumulate

'Ashwa'iyyat in Al Haraneya

benefits from minimal knowledge, experience, or legal right in any given context'. According to Ahmed Elewa, *fahlawa* is the skill to survive in a modern world you are not prepared for, by using the pre-modern skills that you have learned naturally. Untranslatable (for example the way *gezellig* is untranslatable from Dutch, due to its cultural entanglements), *fahlawa* is a combination of intuition, horse sense, experience, denial, and wit. It is not knowledge obtained from formal education and methodical pursuits. In short, *fahlawa* is when you seek sufficiency instead of perfection.[4] Applied to architecture and urbanism, the concept of *fahlawa* can help to conceptualize and create new building typologies and urban developments that allow for appropriation by users who lack the knowledge and resources to design or finance a formal and sustainable house. This approach was first promoted in the 1972 essay, 'Housing as a Verb' by architect John F.C. Turner,[5] who made the case that housing should be conceived of as an ongoing project wherein residents are co-creators. This concept was later popularized in projects like Charles Correa's unfinished 'Artist Village' and Alejandro Aravena's 'half houses'. These real-life experiments with incremental and 'open source' housing, fuelled by the spirit of *fahlawa* and combined with a more democratic urban governance structure, prove the potential of tabula scripta. The DIY-mentality of the people in Imbaba and their *fahlawa* give us the courage to change.

If a donkey's leg is enough to weave and sew, one family home can re-write architecture.

## SELF-ORGANIZED COHABITATION

The Workers' City is one of the few planned neighbourhoods in Giza. When you start moving westwards, away from the Nile and towards the pyramids of Giza, the cottage-style architecture and tree-lined streets soon give way to imposing apartment buildings with red brick infill and narrow, dusty alleys. Here, in Giza's vast and self-built *ashwa'iyyat*, the idea of *fahlawa* is pushed to its limits. Squeezed between the Nile river, the Sahara Desert and Cairo's ring road, millions of migrants are using their intuition, horse sense, experience, denial, wit and their own hands to collectively create an extremely dense and dynamic environment they can call home.

Rendering of the proposed temporal skeleton

In 2017, students of the Academy of Architecture in Amsterdam and the German University in Cairo explored the peri-urban landscape of Al Haraneya at the southern edge of Giza. This collaborative studio viewed the rural-urban fringe as a landscape in its own right, a place to forge new coalitions between 'nature and culture'. Environmental issues, 'water wars' and global climate change make redefining the relationship between Cairo and the Nile Delta a matter of urgency. Students tried to reconnect nature and culture by adding new layers to the city, while using their own skills and ideas to support the needs of the people (and non-humans) they met. The result is a wide range of—realistic or more speculative—design proposals that tap into the dynamic nature of the neighbourhood, and the *fahlawa* of the people living there. For example, Quita Schabracq proposed to provide residents with simple solutions to use and integrate the natural quality of the wind for cooling and circulating air in the cramped streets and apartments. Tobias Kumkar imagined flexible and temporary systems to, for example, grow vegetables, which can be attached to the concrete skeleton of existing buildings and invite people to access and inhabit empty plots, underutilized roofs, spaces between apartments, and other unused 'urban niches'.

The cutaway drawing of an imaginary building in Al Haraneya, created collectively by students from both schools, reveals the ingenuity of these radical forms of self-organized cohabitation. Humans, animals, plants, satellite dishes, old traditions, and new forms of life, all competing for space in a makeshift ensemble of handmade materials, as a physical manifestation of *fahlawa*.

Parts of this article were first published in Lodown Magazine (Fall edition 2018). The image of the student project was taken from Delta Strikes Back, nine projects for El Haraneya (2017), a joint publication of the Academy of Architecture in Amsterdam and the German University in Cairo which resulted from a research and design studio led by Lada Hršak, Jana Crepon, Billy Nolan and Holger Gladys. We also want to thank René Boer for sharing his knowledge of Cairo and his local network. And we want to express our gratitude to Amr Abotawila for inviting us to his home in Imbaba and for showing us around his neighbourhood and hometown.

1 'Cairo has started to become ugly: why Egypt is building a new capital city', *The Guardian*, 8 May 2018.

2 Imbaba, ETH Studio Basel, Contemporary City Institute, 2010.

3 Ahmed Elewa, 'What is Fahlawa?', *alBostoni*, August 2010.

4 Nael M. Shama, 'The decline of knowledge in Egypt', *Saudi Gazette*, 30 April 2013.

5 John F.C. Turner, 'Housing as a Verb', in *Freedom to Build: Dweller Control of the Housing Process*, ed. John Turner and Robert Fichter (New York: Collier-Macmillan, 1972).

# AMSTERDAM—FOREVER YOUNG

Jarrik Ouburg

'We need to change everything, so that nothing changes.'

Giuseppe Tomasi di Lampedusa

I'm writing this in the library of the Amsterdam Academy for Architecture, in a seventeenth-century block on Waterloo Square, right in the heart of Amsterdam. It used to be the premises of an organization for relief of the poor, where people could come for cheese, bread, peat, and, if the need arose, a coffin. In the warehouse, which is part of the block, the goods were stored. The adjacent, stately building housed the Board of Governors and the administration and from here the goods were distributed. Since 1946 the Academy has been located here. The spatial qualities (and limitations) of the building still determine, to a degree, how the study programme is organized. The board and administration are still in the same spot and the place from where once goods were distributed, the so-called 'Hoge Zaal', is now used for giving lectures; inspiration has replaced bread and peat. Where I'm sitting, in the former warehouse, I am now surrounded by bookcases, maps, and magazines: stacked knowledge.

The inner courtyard with its big chestnut tree is the centre of the Academy's premises. In the old days, people would enter here via a narrow, covered passageway at the back and walk around the courtyard, past the distribution windows and then exit again. This allowed the poor to arrive and leave unseen, causing them no shame. It explains the introvert character of this block in the centre of town, in the eye of the hurricane. The Academy's gaze is turned outwards, but the introvert nature of its premises provides students with the quiet and concentration to study the hurricane itself, from the inside. When I was head of the Architecture department, I always regarded the city as the most important teacher, since almost all of the subjects and themes that are taught at the Academy can be found in its immediate surroundings.

But good students are cocky, testing the teachers' knowledge, posing questions, dilemmas, alternatives and trying to rival the teachers whenever they can. The question of what the Academy can learn from the city is an important one, but equally important is what the city can learn from the Academy. Time and again, with each design, with each course, within the walls of the institute people are working on a parallel reality with a power of expression that is in every sense a match for the world outside. Their ambition is not just to study the hurricane, but to take part in changing its course as well.

The historical centre of Amsterdam with its famous ring of canals was declared a UNESCO World Heritage Site in 2010. The UN organization praised it as an 'outstanding example of a built urban ensemble, civil engineering, town planning, construction and architectural know-how'. Of course, as an architect or urban planner one can only be proud of this appreciation of the city where one lives, works, or studies until one realizes that this status of world cultural heritage comes with conditions for keeping it. New developments, for example across the waters of the IJ, were strictly supervised because of 'the visual impact of tall

Amsterdam Academy of Architecture

Herengracht 148a t/m 82

Keizersgracht 97 t/m 157

1776 ——
2019 ——

Actual situation of facades of houses on Herengracht and Keizersgracht projected on renditions of drawings by Caspar Philips (1768).

buildings on the urban landscapes of the property'. On the one hand the city is praised for its urban planning and engineering of the past, but on the other hand it is being punished for showing that same ambition for the future. Integrity and authenticity are the core values UNESCO aims to protect with its listings but these are the very same values that come under pressure in a living city. Is image displacing identity here? Is the slogan 'I AMsterdam' slowly but surely changing into 'I WASterdam'? That Amsterdam is not a finished 'product' but rather a continuous 'process' also becomes evident when we take a good look at its appearance now and in the past. In 1776, Caspar Philips minutely sketched all the facades of the properties on the Keizers-, Heren-, and Brouwersgracht. If we make the same drawings now and superimpose them over the ones Philips made, the differences outnumber the similarities. Some of the buildings are still 'original', but all of them, from all ages and styles, contribute to the overall picture. Change proves to be the only constant and the city's capacity for transformation is also its strength and it is essential that it can continue to do so in the future.

The city of Amsterdam is not only defined by its buildings, streets, and parks, but of course just as much by the people who live there. The many debates about the city show that it is not just a physical but also very much a social construct, which is passed on from generation to generation. The generation of the 1970s and 80s have saved the city from both material decay and the wrecking ball. The generation of the 1990s and the first decade of the new century have helped the city to grow and flourish. Today, the city centre's popularity threatens to put its liveability at risk. The present generation complains that there are too many tourists, that it has become a platform for noisy entertainment, and that only rich expats can afford to live there—that the city is no longer the symbol of meeting and fraternizing, but rather of loneliness and alienation. In the workshop 'Forever Young', which the Academy organized in 2016, we gave a new generation the opportunity to respond to this. We asked the students to find inspiration in the past for the challenges of today and to come up with spatial solutions that would allow the historical inner city of Amsterdam to go on innovating but at the same time have meaning for present and future generations.

Opening of Forever Young workshop in Amsterdam's Old Church

The workshop started with a series of lectures on winter nights in the Oude Kerk, from 1306, which makes it the oldest building still standing in Amsterdam.

This location was chosen on purpose, perhaps even more for its recent history than for its rich past. Six months earlier, in the summer, the artist Taturo Atzu had created his work *The Garden Which Is The Nearest To God* there, not inside the church, but *on* it. He had built a snow-white platform on the roof, with a view of the city. On this platform was a strange, little white house with an interior that was not surprising at first sight. A standard IKEA interior with a few cupboards, chairs, and a small coffee table with a statuette of an angel blowing a trumpet. Everything changes once you realize that the statuette is 'really' the church's wind vane and that the little house is built around it. Exterior has become interior. Obviously,

Taturo Atzu, installation with wind vane on top of the Old Church in Amsterdam

this new context robs the vane of its function, as it is hard to show which way the wind is blowing inside. This new context suddenly provides a totally different look at elements that have been on that same spot literally for ages. You not only look at them differently, it's only now that you see them.

An intriguing work that demonstrates that a new modern addition can be in symbiosis with what is centuries old, both profiting from each other's presence. And a great source of inspiration to start the workshop with as well.

Puzzle of Amsterdam

Puzzle pieces

For this workshop all the Academy students were divided into eighteen interdisciplinary groups. The inner city was likewise divided into eighteen sections. After all, *the* inner city doesn't exist; it is made up of various neighbourhoods with distinctive qualities. Each group was assigned one section of the city centre and was given a matching bottom plate for building a model on a scale of 1:750 that was to reflect the two weeks of research and design.

The outcome of the workshop revealed the power of interdisciplinary work. In one of the plans, The Low Line, the inner city's outer canal Singelgracht is filled in. Not for traffic, as was done so many times in the past, but in order to create a sunken park that connects various other parks in the city. In another landscape proposal for the area around Artis Zoo, Welcome back, Darwin, not only are the fences around the animals removed, but also the fence around the zoo itself. Man, animal, and nature are thus encouraged to live together in a new and more harmonious manner.

Live and let die is an urban development plan for a neighbourhood where many of the historical buildings were demolished when the underground was constructed in the 1980s. This urban scar of new houses amidst the old fabric is regarded by the students as an opportunity because it doesn't have to be preserved because of its age and can therefore be renewed time and again. An urban testing ground, right in the middle of the city.

Other architectural plans focus on new habitation in empty storage spaces over shops, or connecting roof terraces to make one collective space for all the residents. Equally impressive is the Diaspora plan, which takes the insufficiently exposed past of the inner city as its central theme. The place that originally was the harbour for the VOC fleet is not just a symbol of trade and prosperity but also of slave transport. The plan transforms this neighbourhood into an anarchistic port of refuge, a haven where all residents and all cultures of the city can meet. And then there is the Spoken Heritage plan, which makes no physical intervention at all but focuses on the oral history of the city by interviewing as many people as possible during two weeks to collect as many stories as possible about the neighbourhood.

After two weeks of blood, sweat, and spray paint the students present their ideas and bring the puzzle pieces with their vision for a particular part of the city to the Academy building's Hoge Zaal, the erstwhile distribution point. Piece by piece, they build a scale model of the city that hardly fits into the space. A collective work with diversity as its main quality, especially because of the differences that are revealed.

One might ask oneself whether it wouldn't be more socially relevant for a progressive school of architecture to think about the future of the neighbourhoods outside the city centre, where most people live and where most construction will take place. Isn't this look at the centre a form of navel gazing in which the inner city, just like the navel after the umbilical court is cut, is no more than a scar, a shadow of its original function?

The Low Line
Students' work

Live and let die
Students' work

Final model

The workshop and the commitment of a young generation do however present a different image of the navel, one that, as with Leonardo da Vinci's Vitruvius Man, still occupies the central place in the corpus of the entire city. A central place for a young generation that doesn't have a tunnel vision of the physical appearance of the city and does not see it exclusively as a product of the past. A generation that regards the city as a continuous process that has topical meaning for the current residents. If every generation is allowed to contribute to the city—which thereby constantly rejuvenates itself—it will not perish but age in a valuable manner. The place where I wrote this text, a centuries old warehouse as well as a progressive school of architecture is the living example of this.

# AFTERWORD

Madeleine Maaskant
Director Amsterdam Academy of Architecture

In times when almost the entire economic system is based on a continuous acceleration of the consumption cycle, when 'new' is tantamount to 'better', a revaluation of how things are is an act of resistance. This applies not only to items of everyday use, such as clothing and furniture, but also to the built environment. Old town centres are generally popular, but everything surrounding them less so. Certainly in the Netherlands—with its rather unscrupulous spatial planning culture and where buildings are often regarded as an investment with a depreciation period—developers prefer to start a new building project with a clean slate.

The Tabula Scripta research group, led by Floris Alkemade, Michiel van Iersel, and Jarrik Ouburg, at the Academy of Architecture Amsterdam from 2014 to 2019, has come up with alternative ways of how to deal with what is already there by regarding the context of a building task not as an anecdotic pretence for accounting for a design after the fact, but as the *sine qua non* of a good design proposal. Based on their research—which not only concerned architecture but various related disciplines as well—the research group formulated eleven strategies for relating to the existing environment. In this book, they clarify and elaborate on these strategies from a variety of perspectives.

The Academy of Architecture is attaching more and more importance to doing research. In the first place, it is important that new generations of designers not only develop design skills, but learn research skills as well. The latter will become increasingly important in the professional practice, as clients more and more frequently ask designers to contribute to thinking about the design brief. Designers then first have to clearly define or rephrase the client's wishes before they can start on a design.

The Academy also hopes, by carefully selecting research themes, to contribute to currently urgent issues in society, such as sustainability, circularity, healthy urbanization, and the energy transition. The three research groups within the Academy (in addition to architecture also in the disciplines urban planning and landscape architecture) have research programmes that, each in its own way, are linked to these issues. The Tabula Scripta research group is no exception.

The Tabula Scripta research group has also made an excellent contribution to the international goals of the Academy: students have taken part in design studios in Mumbai and Cairo and the admirable results are documented in this publication. The many international references also demonstrate how the relevance of this subject extends far beyond the Netherlands. This large scope is not just in terms of geography but also in terms of disciplines. The researchers did not restrict themselves to their own disciplines but also used insights from, for example, visual art, psychology, and biology. It is this interdisciplinary and 'crossing-borders' approach that makes this research so appealing.

I am therefore very proud that the Academy has been able to facilitate the research of which this book is the result. I'd like to thank editor Mark Minkjan and graphic designers Sonja Haller and Pascal Brun for their excellent work, and all others who have been involved in the Tabula Scripta research group. I hope that this book reflects the joy the stimulating collaboration with all of them has given the Academy.

INDEX

CREDITS OF THE IMAGES

With all images in this publication, the architects, designers, artists, and original makers are mentioned on their page/s. They hold the copyright of their images, and are not repeated here. If a (reproduction) photographer, institute, photo news agency, press agency, or archive is involved, these are mentioned on this page.



For works of visual artists affiliated with a CISAC-organization the copyrights have been settled with Pictoright in Amsterdam, 2020.

The editors have made every effort to secure permission to reproduce the listed material, texts, illustrations and photographs. We apologize for any inadvert errors or omissions. Parties who nevertheless believe they can claim specific legal rights are invited to contact the Amsterdam Academy of Architecture: avb-info@ahk.nl.

Position on page: l=left, r=right, t=top, b=bottom, m=mid

ADAGP, Paris; Hérold Jacques (dit), Blumer Herold (1910–1987); Paris Lam Wifredo (dit), Lam y Castilla Wifredo Oscar (1902–1982); Breton André (1896–1966); Paris Localisation: Centre Pompidou–Musée national d'art modern–Centre de création industrielle, Photo © Centre Pompidou, MNAM-CCI, Dist. RMN-Grand Palais / Philippe Migeat, p. 71t
Aerodata, photo p. 361
Aerodata/Vizualism, photo p. 362t
Amsterdam City Archives pp. 58b, 334, 369
ANP, photos pp. 264–265, 343b, 376b
ANP/AFP/Jewel Samad, photo p. 38b/l
ANP/Fethi Belaid, photo p. 273b
ANP/dpa Picture-Alliance/Boris Roessler, photo p. 38b/r
ANP/Jean-François Monier, photo p. 173b
ANP/Ed Oudenaarden, photo p. 362b
ANP/Reuters/Amr Abdallah Dalsh, photo p. 174b
ANP/Reuters/Darren Staples, photo p. 171t
ANP/Marcio Jose Sanchez, photo p. 377t
Marcel Antonisse/Anefo/Dutch National Archives Collection, photo p. 137b
AP|Associated Press, photo p. 35b
ARS (Artists Right Society), photo p. 186
Christian Åslund, photo p. 239t
Andrea Avezzù, photo p. 241t

Iwan Baan, pp. 127b, 133, 328, 329b, 332–333
Fethi Belaid/ANP, photo p. 273b
La Biennale di Venezia (Courtesy), p. 241t
Menno Bouma, photo p. 140
Boijmans Van Beuningen Museum Collection/ARS, p. 103t
Yvonne Brandwijk, photo p291
Zweer de Bruin, Flickr, CC BY-NC-ND 2.0, photo p. 69b
Harry Burton, photo p. 378

Cambridge University Library, p. 344t
Canadian Centre for Achitecture, Gift of Estate of Gordon Matta-Clarck © Estate of Gordon Matta-Clark/ Artists Rights Society (ARS), New York, p. 55b
Paul Carstairs for Arup, photo p. 326
CBS 17, https://youtu.be/6UhhqCy9yls?t=96,1.36/2.46, p. 38t
CERN, photo p. 206t
Joost Conijn, photo p. 171b
Pauline Conolly, photo p. 172b
Lee Craker, photo p. 341t

Jean-Pierre Dalbéra, Wikimedia, CC BY 2.0, p. 202b
Amr Abdallah Dalsh, Reuters/ANP, photo p. 174b
G. Th. Delemarre, Cultural Heritage Agency of the Netherlands, CC BY-SA-4.0, p. 58t
Walter Dhladhla, AFP, photo p. 342t
Quinn Dombrowski, Flickr, CC BY-SA 2.0, photos p. 189
Ossip van Duivenbode, photo pp. 358–359
Filip Dujardin, photos pp. 47–49, 183m
Sarah Duncan, photo pp. 256–257

ETH Zürich/Department of Architecture: Alex Domin, Marcel Fässler, Klaus Platzgummer, Pascal Tschumper, Adam Caruso, p. 223t
Aldo+Hannie van Eyck Foundation, p. 335b

Thomas Fabian, Flickr, CC BY-SA 2.0, ARS, photo p. 124
Faris (Knight) aka Faris El-Gwely, CC BY-SA 4.0, photo p. 372b
FCG/Pond5.com, video, p. 37b
Fitness Functions Floors, p. 274t
FLC (Fondation Le Corbusier)–ADAGP, p. 258–261
FLC (Fondation Le Corbusier)-ADAGP/Paul Kozlowski, p. 259b
Tom Flemming, Flickr, CC BY-NC 2.0, p. 262b
Fotomuseum Antwerpen Collection, B/2007/2186/1, © Filip J. Tas/ SABAM 2019, photo p. 72b
Roger J. Frank, photo p. 51

Gladstone Gallery (Courtesy), pp. 164–165
Jean-Pol Grandmont, CC BY 3.0, photo p. 270t
Griffith Institute, University of Oxford (Courtesy) p. 378
Francisco Guillan y Suarez, photo p. 289b
Gérard Guillat, Fonds Patrick Forest, photo p. 85t
Gym&Classics, photo p. 138m

Wim Hanenberg, photos p. 297
Carol M. Highsmith, photo–U.S. Library of Congress, Highsmith Archive p. 300t
Rasmus Hjortshøj, photo pp. 128–129
Allard van der Hoek, photos p. 155
Dave Hogg, CC BY 4.0, photo p. 310t
HOH Architecten, pp. 381, 382, 388t (photo editing), 389 (drawings), 390 (drawings), 396 (drawing), 398
Jordi Huisman, photos p. 82, p. 83t, 91–93b, 166b

Michiel van Iersel, photos pp. 61, 387, 391

Tadeusz Jalocha, photo p. 89b
Jan Willem Kaldenbach, photos pp. 298–299, 397b

Yevgeny Kondakov, photo p. 274b
Luuk Kramer, photos p. 222
Andrew Kreps Gallery (Courtesy), New York and Esther Schipper, Berlin (Courtesy), © VG Bild-Kunst, Bonn, 2020, pp. 104–105t
Tobias Kumkar, rendering p. 392b

Ian Lambot, 1989, photos p. 231
André-Pierre Lamoth, Document Nederland, Rijksmuseum Amsterdam, p. 364t
Markus Lanz, 2012, CC BY-NC-ND 2.0, photos pp. 199–201
Tyler Lastovich/Unsplash p. 208t
Steven Lawrey, AIA, photos p. 262t
Andrew Lee, photos p. 338
Thomas Lenden, photos p. 397t, 400
Christopher Little, Western Pennsylvania Conservancy, ARS p. 301b

Alex Maclean, photo pp. 52–53
Eric Mairiaux, photos pp. 153, 154
John Marchael (Courtesy photo) p. 367t
The Estate of Gordon Matta-Clark ©/Artists Rights Society (ARS), New York Courtesy The Estate of Gordon Matta-Clark and David Zwirner, p. 55t
Thomas Mayer, photos pp. 190b, 193
Leechant Mcarthur CC BY 2.0, p. 341b
Geneviève Michon, Globe-Democrat Collection, p. 205t
Jean-François Monier/ANP p. 173b
Philippe Monteil, photos p. 266
The Henry Moore Foundation/ Henry Moore Archive p. 35t
Ernst Moritz, photos pp. 227–229
Federico Moroni, Flickr, CC BY-NC-ND 2.0, photo p. 337t
Keith W Muir, photo p. 59t
Osamu Murai, photos pp. 292b, 293

NASA, photo p. 309
National Collection of Aerial Photography (NCAP), p. 273t
Maarten Nauw, photos p. 327
Nederlands Fotomuseum/Cas Oorthuys, photo p. 335t
Tiksa Negeri/Reuters, photo p. 59b
Nike/Abloh p. 139t

Sue Ormerod, photo p. 50
Jarrik Ouburg, photos p. 126, 263t/l, 304b, 310b, 381, 384t/b, 392t
Corry Ouburg-Heijne, photos p. 241b
Ed Oudenaarden/ANP, photo p. 362b
Cristobal Palma, photo p. 88t
Frans Parthesius, photo pp. 86–87
Pam Penick, p. 205b
Sandra Pereznieto, pp. 98–99
Lars Plougmann, Flickr, CC BY-SA 2.0, photo p. 372t

Robert Rauschenberg Foundation p. 36b
Christian Richters, photos pp. 122, 123, 395
Boris Roessler, dpa Picture-Alliance/ANP, photo p. 38b/r
Rogers Fund, Library, CC 0 1.0 Universal Public Domain Dedication, p. 100t
Fred Romero, 2018, Flickr, CC BY 2.0, photo p. 100b
Rotterdam City Archive, p. 167
Philippe Ruault, photos pp. 79–81, 184–185, 268t, 269, 290t

Arto Saari, photo p. 172t
Lauren Saldana, Takeyama Center for the Study of Japan and Japanese Culture, photo p. 104b
Jewel Samad / AFP/ANP, photo p. 38b/l
Marcio Jose Sanchez/ANP, photo p. 377t
Hp Schaefer, www.reserv-art.de, CC BY-SA-3.0, photo p. 84b
Schizar, Flickr, CC BY-2.0, photo p. 189b
Johannes Schwartz, photo p. 173t
SFMOMA Collection/Accessions Committee Fund: gift of Frances and John Bowes, Collectors Forum, Pam and Dick Kramlich, and the Modern Art Council © Estate of Gordon Matta-Clark/ Artists Rights Society (ARS), New York, p. 54
Sharjah Art Foundation (Courtesy), photo pp. 120–121
Kartikeya Shodha, photo p. 267t
Siggi, Huld & Co, CC BY 2.0, photo p. 344b
Maarten Smit, CC BY-SA 4.0, photos p. 270b
Darren Staples, Reuters/ANP, p. 171t
Matthieu di Stefano, Flickr, CC BY-NC 2.0, photo p. 337b
Students' work, Amsterdam Academy of Architecture: Sebastiaan van Heusden, Chrysafenia Lagouda, Robert Younger, Heleen Bults, Marilu de Bies, Hoeshmand Mahmoed, Florian Fakkert, Leo Taylor, Thomas Wolfs, p. 399t
Students' work, Amsterdam Academy of Architecture: Daan Foks, Anna Zan, Veronika Skouratovskaja, Manon den Duijn, Ries van den Bosch, Paulina Kapczyńska, Corinna Wassermann, Midas van Boekel, Ramses van der Dussen, Aleksei Kanin, p. 399b

Tate, p. 307
Sander Tiedema, photo pp. 36–37t
Tsugi.de p. 71b

Johnny Umans, photo p. 196t
Francesco Ungaro/Unsplash, p. 207b
United States Geological Survey, United States public domain, Wikimedia, photos pp. 60tb
Unredacted.com/2010/07/23/what-if-nixon-had-become-a-g-man/, retrieved September 17, 2019, Public domain, p. 106t
Tomas Utsi, photo p. 371m

Arild Vågen, Flickr, CC BY-SA 2.0, photo p. 371t
Matthias Van Rossen, photos pp. 287b, 289t

Ce Wang, photos p. 360
Tony Webster, CC BY-SA-4.0, photo p. 106b
Eresh Weerasuriya, photo p. 267b
Hans Werleman, photo p. 302b, 331b
Western Pennsylvania Conservancy, CC, ARS, pp. 300b, 301tb
Jeroen van der Wielen, photo p. 160b
Natalie Wright, photo p. 207t

Changheng Zhan, photo p. 233t

# CITIES OF THE FUTURE—PEOPLE AND PLACES THROUGH THE LENS OF IWAN BAAN

Iwan Baan in Conversation with Michiel van Iersel

MvI Dutch photographer Iwan Baan studied at the Royal Academy of Art in The Hague and is known primarily for images that narrate the life and interactions that occur within architecture. With no formal training in architecture, his perspective mirrors the questions and perspectives of the everyday individuals who give meaning and context to the architecture and spaces that surround us. Examples of this can be seen in his work on informal communities where vernacular architecture and placemaking serve as examples of human ingenuity. For this book we asked him to select photos of places that reveal the complexities and conflicts of our urban age and show the myriad ways in which humans (and non-humans) manage to co-create and co-exist in the face of environmental emergencies and resource scarcity.

IB LOOKING WITH NEW EYES

When you live in a place for a long time, you often overlook a lot of things or take them for granted. However, when you stumble upon a situation as an outsider, you see the special beauty of these places. And it often happens that when I show locals my photos, and give them this other perspective, they start looking at their environment in a different way and see it with new eyes.

P-1 BAKU, AZERBAIJAN, 2011 This is one of the shopping streets in the centre of Baku. As you can see on the right side, there is this Parisian looking facade, which was built right in front of these buildings from the Soviet era. Behind the neoclassical arcade is the old residential building from the 1950s or 60s. Over time, the occupants upgraded their homes, turning the facade into a patchwork of self-made additions and modifications against a greyish concrete background. The recent makeover was part of a big push to bring the country in line with 'Western standards'. They added only a thin veneer, leaving the original balconies and windows untouched in the space between the old and new layer, where daylight hardly enters. On the left you see a more extreme version of this veneer in the background, where they placed a large print over the scaffolding to cover up this construction site in what is supposed to become the new heart of Baku. In a way, these prints are more honest, because they actually reveal the thinly veiled attempt to hide history from view.

P-2 BAKU, AZERBAIJAN, 2011 These massive walls of residential buildings are in a part of the city that was built in Soviet times in, I believe, the 1950s. They consist of rows and rows of boxes right next to each other all the way up the hills. It's fascinating to see their density, and how they are taken over by residents who add balconies and entire rooms that grow out of these rigid structures.

Baku was the first place where oil was discovered and it went through three oil booms over the last 120 years. Under the Russians, and now as a sovereign state, the country went through another boom over the past few years in which the city trans-
P-6 formed tremendously. As in other places where oil is found, the revenues shape the city and society at large.

The buildings were privatized, after the collapse of Communism. Now there is another authoritarian regime, and the current ruler felt that the city was ugly and needed to be beautified, so he ordered that all the apartment buildings from Soviet times along the main roads had to be newly cladded and covered with neoclassical facades. A whole new layer of a kind of sandstone, with decorations that make it look like Paris. It creates a thin layer in front of the original facade, to cover up the concrete. The new windows are much smaller and block people's views from the balconies, which are hidden behind the sandstone.

P-4 LIMA, PERU, 2015 This is an incredible area on the outskirts of the city. On these hills a cemetery is intertwined with unpaved walkways. It's difficult to understand the enormous scale of it when you see the picture. Only when you look very closely you can see someone walking around or sitting on the small mausoleums. They are painted in almost the same colours as the houses, which are laid out in a very similar way on the other side of the hill. The architecture for the dead mimics that for the living. I'm
P-8 not sure if it was planned, because different types of graves in various stages of construction stand next to each other in a seemingly uncontrolled way.

TOKYO, JAPAN, 2011 When you look at graveyards you often see a microscopic version of the city. In the case of Tokyo, you can clearly see this idea of 'pixelation', or the fact that every plot and house has to be detached from the neighbouring ones. And that all the plots have become smaller and smaller over time. The same happens in this cemetery, where all the graves have the rectangular shape and the same dimensions and distance between them. It becomes almost a mirror image of the city. In Tokyo, or in Japan in general, all the buildings have the same grey patina, which is also reflected in the granite gravestones. Usually the cemeteries are connected to a small shrine, with people passing by to pay respect or pray. These shrines and holy places are very much part of everyday life in Japan. This photo was taken just after the major earthquake and the ground was still trembling due to the aftershocks. But because everything is extremely well-built, hardly anything came down in Tokyo. As in the rest of the Tokyo, the cemetery was hardly affected. Therefore, it was shocking to see the devastation in Fukushima, where a nuclear power station flooded as a result of the tsunami. Where Japan is completely about control, that control was completely gone in Fukushima.

MUMBAI, INDIA, 2018 There is this incredible infrastructure in the middle of the city. They have built elevated highways right between existing housing blocks. When people open their windows, they can touch the cars that are passing by. All kinds of things are happening underneath these highways. But only late in the day, when the sun is low on the horizon and the light enters the city almost horizontally, you can see what is going on. During the rest of the day the people there live in the dark. I don't expect that these roads will be removed anytime soon, because they are all part of government-led programmes to improve the flow of traffic. Many of the roads are doubled or tripled. It's hard to imagine what it is like to live in these conditions, where all the air pollution is trapped.

CAIRO, EGYPT, 2013 I've only been to Cairo once, and this was just at the moment when the Arab spring began to fade away and the streets were busy again. This photo shows a clash of everything: a truck is driving through, people are selling food from a stall, while in the background a massive concrete building without any windows is trying to reference some kind of traditional Arab architecture. It shows the blandness of urban development in Cairo, which grew exponentially and totally uncontrolled over the last few decades. All around Africa the streets are always so full with young people, and it's so incredibly energetic that, despite all the difficulties, it also fills them with a lot of hope and possibilities for the future, when this younger generation can take over.

PORT-AU-PRINCE, HAITI, 2014 This photo shows a part of the outskirts of the city, which has an incredible density. People are building everything right on top of each other on these hills, waiting for the next earthquake to happen. The downtown area of Port au Prince is still in shambles after the earthquake of 2010, but these informal places (like the one in the photo), are completely rebuilt. Each corner, and every nook and cranny are used to make a staircase or walkway. Kids play on the stairs and people have to carry water up the hill, while grey wastewater comes down in an open sewer. At the same time people try to make the best of the situation. Each house is painted in a different colour, people decorate their homes, and take real pride in their self-built living spaces. But obviously there are no structural engineers involved, which makes me wonder what will happen to these dwellings. You see that house balancing on one column, and a thin concrete staircase winding through it. I'm afraid that all these houses will come down during the next earthquake. Before the previous earthquake these houses were built much lighter, P-10 from found materials. But these new structures are made from concrete, which is being imported and is used because it allows for quick construction.

DHAKA, BANGLADESH, 2017 I think P-14 Dhaka is the city with the highest population density in the world. Every inch of land is used. I spent half a year there in my last year of art school, nineteen years ago. Back then you could already feel the density. But when I went back in 2017, the population explosion was even much more apparent. In the meantime the population had grown by almost one third, from 120 to 180 million people. At the same time, the land is only shrinking. Dhaka is situated in a delta, and the rising water is threatening the city and all parts of society. This image really encap- P-12 sulates all of that. On the left, you see posters for new housing developments. There's an unbridled development everywhere, even in places that are flooded twice a year. New high-rise buildings are going up, and because of a lack of planning, on the roads between them two rickshaws can barely pass each other. It's difficult to imagine how this can continue to grow. And literally everything is held together by a spider's web of electricity cables. The political situation in Bangladesh is quite difficult at the moment and there is no overall urban planning. During the monsoon, the streets are almost constantly flooded by a foot of water, with people stuck in their cars. However, it feels like the future of cities around the world. If you consider the impact of sea level rise on the planet, this is how a lot of other places will look like in the coming century.

P-16 KAMPALA, UGANDA, 2019 The capital of Uganda is an incredible chaos, where anything goes and everything happens outside in the streets. Compared to, for example, Dhaka in Bangladesh, where roads are narrow, here there are places right in the centre where tens
P-416 or hundreds of buses are snarled up in traffic while they are trying to get to the main bus station, which extends far beyond its location on a map. And all the street vendors and little shops turn this place into the main economic hub of the city. Like in other cities across Africa, there is a capacity to self-organize in any situation. And although change is happening, with China building highways and railroads all around the continent, corruption and informality will probably prevent cities from changing fundamentally.

P-415 TOKYO, JAPAN, 2011 This was an important project for the architects of SANAA, which they finished around the year 2000. It was designed for HHStyle, a shop selling designer furniture. The furniture would be visible through the milk-glass windows. But like everything in Tokyo, the function of this kind of building has a very short lifespan, especially in retail. After a few years, it became a fashion store and when I visited again in 2011, it had become Kiddy Land, a large and popular toy store. It was chock-full of flashy, plastic fantastic toys and it was hard to see SANAA's original design. Since then it has probably changed again. When I showed this photo to Kazuyo Sejima, one the architects, she had to laugh. It's interesting, because people here in Japan worship architects, but at the same time everyone seems to accept that buildings are being changed so often and so rapidly. Right now, it serves as a branch of Ragtag, a chain of fashion stores that specializes in second-hand designer clothes. And given the building's history, this seems quite appropriate.

KIBERA, NAIROBI, KENYA, 2016 Kibera is the largest urban slum, or informal settlement, on the African continent. There are an estimated two to five hundred thousand people living there. From a distance it looks like a sea of corrugated steel roofs and everything is built from found and recycled materials. At the same time, it's a thriving community where everybody has a small job and is doing something to make a living. There are a lot of shops, like the hairdresser in the photo, which doubles as a shop where you can recharge your phone and probably ask for any other service you can think of. The barber perhaps had others helping him construct the shack, but he must have decorated it himself. Kibera started when migrant workers from the countryside settled there during the construction of the railroads in colonial times and they stayed there after the work was finished. Now Kibera is surrounded by office buildings and tennis courts and cannot expand, so people start adding floors to their homes and shops and add density to an already overpopulated part of the city.

MOPTI, MALI, 2011 In the background you see the mosque in Mopti, which is an incredible piece of mud architecture. It sits next to the road to Timbuktu, which is historically an important trade route. It has been there for many centuries. But it became UNESCO World Heritage and, unfortunately, in an attempt to preserve it, it was covered with a layer of concrete. This gives the mosque a tacky, strange feel and makes the softness of the mud invisible. At the same time the few remaining mud structures around it are also disappearing rapidly. With incomes rising just a tiny bit, people start buying concrete and corrugated steel. Mud structures need a lot of maintenance and people don't want to make that effort anymore. The old streets are not treated any better. They serve as storage space for street stalls and the trees with their trunks painted white reflect the headlights of cars passing in the night.

AHMEDABAD, INDIA, 2016 All layers and levels of life come together in Indian cities. Every apartment, every person, the display of fruits and vegetables, they all have their own distinct colour. There is this seemingly incredible chaos, but at the same time everyone is taking care of their own little environment. This photo captures the moment when I walked through the city and encountered this incredible density of life, and everything is happening at the same time. You have the people who are selling in the streets and the houses around it. This centuries-old sacred tree is an important meeting point in the city. There is a shrine connected to it, with an altar, which is still functioning and is used every day by people who come here to worship. For generations, people have been taking care of these places, which remain part of daily life despite the big urban developments.

 P-418

BAKU, AZERBAIJAN, 2011 The oil in- P-422
dustry is visibly present wherever you go in Baku. While the 'beautification' of the city took place over the last decade, gas pipelines are running through the city, crossing roads and parks. This incredible oil and gas infrastructure is part of everyday life. Kids play on pipelines, while trains pass by and shepherds let their sheep graze right next to them.

LAGOS, NIGERIA, 2018 This photo was P-424
taken just outside of Nigeria's National
Stadium, which seems to be too big to be
used properly and was closed each time I've
visited it. All around the stadium, underneath the main structure, there are all kinds
of sports activities taking place throughout P-420
the day and night. People go there for fitness and boxing classes or, as you can see in the photo, kids can learn to roller skate on a ramp that leads up to a parking lot. All the infrastructure that was intended to get people into the stadium is always open and is being used intensively most of the time. I'm pretty sure that in all the nooks and crannies of the vast concrete structure there are people living as well.

P-426
P-430
TOKYO, JAPAN, 2011 This is a very characteristic image of Tokyo. It shows the typical whitish-greyish patina that covers the entire city, and the windowless utilitarian infrastructure that seems to be everywhere, creating all these anonymous spaces. These narrow highways wind between the buildings and are completely closed off from the rest of the city by big noise barriers. You have no idea where you are going and the only way to navigate is using GPS, because everything looks the same.

P-428
HANGZHOU, CHINA, 2016 Hangzhou is dominated by massive urban developments, either initiated by big corporations or the state. This photo shows the view from a restaurant on the top floor of a hotel. I don't really remember where it was exactly, because everything is so generic and looks the same. You literally cannot see the end of it, everything disappears in the thick smog. These two girls are having tea, while overlooking this completely generic city, where all the buildings look like they were cloned or replicated, row after row. Within one or two generations, China managed to move from massive famine to prosperity for the majority of the population. These urban situations are in a way very depressing, but they are places where people can enjoy their collective achievement and where the promise of the future manifests itself.

MAPUTO, MOZAMBIQUE, 2008 In the front you see a building by Pancho Guedes. He was a Portuguese architect who designed 350 buildings in the city in the twentieth century, so approximately half the city, during the time when Mozambique was a colony of Portugal. When the Portuguese left, Guedes also left. This photo of one of his buildings was taken on a nice afternoon and you see life happening on all these different levels. Kids are playing football on top of the roof, because every inch of the city is being used and the top of a building all of a sudden becomes a playground and public space.

THE FUTURE OF (AFRICAN) CITIES

Looking at photos by Joost Guntenaar, a photographer who, in the 1960s and 70s, documented many of the places I have visited across Africa later, you see a continent with a lot more hope and possibilities than you see in my photos. Now it seems almost impossible to improve things for the millions of people who live in the rapidly growing cities. At the same time, there is a very large and young population that wants to do things differently. Of course, there will be massive problems, but people will figure out ways to make it work somehow. They show great ingenuity and an ability to change their conditions without the help of an architect. Looking at the larger picture we can see the multitude of ways in which people deal with challenges in their city, from the importance of rules and regulations in Tokyo to the creative power of chaos in cities such as Mumbai.

Iwan Baan, Tokyo,
Japan, 2011

Iwan Baan, Kibera,
Nairobi, Kenia, 2016

PHONE
charging
Try
us
now
Xperts

Iwan Baan, Mopti,
Mali, 2011

Iwan Baan, Ahmedabad,
India, 2016

રાજહંસ
છડેલા ઘઉં
HONDA
Activa

Iwan Baan, Baku, Azerbaijan, 2011

Iwan Baan, Lagos,
Nigeria, 2018

NATIONAL INSTITUTE FOR SPORTS

Iwan Baan, Tokyo,
Japan, 2011

配・急カーブ
車は大回り

Iwan Baan, Hangzhou,
China, 2016

Iwan Baan, Maputo,
Mozambique, 2008

## BIOGRAPHIES

### EDITORS

FLORIS ALKEMADE (1961) is an architect and urban designer. After completing his studies with Rem Koolhaas at Delft University of Technology (NL) he worked at the Office for Metropolitan Architecture (OMA) for eighteen years, the last eight years as a partner. Since 2008 he has been heading FAA (Floris Alkemade Architect). In 2015, Alkemade was appointed the Chief Government Architect of the Netherlands. He monitors and promotes the architectural and urban planning quality of government projects, and advises on major spatial and architectural issues. Floris Alkemade has included the ambition to search for the added social value of every design challenge.

MICHIEL VAN IERSEL (1978) works as an independent urbanist, curator, writer, and teacher at the intersection of the arts, architecture and related fields. He is the founder of Non-fiction and Failed Architecture and holds the position of Program Lead of the Chair of Architecture and Urban Transformation at ETH Zurich. His practice stretches from museum exhibitions to interventions in public space. He was a 2018–2019 Loeb Fellow at the Harvard Graduate School of Design and continues to teach at the Rietveld Academie and the Amsterdam Academy of Architecture. failedarchitecture.com; Newrope.world; non-fiction.nl; @michielviersel

MARK MINKJAN (1986) is an urban geographer and writer about architecture. He is Editor-in-Chief at Failed Architecture and produces the Failed Architecture Podcast. Mark has written for publications including *VICE*, *The Guardian* and *The Architectural Review*. In 2016, he received a talent grant from the Creative Industries Fund NL to develop new forms of architecture criticism and he received the Geert Bekaert Award for architecture criticism in 2017. Mark currently teaches at the Amsterdam Academy of Architecture, the Gerrit Rietveld Academie and the Rotterdam Academy of Architecture. failedarchitecture.com; non-fiction.nl; @markminkjan

JARRIK OUBURG (1975) is an architect and urban planner. He studied at TU Delft and the ETH Zurich, his graduation project was awarded the Archiprix International. He was a researcher at the Tokyo Institute of Technology. After having worked in Switzerland, Japan, and Belgium he founded HOH Architecten together with Freyke Hartemink and Carsten Hilgendorf in Amsterdam. He was Head of the Architecture department at the Amsterdam Academy of Architecture from 2012 until 2016 and initiated the research programme Tabula Scripta. hoh-architecten.com; @hoh_architecten; @jarrik_ouburg

### IMAGE EDITOR

SARAH VAN DER GIESEN (1989) is an architect. She studied at the Gerrit Rietveld Academie in Amsterdam and Universität der Künste Berlin before graduating at Delft University of Technology (NL). Sarah has worked for several architecture firms, taught newly arrived migrant youth in Rotterdam, and organized design workshops in Rotterdam and Brussels.

### DESIGNERS AND PUBLISHER

HALLER BRUN is an Amsterdam-based graphic design studio run by Sonja Haller (1977) and Pascal Brun (1974). After graduating in Switzerland, they moved to the Netherlands where they established their own studio in 2011. They mainly work in the fields of art, culture and design, with a focus on editorial design. The work of Haller Brun is characterized by a combination of the Swiss tradition of precision and typography with Dutch directness and playfulness. Their work has been honoured with several international awards. hallerbrun.eu; @haller_brun

VALIZ is an independent international publisher, addressing contemporary developments in art, design, architecture, and urban affairs. Their books provide critical reflection and interdisciplinary inspiration in a broad and imaginative way, often establishing a connection between cultural disciplines and socioeconomic questions. Valiz is headed by Astrid Vorstermans (1960) and Pia Pol (1985). valiz.nl; @valiz_books_projects

COLOPHON

Editors:
Floris Alkemade,
Michiel van Iersel,
Mark Minkjan,
Jarrik Ouburg,

Contributions by:
Floris Alkemade,
Iwan Baan, René Boer,
Elma van Boxel, Xaveer
De Geyter, Lionel
Devlieger, Amie Dicke,
Mona El Mousfy,
Sean Halloran, Michiel
van Iersel, Sharmeen
Azam Inayat, Sam
Jacob, Momoyo Kaijima,
Kristian Koreman,
Anne Lacaton, Madeleine
Maaskant, Arna Mačkić,
Keiichi Matsuda,
Mark Minkjan, Jim van
Os, Jarrik Ouburg,
Freek Persyn, Karin
Riley, Tamar Shafrir,
Tom Simonite, Hito
Steyerl, Jo Taillieu,
Marga Weimans

Image editor:
Sarah van der Giesen

Translation and
copy-editing:
Leo Reijnen

Proofreading:
Els Brinkman

Index:
Elke Stevens

Graphic design:
Haller Brun

Typefaces:
Neue Haas Unica Pro,
Suisse Works,
Monospace 821

Paper inside:
Munken Print White,
UPM Sol mat, Rigical

Paper cover:
Rigical

Lithography:
Mariska Bijl, Wilco
Art Books, Amsterdam

Printing and binding:
Wilco, Meppel/
Amersfoort

Co-publisher:
Amsterdam Academy
of Architecture

Publisher:
Valiz, Amsterdam,
Astrid Vorstermans
& Pia Pol



Amsterdam Academy
of Architecture
www.academyof
architecture.nl

Valiz, Amsterdam
www.valiz.nl



International
distribution
BE/NL/LU:
Centraal Boekhuis,
www.centraal.
boekhuis.nl
GB/IE:
Anagram Books,
www.anagrambooks.com
Europe/Asia:
Idea Books,
www.ideabooks.nl
USA, Canada,
Latin America:
D.A.P., www.artbook.com
Australia:
Perimeter Books,
www.perimeterbooks.com
Individual orders:
www.valiz.nl;
info@valiz.nl

This publication was
made possible through
the generous support
of

the Creative Industries
Fund NL.

**creative industries**
**fund NL**

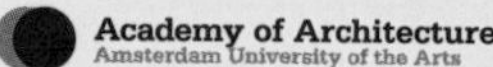


ISBN 978 94 92095 70 1
Printed and bound
in the EU